Dear Ann, Dear Abby

Dear Ann, Dear Abby

The Unauthorized Biography of
Ann Landers and Abigail Van Buren

Jan Pottker and Bob Speziale

Dodd, Mead & Company

NEW YORK

for Andy, for Jack

*Abigail Van Buren uses the registered trademark
Dear Abby as the title of her column.*

1 2 3 4 5 6 7 8 9 10

Library of Congress Cataloging-in-Publication Data

Pottker, Janice.
Dear Ann, Dear Abby

Includes index.
1. Landers, Ann. 2. Van Buren, Abigail, 1918—
3. Journalists—United States—Biography. I. Speziale,
Bob. II. Title.
PN4874.L23P68 1987   070′.92′2 [B]   87–19945
ISBN 0-396-08906-2

Contents

"We've been anonymous and we've been famous. And it's more fun famous."

—Popo Phillips (Dear Abby)

"It'll be about Ann and Abby," said Jan, whose idea it was. We were having lunch, chicken salad, at a Georgetown restaurant.

"Ann and Abby the advice columnists?" asked Bob, not sure he heard Jan correctly.

"Ann Landers and Dear Abby. You know, they're twins," said Jan.

"I like it," said Bob. "Tell me more."

"Well, they're the most influential women in America, and they've never had a book written about them," Jan started explaining. "Not only that, but they are identical twins who ended up doing the exact same thing, and because of it, they didn't speak to each other for years and then . . . ."

Bob remembered that when he was seven or eight he asked his mom if Ann and Abby were the same person. Their photos over their columns looked the same, even though Ann appeared in the morning paper and Abby in the afternoon. "They're twins," she had said. "And they don't talk to each other."

It wasn't until more than twenty years later that Bob thought long and hard about those twins again. But by then, Jan had already started working on *Dear Ann, Dear Abby*. Our collaboration had begun.

* * *

Ann and Abby are history's most famous twins. The Ann Landers and Dear Abby columns together are syndicated in more than 2,000 newspapers all over the world with a reading audience of nearly 200 million people. They are the world's most widely syndicated columns.

Over the past three decades, Ann or Abby or both of them have been named the most admired women in the United States (Gallup), the most important women (UPI), among the one hundred most important women in America *(Ladies' Home Journal),* and the most influential women in America (UPI and *World Almanac).* No other sisters, much less identical twin sisters, have ever appeared on these lists. No other women have remained on these polls over such an extended period of time.

Every weekly news magazine has featured either Ann or Abby. Women's service magazines have profiled these columnists, as have a variety of other publications. But the lives and work of these women, each of whose columns has become an American institution, have not been written about in depth.

A traditional accounting of the columnists' lives would in itself be a fascinating story. But in *Dear Ann, Dear Abby* we not only chronicle lives of extraordinary accomplishment and, at times, spurious glamour, but also illuminate the actual, unvarnished characters behind the image of two of America's most admired women.

At the start of our work, identical letters were sent to Ann Landers and Dear Abby to tell them about the book and to request interviews. Despite the columnists' unending courting of the media in print and through television, both women refused interviews.

Inexplicably, Kathie Mitchell, Ann Landers's top assistant, wrote to tell us her employer could not grant an interview because she was receiving so much publicity. Abby's response, in big handwriting on heart-printed stationery, said she had received a copy of Ann's refusal and that after discussing the request with Ann, she was "not inclined to cooperate. Perhaps one day, but not now."

Then we made a request through an intermediary. A close friend of Abby's, Theodore Bernstein, happened to be a relative of Jan's by marriage. In her twenty-fifth-anniversary column, Abby said she was "filled with gratitude to the late Ted Bernstein of the New York *Times,* who, out of friendship, served as my Supreme Court on word usage."

Ted's sister-in-law, Beatrice Bernstein, followed up our request for an interview by writing a personal note to Abby. Mrs. Bernstein reminded the successful columnist of her debt to Ted and assured her that if he were alive, Ted himself would not hesitate to ask Abby to grant us the opportunity to speak directly with her. Abby's short reply to Mrs. Bernstein was still, "No."

Near the completion of our book, we again wrote to Ann and Abby, attempting to speak directly with them. But again they chose not to cooperate.

Other roadblocks to research were met when we contacted friends and colleagues of Ann's and Abby's. Jules Lederer, Ann's ex-husband, said, "I generally do not indulge in interviews and particularly do not get involved in anything dealing with the former Mrs. Lederer's career."

When Jan arrived in Sioux City, Iowa, the birthplace and home for twenty-one years of the Friedman twins, she was told by the head of a Jewish social service agency, "Word is out not to talk to you." Despite the edict, the director of the agency helped out. And two years later, when Bob went to Iowa for the Friedman twins' fifty-year class reunion, everyone he spoke with was delighted to share his or her memories of their famous classmates.

In Eau Claire, Wisconsin, where the twins lived as married women for ten years, former friends were reluctant to respond to our inquiries. In a town where the public library and park are named after Abby's husband's family, it was not politic to be seen or to be known as someone who was aiding an unauthorized chronicle of the twins' lives.

In Wisconsin, an editor of a newspaper had originally agreed to an interview. He cancelled it after telephoning Ann Landers. He told our researcher that Ann Landers said she had never been informed of our book, and therefore he was no longer willing to be interviewed. Although he was offered evidence to support our claim that Ann Landers had written knowledge about the proposed book, the editor insisted that was impossible: Ann Landers had just told him she never forgets anything.

Reporters and editors for newspapers in Illinois, Wisconsin, Minnesota, Iowa, and California were interested in our project and wanted to be cooperative. But again, most asked that their help be kept confidential. These journalists feared their professional lives could be made uncomfortable if their help became known to Ann and Abby.

Despite their initial timidity, hundreds of close friends and colleagues provided candid recollections of their association with Ann and Abby. In all, we conducted several hundred interviews with people who have known Ann or Abby, or both of them, sometimes throughout their lives. But regrettably, many of these people requested anonymity. As one person jokingly warned, "If you use my name, I'll break every bone in your body."

Ann and Abby crave publicity—when they can control it. Their success at promoting and sanitizing circumscribed versions of their lives and work is no secret. Abby joked about it when she chided Cliff Jahr for supposed inaccuracies in his profile of her twin that appeared in *Ladies' Home Journal.* Following Jahr's explanation that Ann had supplied the information, Abby's off-the-record remark was, "Brother, you were had."

If Jahr, who we later interviewed, was misled by Ann or Abby, he does not stand alone. The many stories, myths, and legends that have sprung up around the columnists had to be untangled. The twins' relentless concern over their publicity was one clue that led us to double-check their anecdotes.

When we began our investigation, we were complete admirers of how Ann and Abby have conducted their personal and professional lives. We still admire them.

In *Dear Ann, Dear Abby,* we have taken a balanced look at the nation's two most popular advice columns and the women who write them. Sometimes we point to discrepancies that illustrate how the columnists would like others to view them and how they really behave. Mostly we highlight the real, the unpublicized Ann Landers and Dear Abby, how their lives have affected their columns and their careers have affected their lives, and how they have remained at the center of America's moral conscience for more than thirty years.

Without the help and assistance of Olga Pottker, we would have found *Dear Ann, Dear Abby* a formidable task. For their discerning judgment, enlightened vision, and constant support, we are grateful to Jack Weiser and Andy Fishel.

Because many people we spoke with requested anonymity, we are able to mention only a very few here, but we are grateful to them all. For their help and cooperation we thank Dr. Robert Stolar; Father Theodore Hesburgh, president of the University of Notre Dame; Dr. Abraham Franzblau; Senators Birch Bayh and Eugene McCarthy; Stanleigh Arnold of the *San Francisco Chronicle;* John P. McMeel, president of Universal Press Syndicate; Katherine Fanning of *The Christian Science Monitor;* Dr. Joyce Brothers; Charles McAdam Jr., president of McNaught Syndicate; Cal Thomas; Tom Cottle; Howard Phillips of the Conservative Caucus Foundation; Diane Crowley; Don Michaels of The Tribune Syndicate; Cathleen Douglas; Cliff Jahr; Harold Senecker of *Forbes;* James Shannon; Stuart E. Schiffer of the U.S. Department of Justice; John Aquilino; Charles and Margaret Lindsay; John Gruenwald; U.S. Ambassador to Italy Maxwell Rabb; Rosemary Bloedorn; Lynne Zerschling of the *Sioux City Journal;* Barbara Flanagan of the *Minneapolis Star & Tribune;* and His Holiness Pope John Paul II.

Tim Sommerhauser went out of his way to help us many times. Richard Zoerink and Sam Daniel provided us their unique perspectives during our work on this book. We are grateful to Darryl Puterbaugh for, at least once in his life, having been in the right place at the right time. For his unflagging interest and guidance, we thank Dotson Rader, and for her picture editing and pursuit of quality, we thank Jane Jordan.

For their heartfelt support and enthusiasm we are deeply grateful to Bernice and Dominick Speziale, Ralph Pottker, Mary Helene Pottker Rosenbaum, Beatrice Bernstein, M Kathleen McCulloch,

Adele and Stanley Fishel, Phyllis Theroux, and Bette and Joyce Speziale. Special thanks to Tracy and Carrie Pottker-Fishel, who allowed their mother time to work, and to Fifi and Bowser, for giving Bob companionship and enough elbow room to write.

Molly Friedrich gave us her unqualified support and the benefit of her professional expertise. Our deepest thanks to Barney Karpfinger for his hard work, expert counsel, and unfailing optimism, to our editor, Cynthia Vartan for her judgement and wisdom, and to our publisher, Dodd, Mead, for bringing *Dear Ann, Dear Abby* to life.

Going Home

One

isterly love wasn't the only reason Eppie and Popo strode arm in arm off Ozark Airlines Flight 989 on a warm summer afternoon in 1976. The two most identical members of Central High's Class of '36 earlier that Saturday had squeezed into the cramped bathroom on the airplane together and traded hushed secrets, much to the delight of the invited retinue of photographers from national magazines and big-city dailies who trailed them.

Starstruck relatives and friends greeted their arrival at the Sioux City airport with a sparkle of flashbulbs. The most famous twins who ever lived chatted politely with the twin nuns who said they used to babysit for them and accepted their gifts of Blessed Virgin medallions, though Popo later stated that both sisters, habits and all, were phonies. The car thoughtfully provided by the reunion committee was sent away, at Eppie and Popo's command, occupied only by their luggage.

Ann Landers and Dear Abby decided to make their own plans, even though the reunion committee had carefully arranged every aspect of the famous twins' homecoming, including scheduling the class reunion on the weekend before the twins' fifty-eighth birthday,

July 4. Spotting their close cousin Henry Greenberg in the crowd, Eppie pushed Popo in and out of focus of a dozen more cameras and into the front seat of his waiting car. The giddy threesome huddled together behind the windshield for one brief moment and then, in a burst of high-pitched giggles, zipped off to the bridal suite of the Sioux City Hilton. The once-animated airport crowd quickly realized that the twins were turning their forty-year high school reunion into a publicity stunt.

Classmates who said they could not tell the Friedman twins apart when they were teens had no such problem at the airport. Despite their nearly identical bouffant hairdos with the identical stiff side flip, Eppie, better known as Ann Landers, had fewer wrinkles and a smaller nose. But both twins still sported big dimples and high-boned bubble cheeks. When either of them smiles, it still comes out slightly crooked looking, and both twins' eyebrows seem permanently arched. "I hope they don't compare us to see which one has held up the best," Popo, or Abby to her readers, confided on the plane. But the comparison was inevitable. Even though Popo had plastic surgery too, classmates said she appeared self-conscious next to Eppie, perhaps because she looked older. Popo says she's convinced she photographs like the late Israeli prime minister Golda Meir.

Press hype for their class's forty-year reunion had gathered speed since their announced homecoming weeks before. Popo explained to the reunion committee that she and "Sissie" planned their engagements a year ahead of time. No wonder. The Sioux City twins are in demand. Their advice columns are not only syndicated in more than 1,600 newspapers in the United States alone but are also translated into as many as twenty languages all over the world. Both Ann and Abby continue to be among the most sought-after and most highly paid speakers in the country, even at $10,000 for thirty minutes. "That's not bad for thirty minutes. It makes you feel, well, quite good," admits Popo.

Entering their third decade as Ann Landers and Dear Abby, Eppie and Popo were worried about being out of step. The world about them in the summer of 1976 was changing, and changing quickly. Against the backdrop of America's bicentennial, a peanut farmer from Georgia was campaigning for the presidency preaching a gospel of human rights while a former encyclopedia salesman was preaching something called est and calling *help* a dirty word. Dozens of religious groups like Sun Myung Moon's Unification Church, the Hare Krishnas, and a group billing itself as the Divine Light Mission were offering guidance of a different sort to America's youth. Ann and Abby were concerned not only that their columns were staid and conventional but also that they themselves were slowly slipping from the public eye. A public display of mutual support would work wonders in reaffirming their status as America's reigning advice queens.

Later that evening at the reunion festivities, their classmates' suspicions were confirmed. A couple who knew the twins well said the event was "almost spoiled because it quickly became apparent the now-famous columnists were using the reunion to publicize their personal unity."

"A little false front," commented a member of the reunion committee as she watched Popo, in her lightning-blue lamé Mollie Parnis, impersonally autograph souvenir programs. Eppie too, in her black, form-fitting Adolfo knit weighted down with thick gold jewelry, rarely troubled to chat with classmates or even glance at their faces as she signed the programs. "I stayed up all night studying the yearbook," Eppie crowed from the dais, in an Iowa twang variously described as alfalfa alto or Middletown mezzo-soprano. "And I wanna tell ya, everyone in this room tonight looks a darn sight better than forty years ago."

Eppie had stories to tell of her trip to China courtesy of the American Medical Association. If her divorce from her husband of thirty-six years just nine months before left her distraught, no one noticed. Eppie's recent surgical sleight-of-hand had made her look years younger than her fellow classmates. Some whispered she had nary a body part left to call her own, while others agreed she looked positively stunning. Sioux City classmates were positive both twins had extensive body surgery, including fanny tucks.

≈ 5

Sioux City classmates also were convinced they were in the presence of celebrities. Though sometimes the Friedman twins get glamour, class, and notoriety mixed up, they gave the impression of having to live up to something. "What politicians," a former boyfriend said of them at the reunion. "The girls had an answer for everything, just like they do in their columns."

It was said the ladies who dispensed advice like so much Kool Aid hadn't spoken to each other for years. Their first public appearance together in many years was carefully orchestrated to prove that the sisters were as close as they'd ever been. A public reconciliation of this magnitude was news. It was the type of story that sold newspapers. For the Friedman twins, it was the type of publicity that convinced newspapers to keep running their syndicated advice columns.

Why did sisters who advised the nation on family and human relations repeatedly and publicly feud with each other? How could identical twins, once so close, become so antagonistic toward each other? Eppie was sore at Popo because Popo became Dear Abby only three months after she became Ann Landers. After years of being overshadowed by her sister, Eppie believed she had achieved something unique and apart from her twin. She was not prepared for rival syndication from anyone, and especially not from Popo.

Popo got angry with Eppie because Eppie never publicly acknowledged her helping the new Ann Landers become so successful so quickly. "Eppie should have given me credit, but she didn't, and I understand her wanting to forget," says Popo. When Eppie took over as Ann Landers, she had no office, no telephone or secretary, and thousands of unopened letters to answer. She called Popo for help. As Popo puts it, she supplied "some cute, quippy, snappy replies, most of which were used."

Popo maintains that her becoming a top advice columnist occurred without planning. What she doesn't say is it's thanks to Eppie that she learned how to make money on her own. Popo doesn't admit that Eppie showed her how to become an advice columnist. Undoubtedly it was Eppie's success that triggered Popo's competitive spirit. It's no surprise that Eppie took offense at Popo's attempt to outdo her in the very same profession that Eppie had chosen for herself. But Popo must have been chagrined too. For in this one instance, Eppie had led and she had followed.

For Popo, money came easy: She married it. If Eppie at times appears the less likeable of the twins, it's perhaps because she had to struggle harder to get to the top of her profession and earn an annual income greater than any of her former classmates at Central High would likely earn in a lifetime—an annual income that in later years Eppie chose to keep, but Popo could afford to give away.

Chances are if it hadn't been writing an advice column that precipitated their disaffection, it would have been something else. As Popo sees it, "I understand why she's disturbed. She wanted to be the first violin in the school orchestra, but I was. She swore she'd marry a millionaire, but I did. I'm not trying to be the champion. It's just like playing poker. If you don't *have* to win, you get the cards, and she's always wanted to win." But Popo probably has it a little skewed. It wasn't that Eppie loved winning all that much, it's just that she hated losing.

For both twins, the eight years they didn't speak to each other is a time neither is very proud of. Yet their avowed reconciliations, first in the spring of 1964 and then in June of 1976, were only temporary. America's two preeminent advice columnists have never been able to resolve their differences completely. The twins' actions and words keep everyone guessing. They contradict each other even in print. Eppie says, "There were some years we didn't speak." But Popo, just as solemnly as Eppie, declares, "There was never a time when we weren't speaking to each other."

Both twins seem to revel in their public display of sisterly disaffection. Keeping their stars in ascendance demands that these fifties-era housewives set themselves apart from the normal, vulnerable, and undramatic life they left behind. Their public spitefulness is a way of validating their status and asserting the prerogatives of fame through their own style of glamour, high drama, and even malevolence. Popo, however, sees it differently. She blames the media for misrepresenting her and Eppie. "Happiness doesn't make news. We were both abused by the press. There is some jealousy because we are so successful," she sniffs.

Despite their failings, both sisters are perceived as possessing innate wisdom and insight. Together Ann and Abby receive as many as 15,000 letters each week. "When I started writing the column at thirty-seven, I thought I was worldly and sophisticated. I knew what life was about. Let me tell you, I didn't know anything," says Eppie.

Neither twin has had formal training in social service work or journalism. To deter lawsuits, their contracts bar them from offering prescriptive advice, so many of their printed replies take the form of personal opinions or referrals to social service agencies. In recent years, the twins have confronted such volatile issues as abortion, birth control, and gun control head-on. Eppie chooses to use her column to educate the American public. "I admit it," she says. "Most of my fans only read the horoscope, Ann Landers, and the funnies. I use my clout judiciously and effectively. I realize the fact that my answers have a tremendous impact on people."

It's more than Ann's and Abby's strong stands on today's social issues that attracts a loyal following. Eppie may believe she's popular because "People want somebody they think is strong, somebody they think is dependable." But to many people, both Ann and Abby represent something much different from the last word on complex social problems. To many people, Ann and Abby personify generosity and human kindness. They reaffirm the importance of kindness and the virtue of boldness. Because they are trusted to articulate how sensible and caring people should act, Eppie and Popo have helped many confused and lonely people choose how they may best live their lives.

Ann Landers and Dear Abby are American institutions. As Popo points out after more than thirty years of advice giving, "Eppie and I must be doing something right. There must be some reason we're still here." Syndication ensures their daily exposure to a vast reading public that can be counted on to catapult Ann and Abby onto any list of the most influential Americans, male or female.

* * *

For two girls called peppy and cute (Eppie) or cute and peppy (Popo), raised in an immigrant family of modest means, the syndication of their advice columns was a crowning achievement far surpassing their parents' expectations. It was the culmination of their efforts and talents, and a tribute to their family. And once Esther Pauline, as Eppie was named, became famous advice columnist Ann Landers, and Pauline Esther, as Popo was named, became famous advice columnist Dear Abby, the twin sisters were going to trumpet their celebrityhood every chance they got.

With their gutsy opinions and down-home womanly advice, it's difficult to describe the twins as anything less than mainstream. In their columns the twins always sound sincere because they take their advice giving seriously. But sometimes they take themselves as seriously as the advice they give. When they appear in public they are often seen as Ann Landers or Dear Abby, not Eppie Lederer or Popo Phillips. When they impersonate their column namesakes and tend toward self-congratulation and grandiosity, their conduct seems comical.

Regardless of their occasional posturing, the twins will always seem authentic. Whether they're attempting to upstage each other by giving catty understatements to reporters from national magazines or publicly reaffirming their sisterly affection, they have an oddly reassuring manner that generates trust. Eppie herself confirms her appeal in a sly but ingratiating way. Whenever she's at a loss to explain herself, her views, or her source of wisdom, Eppie frequently resorts to invoking her small-town upbringing and brags, "I'm the original square Jewish lady from Sioux City, Iowa."

At the very least, Eppie gets it half right. She's an original, for sure. But so's her identical twin, Popo.

Before

Two

Sioux City, Iowa, in the heart of the Midwest, was hardly the ideal place to raise a Jewish family during the early part of the twentieth century. Eppie and Popo were born there seventeen minutes apart on July 4, 1918. Abraham and Rebecca, the proud parents of the identical twins, were Russian immigrants. They spoke Russian and Yiddish fluently, but, admitted Abe, they spoke "English with a broken handwriting." The twins were to learn little of their Russian forebears, for once Abe and Becky arrived in America in 1908, they broke their homeland ties and embarked on the earnest task of assimilating American culture.

Originally a supply center for the northern plains and later a center of the expanding meat-packing industry, Sioux City was still a rough town when Abe and Becky Friedman moved there in 1910. Despite its gentle hills and neat stucco-and-clapboard residential areas, a drab pallor seemed to malinger over the neighborhoods closest to the slaughterhouses, railroad yards, and grain exchange. The existence of a Jewish ghetto in a neighborhood called "The Bottoms" fueled the rife anti-Semitism in the city.

As the adopted home of immigrants from many different cultures, Sioux City underwent radical social change in a brief period of time. The Friedmans were among the last wave of immigrants, and they met with resistance from earlier settlers of French-Canadian, German, and Scandinavian extraction. In the hope of driving away its unsavory elements, Sioux City voted itself dry in 1916, four years before Prohibition. But the ban on liquor backfired, and the town became less known for its stockyards and more for the availability of bootlegged Canadian whiskey.

At about the time of Eppie and Popo's birth, hired gangsters still rode shotgun on Highway 75 to and from Winnipeg. Black Cadillacs, the sedans of choice of a Jewish racketeering mob called the Syndicate, contained hollowed-out sections to store illegal booze. Upstanding and hardworking Sioux City Jews like Abe and Becky Friedman wanted no part of the likes of the Syndicate hoodlums. Established Jewish families, sensitive to the charges of lawbreaking, maintained extraordinarily staid and exemplary lifestyles.

Jewish children from all socioeconomic levels were taught that their actions reflected on the entire Jewish community. Despite the substantial contributions and accomplishments of the earlier wave of German Jewish immigrants, bigotry persisted. Even when the nation's economy saw an upturn after the Depression years and prosperity returned to Sioux City, Jews of all nationalities still couldn't get jobs at utility companies, the Sioux City or Toy National Bank, and fashionable stores.

But religion wasn't the only dividing line in Sioux City. Russian and eastern European Jews like the Friedmans met with condescension not only from the Christian community but also from established German Jews.

This stratified Jewish community must have been bewildering to a penniless and unskilled Russian immigrant like Abe Friedman, who paid for his and his teenage wife's passage to America with the sale of a gold watch. Like many other young immigrants from Minsk, Kovno, or Mogilev, Abe sought escape from conscription into the Czar's army during the Russo–Japanese war. The Friedmans traveled west and by 1910 had joined their cousins the Mirkins and the Greenbergs and other relatives in Sioux City.

Abe probably couldn't have gotten a job at Midland Packing or one of the other slaughteryards or packing houses that the local economy was based on even if he had wanted to. Instead, the unskilled Abe peddled chickens from a pushcart. By the time Helen, the oldest of the Friedman girls, was born in 1911, and then Dorothy two years later, Abe had set aside enough of his meager earnings to buy into a grocery store.

Despite the financial demands of his growing family, Abe helped other immigrant families survive the lean years by allowing them to buy groceries on credit. Their ability to pay back what they owed was apparently of little concern to Abe. A short, rotund man with dimples and a sweet smile, he reminded some of S. Z. "Cuddles" Sakall, a popular vaudeville performer of the period who was known for slapping a hand to each cheek and merrily shaking his head from side to side. Abe cut a popular figure in the Russian immigrant neighborhood of tiny rowhouses, second-floor apartments, stoops and hallways cluttered with baby carriages, and a corner delicatessen that sold foreign-language newspapers.

By the time Eppie and Popo were in their early teens, Abe, with the help of relatives who owned shares in the Tri State Movie Association, became part owner of a movie and vaudeville theater in downtown Sioux City. Managing the World, as the burlesque house was called, elevated Abe to a position of financial regard among the recent Jewish immigrants. But the theater wasn't in the high-rent district and was frequented by less-than-well-to-do Sioux City residents.

Assured of some financial stability, if not social standing, the Friedman family moved into a bungalow-style stucco house on a corner lot on Jackson Street, one of Sioux City's major thoroughfares. About twenty blocks north of the theater, the two-story house with a small and open front porch sat on a treeless lot less than a few yards from houses to one side and to the rear.

Becky furnished the house with heavily fringed carpets, an upholstered sofa, big lamps with shades that bore large tassels, and,

≈ 15

of course, the best Victrola her budget allowed. The twins shared one upstairs bedroom, and older sisters Helen and Dorothy shared another.

With the help of a good friend Arthur Sanford, another Tri State shareholder, and the blessing of the Blanks of Des Moines, who owned a controlling interest in the Movie Association, Abe acquired, in rapid succession, the Orpheum, the Capitol, and the Hippodrome. The Orpheum was a step above the World. When it opened in 1927, it became Sioux City's center for "high class vaudeville and the best feature photoplays," according to local history.

Abe soon diversified his business investments and took an interest in a beer distributorship, apartment houses, and an ice factory. As his business dealings began to influence more and more people, Abe's civic stature grew as well. He was justly proud of his accomplishments, and his self-confidence led to an interest in community affairs. He took pride in his sudden entry into non-Jewish circles. Abe had no burning desire to divest himself of his ethnicity. He wasn't a phony. But perhaps because of his immigrant mannerisms, highly inflected speech, and flashy diamond stickpin and big diamond pinkie ring, he fell short of complete acceptance.

Oddly enough, in later years, after they became famous columnists, the twins referred to their father as a philanthropist. It's a honeyed and revisionist reference that has made former neighbors smile. More accurately, Abe was a warm and giving man, always ready to help others less fortunate. He sent a projectionist to St. Joseph's Home for Unwed Mothers to run movies for the girls there, and he lent money to friends and families in need, but he certainly wasn't a name donor to organized charities. "Abe was comfortable," says Don Stone, who received some helpful career advice from Abe and remembers him fondly. "But I doubt he would have been regarded as a social leader."

However, Abe's limited financial means and lack of prominence in the small world of Sioux City didn't mitigate his standing at home. His self-confidence was bolstered by a network of family, relatives and friends who bruited his accomplishments among themselves. His business acumen and quiet authority provided each member of the family with material comforts and a sense of self-worth. In the eyes of his wife and daughters, he was extremely successful.

Popo speaks of how generous her father was and how he taught her the importance of kindness through his own example. "I recall his buying coffee for my twin and me at a coffee shop near his theater," says Popo. "In those days coffee was a nickel a cup, and the bill came to fifteen cents. Father gave the waitress a dollar bill and said, 'Keep the change.' In unison we asked, 'Daddy, isn't that an awfully big tip?' He replied, 'Not for a woman who's working hard to make an honest living.'"

Abe Friedman had gone far in two decades. His ambition and fearless optimism had brought to his family an aura of respectability, and his hard work and business savvy had given him a leg up to that era's middle class. His twin daughters learned from the very start that hard work virtually guaranteed success.

Don Stone calls Abe a promoter. "Theater operators in those days, they really had to be promoters. They were expected to be. He was not as flamboyant as some, but he certainly was outgoing enough." Abe's ability to promote himself and his business ventures aided him immeasurably.

By their early teens, Abe's identical twin daughters were already beginning to attract attention too. Their rounded faces had lengthened and revealed large, twinkling come-hither eyes set off by thinly arched eyebrows and a wide, parted grin that suggested a knowingness well beyond their years. The way they walked, so purposefully, shoulders back and face up, made the best of their slim but curvaceous figures.

The twins' striking good looks, complemented by an intentional duplication from their matching hairstyles to their matching patent-leather pumps, made them a conspicuous and irresistible double bull's-eye for photographers. "We had the edge," says Popo. "When the school orchestra went to the state music contest, we were the girls the photographers always picked out." It was the kind of edge both women would spend a lifetime sharpening.

Three

hile Abe rambled out and about in Sioux City, sallying forth from his theater to pass on a good story or soft sell a new act, Becky remained a homebody. "She was a real Jewish mother," says Eppie. "Her home was her life." But what a home it must have been. Performers from the theater often stayed overnight at the Friedman house. Along with chorus girls and an occasional indigent who traded yard work for a hot meal and a cellar to sleep in, Becky provided hospitality to Abe's business buddies and her daughters' classmates and suitors. With its extended family of friends, characters, and hangers-on, life at 1722 Jackson Street during the Depression era would have tested the resourcefulness of even the most enterprising homemaker. But Becky's domestic hocus-pocus ably orchestrated the cacophony of visitors. She ran the household alone. She didn't have any hired help. Amid the animated informality, family life thrived.

Becky stood 5'3" in heels. She was a heavyset woman with a round face, blue-green eyes, and a lovely olive complexion that her children inherited. Becky and Abe had six children. A little girl and boy died in infancy. Helen, the oldest of the four girls, was called Kenny. Dorothy, the second girl, was nicknamed Dubbie. As the family grew, the odd nicknames reinforced the inseverable ties among the girls and their parents. Esther was not only Eppie, she was also Eppela. Becky referred to her older twin daughter as "Eppela with the *kepela*." (*Kepela* is Yiddish for "little head.") Pauline was Popo and Pesheh. Abe wasn't called Abe by his family, or even Father or Dad—he was always A.B. To an outsider, the names they called one another might have sounded dumb. But to them, the names confirmed their intimacy and their affection.

Becky often depended on her older daughters to take care of the twins. She was prone to bouts of illness that left her unable to manage the affairs of the household, let alone supervise the activities of two spirited little girls. Helen was entrusted with watching over the twins.

Becky distanced herself from the twins in other ways too. She shunned physical displays of affection. In addition, communication with her children was limited to the routine. Eppie says, "Actually, I don't remember any conversations with my mother." Abe, on the other hand, drew the twins to him and sat one on each knee while they pinched him all over and mussed up his hair.

By the time the twins were in high school, both Helen and Dorothy had married. Helen, a talented pianist, attended the Goodman Theater School in Chicago and was swept away by David Brodkey to Omaha, where his family owned a jewelry store. Dorothy settled closer to home with Morey Rubin. The age difference between Eppie and Popo and their older sisters stemmed any jealousies that might have sprouted over the pampering given the twins. It was a loving family atmosphere. Abe and Becky truly adored each other. Popo describes her childhood as being "rich with love. We never heard our mother call our father Abraham. And he never addressed her as Rebecca. It was always Darling, Sweetheart, or Dear."

From the time of their birth, the twins were treated exactly alike by their doting parents. From their transposed names, Esther Pauline and Pauline Esther, to their shared baby bottles, they were treated as two halves of a whole, rather than two daughters with distinct personalities and interests who happened to look alike.

Dressing twin children identically was a popular pastime for many parents of that era. In the Friedman household it was a preoccupation. The stylish clothes each twin wore were not designated as belonging to Eppie or to Popo but rather to the twins.

After they outgrew adjoining cribs, the two little girls with short jet-black hair and bangs shared not only a bedroom but a bed. Thereafter, from their toddler months through their adolescence and until they married, the twins slept side by side, often with their arms wrapped around each other. Popo recalls, "When we were thirteen our parents got us twin beds. Know what we did? We put a violin case in her bed, covered it up, and the two of us slept in mine. By fifteen, it got doggone crowded in there." It is a tender reminder to both Eppie and Popo of how much they depended on each other. The extent of the twins' bonding at that early age persists to this day. Popo continues, "When we are together we still sleep curled up in each other's arms like we always did. We talk and laugh all night."

Parents today are advised to give twins dissimilar names and separate bedrooms, to refrain from dressing them alike and to take photographs of them separately. In addition, twins are now often encouraged to make different choices about friends, toys, and play activities. Instead, Eppie and Popo were encouraged to look, act, and think alike. When the twins were enrolled in school, Abe and Becky insisted that they be placed in the same classes, develop the same hobbies, and cultivate the same friendships. Eppie recalls the pressure they felt to conform as twins, even in trivial matters. "I remember the sense of guilt I suffered when, at the age of eleven, I screwed up the courage to express a preference for Shredded Wheat over Puffed Rice. I had been brought up to feel that everything with twins should be alike."

Enlightened teachers recommended they be separated in their second year at North Central Junior High School. Eppie and Popo complained to the principal, declaring they'd "rather die" than be apart. "We cried all day," says Popo. A compromise was worked out involving different homerooms but some of the same classes. When Popo was elected president of her homeroom, it marked the first time either twin remembers one receiving recognition the other didn't. Eppie says, "I think we secretly enjoyed it, but to have admitted as much would have been traitorous."

It was Eppie who first attempted to authenticate her own existence apart from her twin. Perhaps because Popo excelled at the activities they both took part in, Eppie sought ways to distinguish herself. Constrained to join Popo in violin lessons, Eppie was clever enough to compensate for her lack of musical talent by having Popo take lessons for her. Later, in high school, Eppie would have liked to become active in debating and writing clubs, but she wasn't ready to go it alone. Eppie talked Popo into joining her in their first attempt at journalism, a junior high school gossip column titled "North Junior Breeze." She says, "I loved to write, I loved to talk. . . . But it wasn't until many years later that I was able to break up the vaudeville act and function as a whole person." While Eppie, as an adult, has referred to the difficulties of being raised an identical twin, Popo has never indicated that she found twinhood disturbing. "Being a twin was wonderful," she says.

The twin act received even more reinforcement at home. Abe was delighted both girls took violin lessons. With the slightest provocation the twins could be counted on to entertain houseguests. Popo says, "We memorized nearly every song the Andrews Sisters had recorded and meticulously imitated their style and arrangements. And as if that weren't enough, we also played the violin!"

The constant emphasis on appearance at home and in public would serve them well once the twins achieved wider recognition. "We were so used to being stared at as children," Eppie observes, "that being celebrities has never seemed any different." The twins would get their larger audience later on. In the meantime, they'd have to settle for Central High, a mere five blocks from home.

By the time they entered Central High in 1932, the twins had shed the childhood pudginess that had rounded out their faces and hid their prominent and distinctively shaped noses and cheeks. Their dimples were more pronounced, and their soft black hair, worn somewhat longer, set off their flawless olive complexions. The twins' striking good looks were the kind that relied on dazzle and expression but under closer examination didn't entirely hold up. Pulling back for a long view, a photographer might have said the package was of ideal proportions. Both twins move with an almost feline gracefulness. But moving in for a close-up, one might notice that the mouths were slightly crooked, the noses a bit large, the chins a trifle weak.

Classmates remember the twins as attractive and popular. Twins weren't that much of a big deal in Sioux City anyway—there were ten sets of twins in high school at the same time as the Friedman girls, with seven sets more in junior high. Sioux City teens had grown adept at differentiating twins from each other.

Popo was regarded as the leader of the two, as well as being the wittier and more high-spirited, but not necessarily the more intelligent. "Even in high school you could tell they were going to make something of themselves, just by the way their minds worked," says Levi Jacoby, who was a classmate of the twins in junior high as well as high school and college.

They must have suppressed their gratitude at being separated in junior high school because at Central High, they chose the same subjects and teachers so they could be together again. "We selected every course together, casting ourselves in the roles of Kate and Dupli-Kate," says Eppie. "We were side by side in every class, confusing the teachers, overwhelming the boys, antagonizing the girls, and playing the double exposure for all it was worth."

On their fourteenth birthday, the twins received their first pair of high heels. "Minnie Mouse shoes," Eppie called them, and the black patent-leather pumps were handed over with a jar of Vaseline to keep them bright and shiny. Two years later Becky allowed them to date. Both Eppie and Popo were always interested in sex and boys. Popo had been keeping tabs on Dorothy Dix lovelorn columns for information about sex, but Dorothy Dix had little of value to say on the hazy topic.

Eppie took matters in hand and sent a dime for the mail order pamphlet, Margaret Mae's Twelfth Birthday. She policed the mailbox every day until it arrived, then stuffed it up her sweater sleeve and repaired to a corner of the cellar to read it. Margaret Mae's Twelfth Birthday was a gyp. No surprises. Eppie knew it all already. Becky wasn't any help either. Typical of mothers of that era, Becky viewed basic information on sex and reproduction as unfit for children. With no older brother to nag and Kenny and Dubbie out of the house by the time the twins were all agog over such matters, and with Abe the type of dad who'd likely skirt the issue, the twins had to be more cunning.

The chorus girls who hung around Jackson Street were more than willing to divulge the mysteries of sex to the twins. Eppie vouches for their accuracy. She says, "I learned the facts of life from the girls in the chorus line." To the twins, knowledge of this import was a high-priority intelligence that bore repeating. Next morning before the first bell, the informed siblings appropriated the top slats of bleachers at the high school gym and summoned their classmates. "They always knew everything first," a classmate remembers. "When they told me babies came from between the mother's legs, why, I fell off the curb."

Once the initial shock faded, the girls' interest in sex assumed a conventional posture. "All the nice little Jewish girls in Sioux City got married and had a family," says Eppie. "A woman's role was to raise the babies, keep house, and be a useful and dutiful companion to her husband." Becky certainly fit Eppie's description. It's likely that the twins' early attitude on sex and marriage reflected their mother's homebody status. Both twins have characterized Becky as "unliberated."

Popo claims Becky's message was succinct: "The way to get a boy interested in you is to bone up on what he's interested in." Apparently both Eppie and Popo boned up thoroughly on what interested any boy, Jewish or Christian. High school classmates remember clearly that the twins dated outside their faith. Their recollection, they say, is strengthened by two facts: that many teens of that era were not allowed to date at all, and that Jewish girls who dated Christian boys were especially rare. Eppie and Popo's behavior proved conspicuous and noteworthy.

It's not surprising the twins chose to date Christians. One ex-boyfriend believes the twins went out with him and his friends "just for the shock value." Above all else, Eppie and Popo loved the attention.

Whatever the religion of the boys they dated, both girls abhorred liquor, drugs, and cigarettes. "I liked myself and I had no desire to change my personality," says Eppie. Her friends may have joked about her rigidity and dubbed her Carry Nation, but it shielded her from the type of derision that could besmirch her reputation. It also kept her out of trouble. The twins had good sense even then.

Since naturally they always double-dated—carrying only one purse, "one lipstick, one comb, one set of keys," according to Eppie, "it was a scream"—they realized that their twinhood provided a built-in restraint. When things began to get heavy, Popo says, "Sometimes Eppie would look at me or I would look at her." Apparently a warning look from one to the other was enough to hold their wilder emotions in check.

Although they boast about good grades in school, neither twin was ever honored for academic achievement. In fact, the twins were enrolled in the general curriculum, which included typing and bookkeeping classes as well as some college prep courses. They avoided the more rigorous courses taught in the classics curriculum.

Former high school chums doubt either girl would have been accepted by a top-ranked university. Eppie claims they chose Morningside College on Sioux City's east side because it was close to home. She implies she could have gone to a school like Wellesley, but her parents insisted on the twins living at home. Popo, more realistically, says they "had dreams of going to Northwestern University but were told we couldn't afford it." Popo, unlike Eppie, must've had a secure grasp of the family's financial situation and their own lackluster high school record.

The twins had priorities. They had little ambition beyond doing respectably in school and being popular. But the twins craved acceptance into the selective girls-only social clubs that were all the rage at Central High. Patterned after college sororities, these restrictive social clubs, the kind that have doubtless been outlawed since in every public high school in the United States, set the tone for social life at Central High and added a chummy cachet to school events.

The selection process was simple and primitive. Potential members signed their names on rosters posted for each group. Decisions on acceptance were agreed upon by a specific date, usually early in the school year. On the fateful day, shortly after classes ended, a carload of committee members would pull up to a student's house, and she would personally be invited into the fold.

Jewish kids at Central High knew their chance of belonging to one of the clubs was remote. Still, the well-liked and popular Friedman girls gamely signed their names to the rosters. But even they were not pledged.

Becky comforted them by saying that the other girls were jealous, that the twins' religion had little to do with being blackballed. The twins' self-confidence, self-confidence that bordered on brashness, probably had much to do with their exclusion from the girls-only clubs. The twins expended enormous energy culling the favor of boys. They were masterful at it, alienating their female classmates who were competing for the attention of the same set of boys. Regardless, club acceptance would have been guaranteed had the twins been Christian, and because of their eagerness to grandstand, acceptance would have guaranteed two new club leaders. Perhaps fear of these new leaders and their propensity to bedazzle led to their rejection.

When they splashed onto the Central High social scene, the twins left others in their wake. Becky probably was right. The other girls were envious. The twins may have swamped them once too often, and they weren't going to grant them the opportunity to do it again.

But the experience of not being pledged to a club was painful to the twins. Nearly fifty years later Popo refers to the incident as a "terrible injustice. We were hurt for many, many years." As a young woman, Eppie spent hundreds of hours discussing her early life with her physician and mentor, Dr. Robert Stolar, a man who would later provide much wanted counsel to Eppie and to her daughter, Margo, through both happy and troubled times. Being rejected for a high school sorority because of her Judaism was a distressing memory, she told Stolar.

Eppie and Popo rebounded from the affront. They could commiserate with each other. Wiser counsel may have whispered that social institutions like girls-only clubs are hardly significant enough to get all worked up over. But Eppie and Popo weren't girls who could forgive and forget. To them a dominant style wasn't just a habit, it was a presence that held them accountable. Popularity was an opiate for them. They may have encountered a slippery foothold on the climb to popularity, but it wasn't going to thwart them. With characteristic self-dramatization, the twins told friends that one day they would show their hometown they were as good as anyone else.

Four

"'R obust but choice" is how a Morningside College alumnus describes Eppie and Popo the first day they arrived on campus in 1936. "The two girls were built like a brick outhouse. They showed up in a pair of skunk coats. The black and white stripes advertised them like road signs. The two of them together were pretty startling; they were about as gaudy as you could get. They looked like a pair of angelfish."

If the twins were aiming to be big fish on the twenty-seven-acre Morningside Campus, it's likely they had little competition. The mini-glitzkrieg the fur-clad twins launched could be matched in sartorial excess and unabashed brio by only a handful of other students. The country was just trying to pull itself out of a long and severe Depression. Many families were still struggling. Eppie and Popo were just plain lucky that their father ran a movie house where for a few cents, people could forget their troubles.

Certainly there were sons and daughters of well-to-do parents at the Methodist-affiliated college, but the majority of the nearly 800 students, three-quarters of whom were in-state residents, held down one and sometimes two jobs to meet the $85-a-semester tuition. Being Jewish at a Methodist school also made the twins stand out. Students were expected at chapel services three times a week. Degree requirements left little time to fool around.

The twins were scads more worldly than other coeds. They traveled to California and Florida with their parents on vacations. At home, they'd been exposed to a substratum of the entertainment world and been shown firsthand how to amuse, impress, or surprise. At the fairly staid and conventional, and somewhat drab thirteen city lots of the Morningside campus, they stood out because they chanced being showy, aggressive, and outspoken.

Undoubtedly their hijinks—like patrolling outside the boys' locker room with a loaded camera—provided a refreshing contrast to the demands of academic life. They were oblivious to the wag of tongues that followed them, and all the more popular because of it. Their flashy outfits and dance-hall sociability projected a putative glamour they hoped others would enjoy envying. The twins, in fact, were so well known on campus that they were talked about by succeeding classes of students. "When I got to college," a later graduate said, "They would talk about 'Whew, those Friedman twins!' What one wouldn't think of, the other would."

As in high school, academics took second place to social maneuvering. For convenience in commuting across town, the twins elected to take similar classes. Both of them concede they chose certain classes, including classroom journalism, because the professors were regarded as easy graders. They candidly admit they took teachers, not subjects. Even then, their performance was average. "I was a good student because I knew getting good report cards was the way to please my parents," says Popo. "I avoided subjects that would pull down my grades, subjects like math and science."

Soon after their arrival on campus, the twins submitted a sample gossip column to James Olson, the editor of the *Collegian Reporter,* the school weekly. Olson rated their first effort good enough for publication, and their double byline, "By the Friedman Twins," appeared in subsequent issues under the heading "Campus Rats." Popo says her interest in advice columns came from writing "Campus Rats." She often cites the column as evidence that throughout her life she has served as an "amateur wailing wall without portfolio."

"Campus Rats" tattled on who was eyeing whom at the malt shop or behind the library stacks. A typical column dutifully poked fun at the captain of the football team, the class nerd, and one or two of the more overmotivated coeds on campus. The twins' breathless journalistic approach often resulted in clips like, "B... and C... believe in pitching a little woo where ever and when ever they feel so inclined. . . . So Cupid slapped an arrow on 'em while they were at the dorm and with the aid of the checker board proceeded to take their fun where they found it. If we wanted to start up a good fuss, we could tell them that they had an audience."

Regardless, the gossip column was an impressive debut for the freshman twins. One college journalist placed "Campus Rats" "head and shoulders above anything else that was written on other college campuses." Morningside alumni remember the shock waves the column caused. It was everyone's favorite column, as long as the titillating topics concerned someone else.

In their eagerness to land a story, the twins occasionally demonstrated a lack of discretion and inadvertently politicized the column by creating trouble for fellow students. Though Prohibition had been repealed a few years before, liquor was expressly forbidden to students at church-affiliated Morningside College. The school's undefeated basketball team frequented one Sioux City saloon and often gathered there for a victory celebration. One Saturday night Eppie and Popo sneaked into the nightspot to chronicle the goings-on. That week a "Campus Rats" poem identified the inebriated athletes by name. The poem was "hysterically funny," says a fellow alumnus, "unless you were a basketball player attending a Methodist college on a scholarship."

Eppie and Popo displayed their spunk and resourcefulness at other times, once in a column that never saw print. Abe Friedman, by the time the twins were at Morningside, ran yet another movie house, the Capitol Theater, where "art" films were shown. The randy *Fields of Alicia,* according to a college friend of the twins, "a film about a nudist colony," was being shown. "At that time it was what passed for pornography. So all us college boys, naturally, had to go down and see the damn thing."

The twins sniffed a scoop. One night while the movie was running, they planted themselves in the shadows of the vacant lobby. When the film was over and the audience filed out, Eppie and Popo jotted down the names of the campus moviegoers for their gossip column. Unfortunately for the twins, two of the patrons they saw leaving the theater were James Olson and John Seward, the editor and associate editor of the *Collegian Reporter*. The item was killed.

The star feature columnists often double dated with their editors, Olson and Seward. Eppie's partner was Seward; Popo doubled with Olson. Both were Big Men On Campus, and dating them granted the twins a heightened visibility and an easy acceptance they might otherwise have had to struggle for. Plus, because they were commuter students, they risked being a beat away from what was happening on campus.

"They wanted to be notorious, in a positive sense. We helped them," says Seward now. "They helped us too, because it protected us from dating girls who would have cost us money." Not that Olson and Seward were cheapskates, but certainly the means to pick up their share of the bill was an asset for the twins during the Depression years.

Seward recalls going Dutch with Eppie to dances and to movies. If the dance or show ran late and the streetcar stopped running, she needed only to call the downtown garage, and a driver would bring the Friedman car round to drop the twins at home and their dates back at school. Having a car at their disposal was a big deal. Few other kids had a car, much less a driver.

Sometimes Eppie and Popo would confuse Seward and Olson by pretending they were each the other twin, continuing the trick they began in high school. One of Popo's other dates studied the sisters, trying to spot a physical difference between the girls. Finally he noticed a brown discoloration, not even so distinguishable as a mole, on Popo's neck. From then on, as far as he was concerned, they were no longer identical.

Seward and Olson weren't the only boys taken by the twins. John Gruenberg, who lived in Philadelphia, met them in 1934 at a Lake Okaboje resort owned by his uncle, and Abe Friedman's business associate, Arthur Sanford. "I was nuts about Popo," says Gruenberg. "She was my first love."

The summer romance over, Popo and Gruenberg maintained contact through occasional visits and frequent letters. When Gruenberg got to Dickinson College, in Carlisle, Pennsylvania, he invited the twins to the junior prom and arranged for a fraternity brother from Columbia University to escort Eppie.

"They took the campus by storm," recalls Gruenberg. "People didn't come to a junior prom from the Midwest very often." That Saturday the foursome left for Philadelphia, and by Monday they were in New York, the twins at the Barbizon, the men at the New Yorker. Says Gruenberg, "At the Barbizon, we couldn't get any farther than the front door.

"Everything was very proper in those days. No hanky-panky, no sexual contact." Despite the times, Gruenberg says Popo was no prude. "I was pretty much in awe of Popo, anyway. I can look back now and see she gave me plenty of openings. But I didn't get the message."

Whatever message Gruenberg was getting, Popo had good reason to temper the relationship and keep it uncomplicated. She already had someone else on her mind. She was getting serious about a long-distance relationship with a young man at the University of Minnesota. Not only was he interested in her, he was eminently eligible.

Though she sometimes doesn't like to admit it, Popo met her future husband thanks to Eppie. Henry Ginsburg, a young man from Sioux City, invited Eppie to a Sigma Alpha Mu dance at the University of Minnesota. Obviously, one twin wasn't going to an out-of-state dance without the other, so Ginsburg asked a frat brother, Mort Phillips, to escort Popo. According to Popo, when she got to Minneapolis, "Morton had decided he didn't want to take me. He said, 'I want to see the girl first.'" Ginsburg got another friend to take Popo to the dance. "Anyway, I went to this dance," Popo continues, "and Morton cut in on me, and I . . . was . . . in . . . heaven. I don't usually do this, but I made a late date with Morton that night."

Why Popo told writer Cliff Jahr a different story in a 1981 *Ladies' Home Journal* interview remains a mystery to her friends. Popo told Jahr that one afternoon while she and Eppie were having their hair done, they saw a man in a brown velvet suit in the barbershop next door. According to Popo, Eppie said, "Oh, that's for me," referring to Phillips, and she retorted, "Uh-uh, that's for me."

One liability of public life is a diminishing memory. Public figures like Eppie or Popo tend to lose track of what they say or don't say. Things that may or may not be true get repeated often enough until even the celebrities themselves have difficulty telling the difference. But it's hard to see how Popo could forget how she met her husband. In spite of her later confusion, it was immediately apparent that Popo wasn't the only girl attracted to Morton Phillips. Eppie fell for him too. After much bickering and harsh words over who was going to make a serious play for Phillips, Popo won out. "He could tell Eppie and me apart right from the start, so I knew he saw something special in me," says Popo.

At first glance it would have been difficult to determine why the twins' feelings for Phillips were so immediate and so intense. He was pleasant, but not outgoing enough to be considered popular. Phillips was somewhat attractive, but he was no matinee idol. Nor was he an athlete or a top student. But Phillips had one profoundly special feature about him that attracted women. By Depression standards, Phillips was very rich. Heir to a multi-million-dollar liquor fortune, he was a top-notch catch for any middle-class girl.

Abe and Becky, jubilant over Popo's prospects for marriage, happily encouraged her long-distance romance. Allowing their daughters to shuttle between Sioux City and Minneapolis was certainly permissive by prevailing standards, but the prize was princely enough. After a three-year courtship, Popo and Mort Phillips were engaged.

Popo's engagement marked the first sour note in the lifelong duet she and Eppie carefully maintained. Popo was in ascendance, leaving Eppie for marriage and in effect abandoning her twin to life alone with Mom and Pop in Sioux City. Eppie was distraught not only over losing her twin, but also that Popo had made out so well in the marriage stakes. Popo was not simply upstaging Eppie, she was upstaging her in grand style. Jealousy, one of the more revealing emotions, prompted the restless Eppie to act and act fast. H. R. Rabinowitz, rabbi of the Friedmans' synagogue, recalls the entire congregation tittered when they heard Eppie declare that she too would find a husband so that she and Popo could have a double ceremony. They couldn't marry the same man, but at least they'd get married at the same time.

On a winter trip with her parents to southern California during her junior year at Morningside, Eppie met Lewis Dreyer, a law student at UCLA. Dreyer fit the bill admirably. Smart and ambitious, he'd make a splendid husband, and besides, his father, David Dreyer, who was a vice president at RKO Pictures, had sufficient prestige to compare adequately with anyone the Phillips family could put forward. After a brief courtship, Abe and Becky announced Eppie and Dreyer's engagement. To no one's surprise, least of all Rabbi Rabinowitz, who'd heard that Eppie herself had done the proposing, there'd be a double wedding after all.

Five

T hough an indulgent father had given Popo luxuries few other women her age enjoyed during the Depression, and she had come to appreciate, even expect some measure of luxury, Popo was not fully prepared for marrying into the wealthiest Jewish family in her future husband's home state of Minnesota.

Today, Popo proudly states that her husband is a successful businessman, but she rarely even hints at the astonishing riches of his family. "A staggering fortune" is the summary of one financial expert. "The Phillipses are today believed to be one of the country's wealthiest families."

The Phillips fortune is based on liquor. The official story begins with an afternoon newspaper route. Jay Phillips, Popo's future father-in-law, who was born in Minsk, Russia, in 1898, was only two years old when he and his brother were brought to the United States by their father and mother, Ed and Rose Phillips. At the age of seven Jay acquired a newspaper route in the small Midwestern town of Manitowoc, Wisconsin, which the family had adopted as home.

Jay and his younger brother Lewis worked diligently and seven years later expanded the market to include magazines. They saved as much of the earnings as they could, and when they learned that their boss was putting his distributorship up for sale, the boys talked their father into making an offer along with two new partners, his teenage sons. On April 13, 1912, Ed Phillips and Sons was established. The distributorship sold out-of-town newspapers and magazines in Manitowoc, and, two years later, candy, cigars, tobacco, and other specialty items were added.

During the twenties, the brothers set about refining the new franchise system of distribution. By 1923 Jay and Lew had moved to Eau Claire to expand their distributorship to northwestern Wisconsin and eastern Minnesota while younger brother Henry opened an office in Wausau. But megamoney isn't made wholesaling candy and cigars.

Newspaper accounts of the Phillips family's rise to prominence state that with the repeal of Prohibition in 1933, Ed Phillips and Sons, reluctantly at first, made the decision to enter the liquor business. "I knew nothing about liquor, its quality or its marketing," Jay Phillips said. "It looked like a hit-or-miss proposition." In due course, despite Jay's somewhat naïve misgivings, the firm opportunely contracted with the Hiram Walker Company, one of the four big distillers at the time, and received its first shipment of Canadian whiskey in 1933.

In 1935, Jay moved to Minneapolis to oversee the family's new business. When Jay's son Mort married Popo Friedman four years later, Ed Phillips and Sons had not only expanded into the largest independent wholesale liquor distributor in the country but had also begun to sell its own line of less expensive booze under the Phillips label.

Having excess millions by the early forties, Ed Phillips and Sons began buying into other companies. Following the death of the head of the National Pressure Cooker Company in 1942, Jay and Lew were approached by Eau Claire business leaders who feared that an out-of-town buyer would move the company's operations out of Eau Claire and create significant unemployment in the community. The brothers responded to the appeal and bought the pots-and-pans firm. The company was renamed National Presto Industries, and, in addition to manufacturing household appliances, it began to produce a panoply of defense items under government contract. In 1944, Mort Phillips became executive vice president.

Also in 1944, Jay Phillips, with his money and that of family members, established the Phillips Foundation, a philanthropic organization. Only three years before, Lewis Phillips had established L. E. Phillips Charities. With assets around $18 million, L. E. Phillips Charities has extensively funded medical research and health causes in northwestern Wisconsin. And the Phillips Foundation, with assets of more than $40 million, today ranks among the nation's top 200 philanthropic organizations.

Popo and Mort's wedding was set for July 2, 1939, two days before her twenty-first birthday. She was marrying into a family concerned with doing good, garnering esteem and fair repute, and correctly fulfilling a public role. Popo's life was about to change and change dramatically. She was about to navigate her way through a level of society she hadn't yet encountered. But Popo was poised for action.

Despite her youth, she possessed the sangfroid and self-assurance to surmount any obstacles barring her way. Living up to the demanding standards of the Phillipses would be challenging. If Popo were to make a few mistakes along the way, so be it. To help her maintain equilibrium, she could rely on money and love. When Popo speaks, later on, of whether she married for love or for money, the unflappable and upfront Mrs. Morton Phillips, nee Friedman, candidly admits, "I married for both."

Six

$\mathcal{E}$ sther Mirkin was going to make sure just everyone in Sioux City knew about her delightful twin cousins Eppie and Popo. That included Jules Lederer, the blond salesman Esther worked with at the T. S. Martin department store.

Lederer, handsome, affable, and single, had just moved to Sioux City from Lansing, Michigan. The salesclerk job at T. S. Martin was a step up from the one at J. W. Knapp, and before that, Herpolsheimers in Grand Rapids. Twenty-one-year-old Jules, aside from being bright, was also ambitious. He must have listened attentively to Esther's chatter about how her twin cousins not only were good-looking, but also how their family was comfortably well off. When Eppie and Popo came shopping for bridal veils, it was Lederer who escorted them through the millinery department.

While Eppie was trying on veils, Jules took Popo aside. He confided that he was attracted to Eppie and would like to take her to a Hadassah dance. But he was reluctant to ask Eppie out because she was engaged. Popo gave Lederer a quick lesson in moral algebra.

"Ask her anyhow," Popo told him. "All she can say is no."
So he did.

"You're the first girl I ever met that I wanted to marry," Jules said to Eppie. "And you're coming in to buy a wedding veil."

Eppie was by no means offended by Lederer's invitation. "Oh, I like this fellow!" Popo remembers Eppie telling her.

"I told Eppie she ought to go," says Popo. "I didn't approve of the other fellow, and I knew Eppie didn't love him. 'You have no business being married if somebody else can still look good to you,'" she recalls advising her twin.

Cousin Esther, the inveterate matchmaker, didn't give up easily either. She told Becky about Jules Lederer and how he was alone in Sioux City and had been casually dating some local Jewish girls. It wasn't until Becky met "this nice Jewish boy," and invited him to Jackson Street for a family dinner, that Eppie began to give in to Jules's advances.

Eppie contends it wasn't Popo but her father who encouraged her to reconsider her hasty betrothal to Lewis Dreyer. Speaking of Popo, Eppie says, "She puts herself in this role where she's instructing me, which is not really the case at all. She was pretty involved in her own Minneapolis situation . . . and actually it was my father who made the difference."

At dinner, Abe wasted no time in establishing Jules's suitability. Although Eppie's date claimed to be Jewish, Abe decided to test him. "Say something in Yiddish," he ordered.

"I vanna go for a valk," Jules responded.

Abe smiled. The kid had pluck.

Jules was indeed charming, and he had a puppydog earnestness Eppie found captivating. But most of all, she was taken by his appearance.

"Just look at that nose, that beautiful nose," Eppie exclaimed later, after the Hadassah dance.

She not only admired his straight nose, but his sandy-hued hair as well. Eppie was completely taken by Jules's non-Jewish appearance. Her ambivalence about her own looks and large nose perhaps led her to dwell on Jules's facial features. Had Eppie chosen to be critical of Jules's appearance, she might have complained about his height. At 5'3", Jules was only a tad more than an inch taller than Eppie, an advantage he immediately lost when she wore high heels.

Shortly after her first date with Jules, Eppie realized she'd made a mistake in getting engaged to Dreyer. She didn't love Lewis Dreyer and couldn't marry him. "Better now than later," Abe remarked to Becky when he was told of the sudden change in his daughter's plans. The wedding announcements had already been posted in the Sioux City papers, and the diamond on Eppie's finger sparkled as brightly as ever. But reassured by her father's reaction, Eppie sent the ring and her apologies back to Dreyer.

Broken engagements don't demand a long period of mourning. Jules found it politic to wait only a few weeks before he asked Eppie. The double wedding was barely cancelled before it was rescheduled for the same day, July 2.

From a purely economic standpoint, Jules Lederer compared poorly with Morton Phillips as a prospective bridegroom. Unlike Mort, Jules didn't come from a wealthy family. Whatever money he had, he earned.

Jules was born on November 15, 1917, in Detroit, Michigan, the third of seven children. His parents, Morris and Gustie, had come to America from Romania, by way of England. Morris, like Abe Friedman, started out as a peddler, not of chickens, but of notions like women's aprons, ribbon and buttons, and other sewing supplies. By the time he was old enough to carry a sample case, Jules accompanied his dad on his sales trips.

Circumstances for the Lederer family were abruptly altered in 1930 when the car Morris was driving crumpled under the wheels of a train at a grade crossing in Jackson, Michigan. Their father's death at the age of forty-nine left the Lederers without a steady source of income. For a time, the family relied on government assistance. Then Jules took over.

"My formal education ended in the tenth grade as a result of my father's death during the Depression," Jules says. Along with delivering newspapers with sister Ruthie, Jules managed to find a job as a stockboy at Kerns department store in downtown Detroit.

He also swept floors and ran the freight elevator. A year later, at seventeen, Jules was living at the YMCA in Grand Rapids, and sending most of his weekly salary home to Gustie. As Jules modestly explains, "I helped to support my family during the years that followed, primarily in the retail business."

"The boy's got potential," was Abe's verdict when Jules came to dinner at the Friedman house. Eppie thought so too. She knew they'd have little money, but she romanticized the early deprivations they'd share as newlyweds. Eppie was confident that scrimping would make their later successes more enjoyable.

In the Friedman household, potential counted a lot. Abe undoubtedly saw some of himself in his future son-in-law. By the young age of twenty-one, Jules had amply demonstrated his mettle. He was deserving of respect.

Chances are both twins were virgins when they journeyed together down the aisle of Shaare Zion synagogue. Admittedly they both were teases and flirted with many boys in high school and at Morningside, but Becky was a sobering influence. The traditional middle-class respectability she drummed into them probably kept them from going all the way, at least before they were engaged.

It's likely both Jules and Mort were virgins too. Mort wasn't exactly a young man about town in Minneapolis. The Sigma Alpha Mu fraternity at the University of Minnesota was hardly a citadel of excess advocating self-indulgence and indiscriminate sex. If it had been, wholesome Popo wouldn't have been interested in dating one of its frat brothers.

A handsome but underprivileged young man like Jules, looking to better himself, didn't want to get the wrong reputation, especially in a small town like Sioux City. The thirties had their share of promiscuous women, but certainly not the marrying kind Jules was looking for.

Big sister Helen orchestrated the event. She was entrusted with the wedding plans because she could be counted on to do the wedding right.

Shirley Rabinowitz Givot, the daughter of Rabbi Rabinowitz and then six years old, witnessed the backstage preparations preceding the ceremony. "They didn't see me," she says, "but I was standing on the landing going down by the restroom. I'll never forget the sight." Popo and Eppie were dressing each other, rearranging their lace-edged tulle veils and tiny hats embroidered with seed pearls. "It left such an impression on me. They were running downstairs, real excited, talking, giggling, laughing. I was wishing I were them."

Dolled up in purest white, in identical gowns of "medieval inspiration," according to the *Sioux City Journal,* and carrying heart-shaped satin muffs, the twins reigned radiantly amid a swirl of Cézanne green, sapphire yellow, cloud blue, ceramic rose, lilac chiffon, and maize organza. The parade of bridesmaids in their pastel gowns looked like so many hothouse flowers lined up to bloom in the intense July heat.

The high estrogen fantasy reached a feverish pitch with the twin brides' appearance at the head of the central aisle, a beaming Abe sandwiched between them. Guests nearly swooned as the Friedman twins slowly made their way to the nuptial canopy. Just shy of 200 guests stood pew-to-pew in the gladiolus- and adiantum-festooned synagogue, almost overtaxing the capacity of Shaare Zion. Outside, oglers and onlookers and shutterbugs swarmed cheek by jowl in the sweltering summer sun, waiting to glimpse or photograph the dazzling twin brides. Police on horseback kept the crowd under control.

Twenty-eight people made up the wedding party, with two maids of honor, big sisters Kenny and Dubbie as matrons of honor, two groomsmen, seven bridesmaids, and seven ushers followed by Mort's parents, Gustie Lederer and her escort, then Abe with Eppie and Popo and Becky with Franz Schwartz, Mort's groomsman from Minneapolis. Pierce Wall, a good friend of the Friedmans and a talented organist, played the processional. Surprisingly, even with a cast of twenty-eight, the ceremony started on schedule, promptly at four o'clock. Rabbi Rabinowitz along with Rabbi T. N. Lewis officiated from the palm-banked pulpit. Since every aspect of the marriage rites had to be repeated for the very conservative double ceremony, the congregation's first double wedding was lengthy.

Few of the guests who witnessed the wedding have forgotten the lavish event. While being shepherded from Shaare Zion to the six o'clock dinner at the Martin Hotel, guests could be heard to exclaim that the festive affair rated five stars. More than 700 friends and relatives, along with many of Abe's business associates, attended the 8:30 reception to offer a toast to the newlyweds and eat cake. The young fogies danced until midnight. One elated but exhausted guest remarked, "Even for a slightly theatrical family, the Friedmans outdid themselves."

Still refusing to be separated, the twins and their husbands left for a double honeymoon. After a two-week journey to Chicago; Breezy Point, Minnesota; Lake Louise, Banff, and other Canadian destinations, Popo and Mort returned to Minneapolis. Unfortunately for Eppie, Jules ran out of money in Chicago, and the Lederers were forced to part company with the better-fixed Phillipses. Both twins swiftly realized that for the first time in their lives, the world each would move through would be vastly different.

Popo Phillips went home to Minneapolis as the wife of a young executive being groomed to take over his family's lucrative liquor business. She was embarking on a life of almost unlimited privilege. Eppie returned with Jules to Sioux City to a one-bedroom apartment and $300 in debt. She was entering a world circumscribed by financial concerns. For Eppie, the end of the honeymoon came quickly.

Seven

Neither twin returned to college after marriage. Dropping out of Morningside in their junior year ended their formal education. The transition from student to homemaker involved many adjustments, not the least of which was setting up a household. Both twins hadn't lived anywhere but in their parents' house. When their parents weren't around, their older sisters took care of them. They didn't know anything about running a household. Neither newlywed was equipped to juggle academics with marriage.

Popo, of course, would have been more able to resume academic life. The Phillipses certainly could afford the tuition on top of all the hired help that establishing and running a household would have required. But, significantly, it's Eppie who later expressed regret at not having gone back to school. "If I had it to do over again," she says, "I'd finish college first."

If Eppie had wanted to go back to school, surely Abe and Becky would have paid the tuition. But it's questionable whether Jules would have allowed his wife to accept money from her parents. Marriage is, after all, one of the traditional ways a daughter breaks free of her parents. Then again, Jules, who had made it only to the tenth grade, might have felt uneasy about a wife far more educated than he.

Eppie, too, may have been reluctant to outdistance her husband scholastically. She may have sensed that Jules was touchy about his decided lack of higher learning. Later, when the self-taught Jules became a successful businessman, he said, "I believe it when I tell people, 'Don't go to college . . . use your brains, your guts, your intuition.' "

Jules used every ounce of brains, guts, and intuition he possessed to make his millinery sales job a success. Eppie provided the encouragement and support Jules needed to carry on when he became frustrated. When advancement at the store seemed blocked, or a customer he'd dealt with had proved particularly nettlesome, Eppie shifted into high nurture. "I was never a dumb kid," Eppie recalls. "I was tuned in. I didn't expect marriage to be paradise. I always knew that it took work." As far as Jules's career was concerned, the two of them were a team. They both believed in the virtues of perseverance and hard work.

To call the Lederers middle class would be stretching their precarious social status. In 1940, 4 million Americans were unemployed, and 7.5 million others were earning less than the legal minimum wage of forty cents an hour. The average work week was forty-eight hours or longer. At best, Jules's meager $35-a-week salary—$10 of which was sent to his mother, who still had school-age children to raise—placed him and Eppie only a step ahead of the poverty line.

Eppie did her own housework and handled a skimpy household budget. They had few comforts. "In the beginning of my married life, I lived with no luxuries at all," says Eppie. "We had no extra money for anything." Luckily, the two-room apartment Eppie and Jules rented at the Bellevue was the right price, if small. The accommodations became even more cramped with the arrival of baby Margo in March 1940, nine months after their wedding.

Where Jules went, Eppie and Margo followed. Every time Jules sensed an opportunity to make a few more dollars, the Lederers packed up and moved. They hustled off to St. Louis, and back to Sioux City, then to New Orleans and Milwaukee, from one shabby apartment to another. Each move meant more work for Jules, and longer hours. "I saw more of a moving van than I saw of my husband," Eppie confesses.

Popo managed to keep track of her twin's meanderings. She faithfully sent Eppie glossy postcards from places like Hawaii and Palm Springs. While she read the sisterly messages, Eppie says, "I vegetated and took care of the baby."

The first peacetime draft in American history was instituted in October 1940. All men between the ages of twenty-one and thirty-five had to register with their local boards and were assigned a draft number. Jules dutifully signed up. With the Japanese bombing of Pearl Harbor on December 7, 1941, life for all Americans changed dramatically.

Wartime housing was scarce. Because of the Lederers' limited means, their living quarters were often drab little cubicles in overcrowded apartment buildings. Life on Jackson Street may not have been luxurious, but life on the road with Jules and an infant daughter was certainly far from what Eppie was accustomed to. One of Eppie's more difficult adjustments came in having to share a bathroom with other families. That dreary, cramped apartment seemed even more confining as Margo's diapers piled up, waiting their turn in the community toilet.

While Eppie stared at dingy walls with only a toddler for companionship, Jules resolutely set out each day, energetically selling ladies' hats for as many hours as the city was awake. Eppie began to question how marriage could make a woman feel so isolated, and so alone. But she was capable of enduring self-sacrifice because she knew that her husband was struggling too. "Doing without, together, never hurt anyone," Eppie later philosophized. "Now, some women can't take it. They are envious of other people and resentful—and their husbands can't help but feel that resentment."

By 1942, Jules's draft number hadn't been called, and he accepted a sales job at Marx Isaacs in New Orleans. Eppie found a small house on St. Charles Avenue. For the first time in her marriage, Eppie had enough time and space to relax. But she soon found sitting home playing mah-jongg or devising makework projects, like decoratively gluing matchbook covers to a cardboard mat, as tedious as housekeeping.

Millions of women were convinced to join the war effort. Many took the paying jobs of men who had gone off to fight. Looking back, Eppie readily sees that World War II had a significant impact on the options available to women. "When the men went off to war, what was the woman?" she asks. "Rosie the Riveter. Women went into factories, they went into offices, they took men's jobs. They had to in order to keep the economy going. This changed everything. Women never went back." But the vast majority of married women served as unpaid volunteers. Eppie at first tried knitting socks for the American Red Cross but was told that she could better serve the war effort by giving her knitting to the Germans.

Eppie made better use of her talents and skills volunteering as a Gray Lady at La Garde Naval Hospital. Her work as a nurse's aide provided a much-needed outlet from the duties of child rearing and housekeeping. Eppie, sociable and outgoing, enjoyed her volunteer work at the hospital. She especially enjoyed meeting people.

Before long, Eppie made friends with Dr. Robert Stolar, a dermatologist who headed one of the wards at La Garde. Stolar, tall, slim, and patrician-looking, was unlike anyone Eppie had ever met. When he spoke, he spoke slowly and with quiet authority. Despite his learned demeanor and stately manner, he could be warm and engaging. Even today, some women who meet Stolar find his courtly manner flattering, and undeniable evidence of their attractiveness to him.

Eager to introduce Stolar to Jules, and concerned that the unmarried doctor needed some exposure to family life, Eppie invited him home to dinner. Although the night happened to be Passover, the invitation hadn't been extended because it was a Jewish holiday. Eppie had assumed Stolar wasn't Jewish. In any case, she and Jules rarely observed Jewish rituals.

During the course of the evening, after Stolar spoke a few words of Yiddish, Eppie realized she had mistaken him for a Christian possibly because of her own stereotyped attitude about fellow Jews. Stolar recalls Eppie's thinking he "didn't behave or act like a Jew" because he was dignified and reserved. In fact, Eppie had met few people like Stolar of any religious or ethnic background.

When Eppie took Stolar to see her two-year-old daughter, Margo stood up in her crib and promptly dropped her pajama bottoms. She was a clown. Embarrassed by her daughter's behavior, Eppie scolded her. Stolar felt that Eppie's reprimand was much too severe, and perhaps a consequence of her own self-consciousness at having a doctor in her home for the first time. He cautioned her that Margo might misunderstand and connect nudity with shame or disgrace.

Despite Stolar's being only a few years older than Eppie, she earnestly accepted the counsel of her new acquaintance, whose cosmopolitan manner and education she held in high esteem. Stolar was beginning to make a strong impression on Eppie. Having known him only for a short time, Eppie still may have apprehended that this man would remain a trusted friend for the rest of her life. Until now, twin sister Popo was the only person whose unsolicited advice she'd listened to and followed. Stolar was beginning to take over the role that Popo previously had played in Eppie's life. In fact, Stolar eventually befriended Popo too.

Although Stolar and her other new friends thought she was attractive, Eppie believed that the shape of her nose set her apart. She believed that her nose barred her from those social circles in New Orleans she aspired to join. Stolar explains, "Eppie wanted to have a straight nose because the people around her had straight noses. This characterizes her." In pursuit of the classic appearance she yearned for, Eppie scraped together enough money for what is ingloriously referred to as a nose job.

Eppie's plastic surgery was a dramatic and uncommon undertaking for a young wife and mother of the early forties. It was also an extravagance, in light of the Lederers' financial condition. Eppie and Popo had discussed their noses with each other, and Popo was all set to go ahead and have it done too, until Mort nixed the idea. "He liked me the way I was," she blithely states.

Eppie's elective surgery not only eliminated the physical manifestation of her ethnic background, it also made her look different from Popo. The twins, identical in appearance for twenty-five years, were identical no longer. The original square Jewish lady from Sioux City, Iowa, didn't look so Jewish anymore.

Eppie's break from identical twinhood probably didn't startle Popo all that much. In many ways, it lacked the element of surprise. Their marriages had started them on different paths. As Popo tells it, they were so close for twenty years that they didn't sleep apart until their wedding night. Just living in different places was a big change for them. Though their physical separation clouded the early years of marriage for the twins, they weren't lost without each other.

Letters rocketed back and forth chronicling this exciting new phase of their lives. The sisters missed sharing their feelings with their parents, so they wrote them often at their new apartment. Abe and Becky had sold the house at 1722 Jackson Street when the twins married and moved three blocks north.

"I got tremendous satisfaction by writing a letter to my parents every day that they lived. And I didn't miss a day," says Popo. Evidently Abe and Becky treasured Popo's letters, for when the twins went back to Sioux City after both their parents died, Popo found the letters neatly bundled and tied with twine, in the order in which they'd received them.

Each bride was beginning to be influenced by her husband's personality. And Jules Lederer and Morton Phillips were vastly different men. Popo quickly acquired a veneer of monied graciousness. But with the country-club suavity came the weariness of too much leisure time and too much unconstructive activity.

"When I got married at twenty-one it never entered my head to be anything but a wife. I played golf and bridge and had lunch with the girls," Popo remembers. "I was bored out of my gourd."

The arrival of daughter Jeannie in 1942 was a joyous and welcome change for Popo. There were baby clothes and baby toys to buy, and a room to redecorate as a nursery. Phillips relatives opened savings accounts for Jeannie and gave her war bonds. Abe and Becky were a receptive audience for stories of their new granddaughter. But soon, Popo's letters home and to Eppie were once again interspersed with other, graver matters, such as the plight of Jews in Europe, and the realities of war.

Popo's anxiety about the war intensified when Mort was drafted into the U.S. Army. By 1944, many of the men who formerly were granted deferments because they were farmers or fathers were called to duty. The war was lasting longer than anyone had anticipated. Manpower was becoming scarcer. Draft-age eligibility was raised to sixty-five, although it still was rare for a man over thirty-six to be called.

Jules was drafted at about the same time as Mort. Jules wanted to train to be an aircraft pilot but was rejected by the Air Force because he was too short. Once again, Eppie packed for her husband, but this time the move was to Army Camp in Little Rock, Arkansas. It wasn't quite the next financial move upward Jules or Eppie had anticipated. After a tearful good-bye, Eppie returned to Sioux City with Margo.

Through an incredible coincidence, Privates Phillips and Lederer were assigned to the same infantry unit at Camp Robinson. Even if before they were just cordial because they were in-laws, Mort and Jules soon became close friends.

A phone call from Sioux City temporarily interrupted their tour of duty. Becky had suffered a cerebral hemorrhage. She was dead. Eppie was with her mother when she died, and Popo came rushing back to Sioux City as soon as she got the phone call. Mort and Jules were granted emergency leave to attend the funeral.

Becky's unexpected death at the age of fifty-six greatly affected Eppie and Popo. If geography had separated them, and marriage had changed them, it wasn't apparent. Becky was the first person close to them who had died. They were wrapped up in their grief, and with each other. They were worried about Abe, wondering how they could help him make the transition from husband to widower. They helped him move out of his second-story flat into the Sioux apartment hotel downtown. For the first time since their double honeymoon, both Mort and Jules vividly witnessed how much their wives depended on and needed each other.

When they got out of the Army in 1945, Mort offered Jules a job selling pots and pans in Los Angeles for a Phillips-owned company called Guardian Service. The job certainly wasn't a prestigious new start for an interrupted career, but with the end of the war and the large numbers of servicemen returning to civilian life, unemployment soared. Jules gratefully accepted Mort's generous offer. He was confident he could do well.

In his first car, a two-door olive Mercury he lovingly dubbed the Green Hornet, Jules peddled the Guardian cookware line. It employed a unique process that cooked food by steam heat. Working nearly seven days a week, as many as fourteen hours a day, Jules bounded door to door demonstrating his wares to housewives by cooking their family dinners.

Housewares were in big demand after the war. Soldiers were reunited with the wives they'd married just before they left home. Couples were starting out anew and starting families. Wives moved out of the factory and back into the kitchen. The need for cookware, coupled with Jules's enthusiasm and natural sales ability, meant lots of business and many sales.

Sometimes the helpers Jules hired to scrub the dirty pots failed to show up, so Eppie pitched in. Up to her elbows in suds in some stranger's kitchen, she'd scrub her husband's demonstration equipment, then return home to cook dinner for her own family and to wash more pots and pans. Referring to her days as a dishwasher, she says, "A lot of women would have resented this, but not me. You see, this was my contribution to Jules's success." Eppie seldom complained. It wasn't her nature. But she was hardly stoic. She may have muttered, under her breath, that Mort could have at least given her husband a job selling toasters.

Mort didn't offer Jules a job out of charity, or just because he was his brother-in-law, though by inducting Jules into the Phillips-owned company, he essentially brought Eppie one step closer to being reunited with Popo. Her twin's presence, he thought, might mitigate Popo's growing ennui.

Mort had seen how much they missed each other when they were reunited at Becky's funeral. There was no mistaking the energy that passed between them. He perhaps reasoned that he'd soon be able to bring the twins together, either by moving out to Los Angeles and one of the family businesses, or by eventually bringing Eppie and Jules back to the Midwest. Mort also knew what a hard worker and good salesman Jules was. He knew that Jules had business savvy and good sense, and concerning women, impeccable taste. After all, Jules had married his wife's twin.

Eight

Mort's brief tenure in the U.S. Army reaffirmed his stature in the Phillips family, especially with old L.E. Uncle Lewis was impressed with Mort, even though his nephew's infantry unit hadn't been anywhere near the front lines. When he got back to Minneapolis from Camp Robinson, the decision had already been made. Mort Phillips would become the new executive vice president of the National Pressure Cooker Company headquartered in Eau Claire, Wisconsin.

Eau Claire wasn't unknown to Mort when he moved there with Popo, Jeannie, and his newborn son, Edward Jay, just a few months old. Mort had spent part of his boyhood in that bustling manufacturing town in the lake region of west central Wisconsin. He had many pleasant memories of the sylvan countryside in northern Wisconsin, and of the rolling hills dotted with dairy farms surrounding Eau Claire.

French for "clear water," Eau Claire in the late eighteenth century was a trading post situated on the Eau Claire River where it flows into the Chippewa. The harnessing of the abundant hydropower brought manufacturers of kitchen appliances, tires, and paper products to Eau Claire. By the close of World War II, Eau

Claire was populated mainly by transplanted defense workers. The town's two major employers were the Gillette Safety Tire Company, today called Uniroyal, and National Presto Industries, formerly called the National Pressure Cooker Company, where Mort's father, Jay, was chairman of the board.

Because of the number of defense workers in Eau Claire, there was a housing shortage that couldn't be immediately resolved even if one's surname was a household word. A series of connecting suites in the Eau Claire Hotel became a temporary home for Mort and family. Overwhelmed by her new status, Popo couldn't help turning the hotel lobby into an extended living room. One year after wartime rationing, while Americans were being told to "use it up, wear it out, make it do or do without," Popo was said to have donned as many as six different outfits and pairs of shoes a day, and head full tilt through the lobby on her way to the hairdresser or the realtor.

Popo's house hunting paid off in the move to a large two-story fieldstone house in a prestigious area just outside of town. She promptly had one of Mort's infantry boots bronzed, ornamented with his keys and dog tags, and displayed it in the living room. The bronzed boot remains one of her prized possessions.

In order to accommodate her large wardrobe, Popo had a mammoth closet built along one side of the house. Huge wall-to-wall sliding glass doors opened on racks of carefully arranged sports outfits, afternoon dresses, suits, evening attire, hats, and other accessories. Popo, of course, loved shoes, especially the kind that are commonly known as hooker heels. Unlike Eppie, she could wear extremely high heels without dwarfing her husband. Popo had wide floor-to-ceiling shelves installed for her cherished and ever-expanding shoe collection.

The Phillipses hired a German governess for Jeannie and Eddie, and a live-in couple who served as cook, housekeeper, and general handyman. A business associate of Mort's learned of Popo's penchant for monkeys and presented her with two. Mort's nickname for his wife was Pete, which had something to do with a Spanish song that ends "with a face like a monkey." David and

Bathsheba, as the simian duo was called, remained only briefly with the Phillipses before they were given away. "I've always loved monkeys," Popo says. "We used to have two real ones, but we had to give them to a zoo. They're just impossible to train. . . . They just wee-wee all over the place."

Married life in Eau Claire was blissful. The Phillipses were and still are an extremely happy and loving couple. In public, they are always touching each other. Popo always speaks of her husband with great affection and love. Their marriage is so secure, she doesn't hesitate to talk about Mort's lovemaking. She says, "He's gentle-gentle, and that's the way he is in bed. Considerate. Very sensual. Completely loving." She adds, "How could you not love a man like that and give him everything you have?"

Jules's sales achievements didn't go unnoticed by the Phillips family. Six months before Mort had been elevated to the executive suite at National Presto Industries, Jules had been made district sales manager of the Guardian line in Chicago. Shortly after Mort settled into his new position at Presto, he offered Jules his first executive job. Within a few weeks of Popo's move to Eau Claire, Eppie was there too, not only as the wife of Jules Lederer, vice president in charge of sales, but also as the twin sister of Popo Phillips, whose husband's family was one of the town's major employers.

At first it went without saying that Mort's offer was the best one Jules had ever had. Jules was good at his job and deserving of the appointment. "We went to Eau Claire," Eppie recalls, "because Jules was the best salesman Presto ever had and because Mort needed somebody solid beside him." Presto managers, however, had their doubts. Jules's entry into the executive ranks caught them off guard, and they soon began asking, "Where'd this guy come from?"

Grace Schute, a friend of both twins, observes that "the feeling was in Eau Claire that Popo had Mort make a job for Eppie's husband." Accustomed to being on equal terms with her twin, that must have been a more difficult perception for Eppie to handle than the difference in their discretionary income.

Eppie and Jules quickly found a house. Fifteen minutes by car from Popo's neighborhood of rolling lawns and majestic shade trees, Eppie's section of town bordered on the outskirts of the working-class town of Altoona. The neighborhood was subdivided into a flat geometric pattern of small, neat houses. The little white house at 1617 Valmont Street, set back only a few yards from the street, had two bedrooms and one bathroom and a back yard the size of a squash court. Tidy aluminum awnings perched over the two windows facing the street, and for the winter months, an aluminum screen door was refitted with storm glass as added protection against the Wisconsin cold and snow.

The contrast between Eppie's and Popo's residences was unmistakable. The Peanut Place, as Eppie aptly named her house, would have been barely large enough to store Popo's clothes. Although Eppie's joking reference to her home reflected a healthy attitude about her lesser means, Popo later claimed that underneath, Eppie was deeply bothered. Popo insists it was her generosity and love of her twin that led Mort to offer Jules an executive job at Presto. "I didn't want a mink coat if she couldn't have one too," Popo says.

The twins were much too aware of the image they projected and the Phillips family's standing in the community to allow real or imagined rifts to surface in public. Eppie enjoyed her lifestyle as a Phillips relation and an executive's wife. She was grateful to her brother-in-law for bringing Jules into a management position. Although Eppie's altered profile made her look a few years younger than her twin, the two women still looked more alike than most sisters and retained many other similarities. Both were always meticulously groomed, with freshly styled hair and beautiful clothes. They were inclined to dress more formally than most other women of the same age and income level.

At every opportunity, Eppie and Popo traveled together to Minneapolis, and via the Chicago and Northwestern Four Hundred to Chicago, so named because the trip took 400 minutes, to have their hair done, to shop, and to escape small-town life. Though they shared beauty appointments, they didn't share hairstyles. Popo stuck with a low-maintenance cut, short and curly, while Eppie indulged in a longer and more wavy hairstyle.

On Chicago's near Northside, operating at Mach 1, Popo would cruise through the swank retailers lining Michigan Avenue's Magnificent Mile with Eppie in tow. Popo always shopped with a tad more intensity than her twin, selecting and buying at a rate that reflected the depth of Mort's pockets. Wired from the day's activities, the twins might hover long enough at The Drake for coffee and cookies before catching the train back to Eau Claire.

"They were both very ambitious, energetic, outgoing, lovely girls," an admirer remarks. The twins were seen as part of Eau Claire society, even if only Popo actually lived the way other people perceived them.

Popo, in her late twenties, slipped easily into a luxurious lifestyle that offered a beautiful home, a doting husband, and abundant amenities. Domestic details were too vexing for active and outgoing Popo. She might bake a devil's-food cake when dinner guests were expected, but other aspects of meal preparation were either very simple or done by others. One friend remarked of both twins, "If they enjoyed cooking or gardening, they certainly deprived themselves of the pleasure." If she wanted or needed something, Popo needed only to ask. Dashing into Demmler's Greenhouse she might leave instructions for the lawn or garden, or at the upholsterer, look over some swatches of new fabrics. On one occasion, Popo called upon a former Presto employee who did odds jobs to travel forty miles just to lay the fires for a dinner party.

Although Jules was making more money than he ever had before, Eppie still was forced to entertain modestly. The dining room of the Peanut Place seated a limited number of guests. Eppie prepared the food and served it herself. But most guests were accustomed to that. The Lederers' style of entertaining was more typical of Eau Claire. Friends were charmed with Eppie's humor and lack of pretension when she warned, "I'm sure this is the first time you've had wieners by candlelight."

Neither hostess drank liquor at her dinner parties. Both women made no secret of their abstention. Even then, Eppie preached about the hazards of drinking, but it would have been impolitic for Popo to carry on about the evils of alcohol. It was no secret in that small town on what the Phillips family wealth was founded.

The Phillips family was near the pinnacle of Eau Claire's upper stratum. The family companies employed a considerable number of people not only in Eau Claire but in the entire upper Midwest. Mort's father and uncle were among the most powerful men in the state, and certainly in town. Popo says of her twin, "Of course in Eau Claire, she was always known as Popo's sister." Other people, however, didn't share that observation, or care to make such fine distinctions. Eau Claire contemporaries believed that both of them represented a way of life that was inextricably identified with ownership of a manufacturing plant, dubbed the "kettle works." Friends and acquaintances firmly state, "They were both Phillips girls."

Dressing up and dining out with their husbands at the Eau Claire Country Club or Austin's White House, a restaurant especially popular with the town's inner circle, was a favored activity. The twins consistently enjoyed taking center stage. It gave both of them the chance to show off the fruits of their plunder from Minneapolis or Chicago. While Eppie might deliberately wear Popo's old red fox stole out of season, Popo might dangle her arm over the back of a chair to flash a new diamond bracelet. In fact, Popo wore jewels in such quantity and of such magnitude that she earned the nickname Sparkle Plenty.

Despite frequent dining out and their fondness for chocolate and other sweets, the twins exercised considerable restraint so they could maintain their enviable figures. The bikini had recently been introduced, and Eppie and Popo intended on being seen in the new fashion. More important, neither twin wanted to be known as the heavier of the two.

Sheltered by their ties to the town's leading family, Popo and Eppie, according to a friend of Eppie's from Eau Claire, "rode roughshod over rules and regulations but got away with it." Wrapped up in themselves, as they had been in Sioux City, they appeared little concerned with how others saw them. On errands in town, if they couldn't find a parking place, they'd double-park. They didn't hesitate at leaving their car for a brief while in the middle of a busy street. Allegedly, Eppie was a far poorer driver than Popo and some say a menace behind the wheel.

Eppie's friend takes credit, but the custodian at the local museum probably more accurately recounts what was troubling about the way Eppie drove. Not only did Eppie speed and drive recklessly through residential areas, according to the man who was also a neighbor of the Lederers, she at times was oblivious to traffic signals and anything beyond the front, rear, or sides of her car. He had many arguments with her about her driving habits, and once, as she roared down an alleyway between their houses, he threw a rake at her windshield and cracked the glass. Eppie never filed charges against him for the damage, he says, because she didn't want him to reveal the extent of her careless driving.

It took little time for their Eau Claire contemporaries to agree with their Sioux City friends that the twins were "flamboyant and aggressive. There wasn't a deliberate bid for attention. They were active, fun people, that's all." Their flirtatious behavior at parties, however, did raise eyebrows. Despite a renewed fascination with sexual conduct, and an eager public that in 1948 sent the Kinsey Report on *Sexual Behavior in the Human Male* to the top of the best-seller list, coquetry within staid Eau Claire was still considered inappropriate. Though the twins, by all accounts, were happily married, they weren't above tugging gently on another man's lapels or listening fascinated to one man's conversation until they elicited what could only be called a rush of feeling. "They came on so strong that they kind of intimidated the men," a friend laughingly remembers.

Friends recall Popo's demanding top-notch service wherever she went. If she didn't get what she wanted, she wasn't shy about speaking up. Just as she wasn't hesitant about flaunting the perquisites of her new status, Popo didn't back off letting help know when things weren't quite up to her expectations. Since Popo only recently had begun to expect all her social desires to be immediately gratified, her impatience with any obstacle to that gratification began to increase.

Typical of her petty annoyances was the time a hotel dining room ran out of dessert. From then on, Popo carried a bag of sweets with her every time she entertained there. Table companions who were served the pastries by Popo as the waiter poured their coffee recall being embarrassed at her unsubtle reminder that once the restaurant had failed her. People long accustomed to dealing with hired help would likely have brushed off the incident and not taken it as a personal affront. Popo, herself only a generation removed from having to use the back stairs, found the presence of service people more visible and felt compelled to teach them a lesson.

Popo and Mort's occasional arrival at a social event in a chauffeured car surprised many of their friends. Once, when a thoughtful hostess suggested to the Phillipses that the driver return for them rather than sit in the car during a freezing cold Wisconsin evening, Popo snapped at her, saying, "What do you expect me to do, invite him in?"

"Neither Eppie nor Popo ever hesitated at doing what she wanted because of social pressure," one of Popo's friends ingenuously recalls. "The middle class was in awe of them." Sometimes, though, Popo and Eppie could push just a little too far, and usually get away with it. Because there was no established synagogue in Eau Claire, and because they shared an interest in other religious beliefs, the twins began to visit various churches on Sunday mornings.

With their flair for making an entrance, the well-known and very well-dressed Jewish women would march down the aisle of the church and seat themselves in the first row of pews. At a Congregational Church one Sunday, in the middle of a sermon they apparently found offensive, both women slowly rose together in their seats and strode the full length of the church and out the front door. After they became famous, the minister whose sermon had been interrupted claimed that despite the regrettable incident, he admired the women for their interest in other religions. The opinions of other churchgoers were not so charitable.

The predominantly Christian community of Eau Claire accepted the presence of a small but influential group of Jewish families. But there were some residents who used Popo and Eppie's brash behavior to typify Jews. Many of the town's blue-collar workers, resentful of their dependence on the Jewish-owned Presto industry, openly made anti-Semitic comments about the Phillipses and the Lederers. A Presto employee recalls, "People had very strong opinions about them."

In light of the atrocities perpetrated on Jews during the war and the international tension over Zionists establishing a Jewish state in Israel, the image presented by the twins to fellow Jews and less affluent townspeople was deemed insensitive. But, as always, Eppie and Popo's actions were not meant to speak for others. The more individualized resources they developed while living apart during very early married life were set aside. Thrown together again, the sisters leaned upon each other and reinforced each other, behaving much as they did as carefree students in Sioux City. In Eau Claire, Eppie and Popo were as close as they'd ever been.

In most ways, Eppie gained prestige from being related to the Phillips family, and she seems to have successfully accepted the disparity in their financial means. Because Popo had it and was not entirely comfortable with having it, she tended to make more of the fact that she had a lot of money. In fact, it is always Popo who seemed to emphasize, in later interviews or magazine articles, how much better off she was and how Eppie resented it. It's Popo, not Eppie, who later feels the need to clarify what money meant in her relationship with her twin. It's Popo who later says, "Talking about money offends me."

Nine

"They were not homemakers. That was dullsville," says an acquaintance of the twins about the countless hours of volunteer work logged by Eppie and Popo. "Doing good," as their father had admonished them, and getting out of the house at the same time, appealed to both twins. Domestic chores were better left to others, as in Popo's case, or given a lower priority.

Popo occupied her spare time by becoming a Gray Lady at Luther Hospital in Eau Claire. Because of the substantial donations made by L. E. Phillips Charities, the philanthropic foundation established by Mort's uncle, Popo was confident she would be treated well there.

The high heels she wore with her Gray Lady uniform may have been strictly nonregulation, but Popo faithfully visited patients and distributed magazines, candy, and flowers. She irritated Red Cross leaders by wearing her uniform outside the hospital. Rules governing Gray Lady mufti stipulated the striped shift was to be worn only while on duty at the hospital. Popo in her uniform soon became a familiar sight on the streets of Eau Claire, a not-so-subtle reminder of her charitable work.

Popo in revolt broke other Gray Lady rules she found not to her liking. When she expressed an interest in wearing the Gray Lady cap, a symbol indicative of thousands of hours of service, she was told by the head volunteer that she was not yet eligible. State rules mandated a specific quota of on-duty time. Undaunted by such nonsense, Popo showed up the next day with the coveted cap squared firmly on her head. Because no one chose to tangle with her, nothing more was said.

When Popo Phillips got behind an idea, she ran with it, and oftentimes it was to the benefit of the community. With Eppie, she became active in the Easter Seal Society and the March of Dimes, recruiting friends and neighbors to help out. When a polio epidemic frightened the nation, Popo spearheaded a local effort to administer gamma globulin shots to schoolchildren, a community health priority before the discovery of the Salk vaccine. Her interest in the cause was no doubt occasioned by concern for her own children and because Mort's sister had been crippled by the disease.

However dedicated she was, gregarious and outgoing Popo couldn't resist turning every volunteer job she took into a social event. Often arriving late to meetings, the mink-clad Popo would interrupt the proceedings by scampering from woman to woman, hugging her friends and hollering her greetings. Still, the hours Popo turned in at Luther Hospital affected her greatly. "In Eau Claire I learned how many people are hurting, and I learned a valuable lesson," Popo says later. "I learned to listen."

Eppie echoes Popo concerning how much she learned doing volunteer work at the hospital. "It was at Luther Hospital I received my basic training in relating to people," she says. "Sometimes I just listened to the agonized, fearful, anxiety-ridden patients and their relations." Eppie's volunteer work was no mere confection to occupy her time. In many ways, she conducted herself more purposefully than her twin. "Eppie was a very responsible person," says a man who knew her well. "If she said she'd do something, it would be done. Eppie is a driving leader. Not for credit, she wanted things to work. She worked for the good of the community."

Although Eppie places emphasis on her work with people, her greater talent lies in her ability to plan and administer. Unlike Popo, who was interested in the hands-on aspect of charitable work, Eppie was a good manager. Active in the National Council of Christians and Jews, Eppie often met with Catholic priests to discuss how to raise money or offer assistance with planning joint charitable events.

At a meeting in New York with Popo, Eppie met Bishop Fulton Sheen, whose dynamic and somewhat self-abnegating approach to Christian charity Eppie found enormously appealing. "He called me Esther," Eppie said, "the only one. He said I reminded him of the biblical Esther when we first met."

Soon, both sisters were corresponding with Sheen, who believed the twins likely candidates for conversion. They began taking formal instruction in Catholicism. Rabbi Rabinowitz of Sioux City learned of their endeavors and wrote to them, warning the twins of the seductiveness of another faith. Popo wrote back, explaining that the lessons were educational, not spiritual, in nature. "I've always been curious," says Popo, "why others believe as they do."

More interested in using her intelligence than her empathy, Eppie was soon welcomed into the Coordinating Council, the organization that directed volunteer efforts in Eau Claire. With social problems resulting from postwar unemployment to solve and an increased need for community services, pulling together and sharing resources helped the volunteer organizations better direct their efforts.

Eppie took the lead in many of the monthly discussions of the Coordinating Council and oftentimes provided a refreshingly enthusiastic approach to that perennial problem of how to provide services despite the paucity of funds. In fact, Eppie proved to be particularly adept at fund raising.

Convinced that Eau Claire was in desperate need of a League of Women Voters, Eppie and an equally civic-minded friend moved to establish a local chapter. The state organization required an initial treasury of $100 as a token expression of community interest before it would certify a local branch.

"Forget it," said Eppie when she learned that her friend had formulated a plan to collect the needed funds door to door. "I'm not chasing around to get a nickel here and a dollar there."

She called in person upon the publisher of the local newspaper and on three leading businessmen.

"Give me a check for $25," she told Marshall Atkinson, the publisher of the Eau Claire *Leader-Telegram*.

"What for?" he chuckled, having met the attractive and petite Eppie Lederer before and knowing full well that her size belied the magnitude of her social self-esteem and pertinacity. Because of her perennial optimism he called her Sunshine.

"Never mind," said Eppie, determined to get a check from Moonshine, her pet name for one of Eau Claire's leading citizens, who was known to tipple some. She knew that along with his ready sense of humor, Atkinson was well respected and took his job as publisher very seriously. "Just make it out to the Wisconsin League of Women Voters."

Armed with a signed check from Atkinson, Eppie made short work of her visits to the other three businessmen. Within an hour, the Eau Claire chapter of the League of Women Voters was certain.

Eppie's entrance into the more political arena of community affairs and Popo's continued work at Luther Hospital exemplify their dissimilar community interests. The bipartisan political concerns of the League of Women Voters intrigued Eppie, while Popo preferred the intimacy of working directly with those in need.

Confident from her fund-raising success, Eppie badgered one of Atkinson's editors until he consented to publish a guest editorial on the need for greater community participation in social service organizations.

"She wanted to write an editorial; it didn't make any difference what it was on," a friend recalls. "She had persuasive abilities." Eppie proudly sent her first professionally published work to her father in Sioux City.

Being associated with the Phillips family combined with her own powers of persuasion garnered Eppie support in many of her endeavors. Because of the Phillips family name, Popo, too, wielded considerable influence and was sought after to head local drives for causes like mental health or United Crusade. She was in a position in town to pressure corporations and companies to spring for a score of tables at a banquet, or underwrite a major portion of the annual campaign. But much of her influence was exercised indirectly. Through Mort, Popo had a say in how the Phillips Foundation, established by Mort's father, spent its money.

An Eau Claire resident remembers that as they became recognized for their community work, Eppie and Popo became more competitive. "They would go to great lengths to best each other, even for the name of charity."

One time Eppie spoke before an annual meeting of the American Red Cross in Eau Claire. Popo, who happened to be in Minneapolis, heard about how successful her twin's talk was. When she got back to Eau Claire, Popo called the secretary of Family Service and asked to be the featured speaker at its annual meeting.

"Popo bought up tickets for the dinner and had friends pass them out," the Eau Claire friend says, in order to ensure a crowd equal to or better than the one her sister had. "She couldn't bear for Eppie to beat her, and vice versa."

The twins' continuing bid for publicity occasionally riled the publisher of the *Leader-Telegram*. Atkinson, who was older than the twins, generally viewed their antics with a mixture of amusement and tolerance. But he also could be irascible when their rivalry, as he saw it, got out of hand. "I told them they would be put on a ration. Only one picture in the newspaper every six months. They were very indignant and said if they did something for the community, they expected to be recognized for it."

In wanting to be publicly recognized for their newsworthy activities, Eppie and Popo opened themselves up to being known in other ways. The mounting tension between the twins, for example, was an undercurrent heard back in Iowa. A friend in Sioux City was sure that Jules's working for Mort created the usual "Eppie is jealous of Popo" syndrome. In spite of their efforts to conceal the friction, their rivalry was apparent to their Eau Claire friends too. As one of their neighbors describes it, "Popo had a nice home, a rather large home, and Eppie started out in a small home and then moved into an apartment. A nice apartment, but Popo had a nice, rather large home she was very proud of."

"Eppie was just one of the people" is how another friend distinguishes between the twins. "Her sister, of course, was married to a millionaire, and there was a big difference. But Eppie lived in a home like any of us would have lived in."

Later, Popo felt the need to drive the point home. "In Eau Claire she had a little tiny place, while I lived in a lovely home with loads of help," Popo says. "Her husband worked for mine. I drove a luxury car; she drove a lower-priced model. And that had to hurt."

Another friend viewed the sisters' one-upmanship as "kind of a joke. If one twin got something, the other one had to have it."

Popo had a mink coat. "Mink coat?" says a neighbor about Popo's furs. "The longer the better." So Popo, who'd always been a very material girl, insisted on giving Eppie one. The fur and other gifts were gratefully accepted by Eppie. It was only later, after Eppie could afford as many minks as a woman could wear, that Popo was criticized for her largesse. Eppie felt compromised and "oppressed" by her sister's gifts, but she chose to accept them at the time they were offered.

Eppie's smaller nose remained a sensitive issue with Popo. If Popo feared she was the less attractive twin because of her more prominent nose, she constantly reassured herself that she, personally, had no need to change her profile. "Mort married me with this nose, so he'll have to live with this nose," Popo declared to all and sundry.

Bickering words between Popo and Eppie were overheard by Presto employees too. One man heard harsh words at various company outings. On several occasions, the conversations between them indicated a deep hostility in their relationship. Robert Stolar, Eppie's confidant, admits that the twins' rivalry was exacerbated by Popo's marriage. "It made a tremendous difference," he says.

72 ≈

Before

* * *

Postwar America, circa 1950, was experiencing the most dramatic industrial expansion in any nation's history. In Eau Claire, Presto production lines hummed with newly hired workers and churned out new products like griddles and can openers. Spurred by the five Army and Navy "Es" for productive efficiency bestowed during the war, the American wartime equivalent of a royal patent, the company diversified from pressure cookers and machine-gun bullets to lithography and precision tooling.

Supersalesman Jules was on the road constantly, scouting new markets for Presto's increased output. The tenth-grade dropout and former hat salesman felt a need to prove himself to his brother-in-law. Mort had plucked Jules from anonymity and given him a shot at the big time. Jules harbored a genuine fear of and antipathy toward failure. It made him work that much harder.

Jules managed his sales force with a big voice and hearty backslaps in the win-by-intimidation style of the fifties go-getter. When he chose to, Jules could be friendly and personable. But he was easily provoked by fellow sales personnel who didn't share his enthusiasm or sense of common purpose. Jules was especially impatient when one of his subordinates, returning from a business trip, expressed a desire to return home rather than report to the office for another four hours of work.

Jules's grueling work week of sixty to eighty hours left Eppie alone much of the time, sometimes for days on end. His frequent absences, Eppie says, "taught me how to be alone without feeling sorry for myself."

Eppie convinced herself that being able to cope with loneliness was an adjustment the wife of an up-and-comer was forced to make. She wanted out of the Peanut Place as much as Jules did. Her vision of married life was shaped by Jules's drive to succeed. "Some women resent the time that men spend away from them," she says. "They complain that their husbands are married to their work. 'I'm second,' they whine. If they only would understand that this is the way life is. A man has to give a great deal to his work if he wants to be a success."

≈ 73

Jules compensated for his absences by being especially attentive to his wife when he was home. Away from the office, the handsome and nattily tailored Jules appeared at Eppie's side, responsive to her needs and consummately charming to her socially prominent friends. He liked being seen with his attractive and curvaceous wife, especially when other Presto executives were present. Her easy conversation and lusty good looks made Eppie a great asset, socially as well as professionally. To their friends, Jules and Eppie were a social elixir, always amiable, always optimistic, and forever game for a good time.

By contrast, Mort in public was quiet, somewhat reserved, and much less eager for high-spirited fun. While Jules was sometimes labeled a bantam, most of his Eau Claire friends called Mort a gentleman. Other people have described Mort as low-key or aloof. Secure in his position at Presto, Mort often took time during the day to squire Popo to social events. On occasion they used the corporate plane for more distant outings. When the two couples went out together, Jules and Eppie often outshone Mort and Popo, impulsively jumping up to form the caboose of a conga line or merrily motioning to other couples to join them for dinner.

Jeannie Phillips, by two years the older of the Phillips children, seemed to take after her father. She was a bit shy and moderately studious. Growing up in Eau Claire, she seemed "aware of her family's wealth and prestige," neighbors recall, and somewhat protective of her family name. Her young brother, Eddie, on the other hand, seldom appeared conscious of his family's position in the town. He was feisty, like his mother, sometimes outspoken, and rarely at a loss for words. One woman who rode a bicycle around town said that once when she said hello to Eddie and his young friends, he remarked, to no one in particular, "Have you ever seen such a fat lady on a bike?"

In one of her few statements of regret, Popo indicates she probably should have done more for Jeannie in teaching her daughter to develop all her skills, not just those that could be considered feminine. "It is to my everlasting shame," Popo says, that she advised girls to be passive and pretty.

Certainly Margo, Jules and Eppie's daughter, was in sharp contrast to her cousin Jeannie. She was characterized by many people in Eau Claire as being "quite aggressive." "A hellion," "sophisticated," and "mature" were other terms used to describe her. Her assertive disposition and devil-may-care attitude were personality traits in direct line of descent from her mother and her Aunt Popo.

All three children were enrolled in the Campus School, affiliated with the University of Wisconsin in Eau Claire. Eppie and Popo shared a common philosophy on child rearing. They both had a liberal hand and a ready wallet. They agreed the single most important consideration in having children was raising them in a loving environment.

"Their concept of being a good mother didn't entail being at the beck and call of their children," a friend said, though it would be inaccurate to say that they didn't provide the attention a growing child requires. Advice, if needed, was provided by Dr. Benjamin Spock's best-selling book on child care. Observers in Eau Claire concur that they were indulgent parents. The twins agreed the way to teach their kids sound, moral values was by providing the example, not by unduly pressuring them or shielding them from the real world.

Because of Jules's frequent business trips, the task of disciplining Margo fell to Eppie. When Dr. Spock failed to address certain subtleties of child rearing, Eppie turned to her trusted friend Robert Stolar. The good doctor's level-headed recommendations were dutifully followed. Despite how she raised Margo, Eppie counsels parents, "If you have to err, err on the side of being too strict, not too permissive. The kid will be better off for it." Eppie insists, however, that "Jules was a little more permissive than I was with our daughter."

Margo seemed a trifle lonely, thought the mothers of her friends, who attributed her frequent bouts with asthma to a bid for attention. Being an only child with a father who traveled a lot and a mother caught up in a whirlwind of activity that soon included party politics as well as the Red Cross didn't leave much time for companionship at home. But Eppie made it up to Margo in other ways. For one, mother and daughter went on many trips together, to Chicago, Washington, and New York, and with Jules on vacation to places like Palm Springs and Hawaii.

"Margo went all over the world with us," Eppie says, referring to her daughter's privileged upbringing. "She had the advantage of traveling with her mother and father." And by the early fifties, when the Lederers moved out of the Peanut Place and into a large apartment, Margo and her parents were traveling to Europe in the spring and California during the winter.

Eppie feels that because Margo was an only child, "she had none of the problems that you have with other brothers and sisters. There was no one with whom to divide the parental love." Eppie questions, however, whether there is a down side to being the sole object of mom and dad's affections.

Regardless, when her only child needed professional counseling, she didn't withhold it or blame herself for somehow failing. With her usual self-confidence, Eppie insists, "I did the very best that I could do with the information and knowledge that I had."

Eppie was there when her daughter needed her most. She felt no need to disguise her lack of interest in homemaking and babysitting. Even at Mothers' Council meetings of the Campus School she would turn the topic of conversation from children to issues like the future of the newly founded United Nations.

Eppie dared imagine a different destiny for herself at a time when even affluent women, with a choice of life's options, had little experience with seeking lifestyles apart from being wives and mothers. Fifties-era values counseled dire consequences would befall women who forgot that they were, in the final accounting, just women. But Eppie was determined to enrich her own life despite what others may have considered proper for her. She seems to have struck a balance in her own mind about how she felt about herself and how others may have perceived her. About her own parenting, she says, "I think I was a good mother, at least I was as good as I could be."

Before

The choices Eppie made seemed extraordinary at the time only because they were unconventional. Alternative female role models worth emulating were virtually nonexistent. Because she understood herself well enough, Eppie wisely decided to limit her family to one child. Postwar birth rates may have soared, but Eppie ignored the norm. "I don't think she could stand still long enough to have more than one child," a neighbor said. "I don't know how she had the one!"

Ten

"Women must have inner resources," Eppie emphasizes, in order to maintain their self-esteem when their husbands become engrossed in their work. She has little compassion for wives who depend solely on their husbands for their identity. "If they'd only do something with themselves," she says. "Stop trying to kill time by playing cards or shopping. Before my job as Ann Landers, I became very interested and involved in politics—that's what I did."

With Jules away much of the time and Margo in school, Eppie had the freedom to do as she wanted. Thanks to Arthur Henning, the cherubic-looking, curly-haired professor of political science she met in 1948, Eppie discovered a means of cultivating her own inner resources. In the process she also discovered that through electoral politics, ambition could be limitless.

Eppie and Popo represented the Gray Ladies and Henning was the spokesman for the March of Dimes at a Coordinating Council meeting. Popo left immediately after the meeting while Eppie lingered on to chat with the bow-tied and tweed-jacketed college professor. Aside from his clean-cut good looks, Eppie was drawn to his intellect and ambition. Henning hadn't started out as a college professor, she soon found out. He had worked his way there from fireman to engineer before joining the staff of the University of Wisconsin at Eau Claire. In addition to his March of Dimes activities, the well-spoken Henning was chairman of Eau Claire's Democratic party.

Eppie listened intently to this man who, like herself but unlike Jules, directed part of his energy to volunteer service. She admired Henning's commitment to a Democratic party that helped the needy and the unemployed. Until Henning came along, the Democratic party platform and its importance hadn't been fully explained to Eppie. Henning must have explained how it was only after the war that Democrats succeeded in extending their power and influence into areas in the Midwest and New England. The coalition that President Franklin Roosevelt forged to back his New Deal reforms included an eclectic party membership of organized labor, farmers, minority groups, ethnic and religious groups, and intellectual liberals.

By depicting the Republican party as "the party of special interests" that "favors the privileged few," Roosevelt's successor, Harry Truman, was able to hold the diverse membership of the Democratic party together. His legendary 31,000-mile whistle-stop tour on a flag-adorned campaign train, the same year in which Eppie attended her first Democratic party meeting, spread the Democratic gospel to every corner of the nation. On election eve 1948, everyone went to bed thinking Truman had lost, despite his "barnstorming" campaign.

But the haberdasher from Missouri had managed to convince the electorate that the social and economic reforms of the New Deal years should be preserved. His warning of a return to "Republican" Depression days had sunk in. Organized labor responded to the call and voted for Truman en masse.

Henning recalls Eppie "thought Harry Truman was a great politician." She looked up to Truman and was inspired by his commitment to the "common everyday man." For Eppie, Truman's dramatic campaign trip, which was the major news story at the time, and Truman's upset victory must have been clear evidence of what her father had taught her all along, that success comes with hard work and dedication. Henning, seeing the potential in this liberal and enthusiastic Truman supporter and zealous new recruit to the Democratic party, invited Eppie to attend a local Democratic party meeting with him.

From Eppie's point of view, involvement in local party politics would enable her to escape being "just a housewife" or hospital volunteer. Politics promised meaningful work that would make use of her talents at organizing and fund raising.

Unlike Eppie, Popo preferred the confines of women's charitable work. Popo, Henning remembers, "was not active in politics, not active in either party." Her family connections had already greased her entree into the charitable and cultural community of Eau Claire that no amount of persistence and grandstanding by her outsider sister could accomplish on her own. Eppie was lured by causes of wider interest where outcomes weren't so clearly defined and where newcomers, willing to perform and be judged, could draw some degree of notoriety to themselves.

At first Jules was amused by Eppie's newly kindled interest in Democratic politics. Like other managers at Presto, and for that matter most of the citizenry of Eau Claire, Jules was a Republican. But whatever made Eppie happy was okay with Jules.

Eppie didn't hesitate at being one of the few Eau Claire women involved in nuts-and-bolts party work. She organized meetings at the Labor Temple, planned Memorial Day and Fourth of July picnics at city parks, and drummed up interest in Democratic candidates. Taking on increasingly sophisticated tasks, Eppie demonstrated a talent for campaign literature. Catchy phrases she coined resulted in more lively and convincing handbills than the usual hackneyed fact sheets.

The main goal was increasing the roster of registered Democrats in Eau Claire County. Despite active efforts and the backing of citizens solidly committed to Democratic goals, only 200 of the 35,000 Eau Claire residents in 1950 paid the modest $2 dues to join the party. The party treasury had hardly enough money to get a candidate on the ballot, much less elected. Eppie and a handful of others equally obstinate refused to see the futility of being a Democrat in Eau Claire. Luckily for the Democratic party, Henning recalls, Eppie was "a leader, and many people followed."

Exhilarated by her newly discovered calling, Eppie wrote to her father in Sioux City saying that this was it, she excelled at party politics, and she described how exciting it was to be out in front on important issues.

Abe told her how proud he was. "My father thought [getting involved in politics], was very neat and very courageous," Eppie says. Abe also must have thought that Eppie was a lot different from her mother or her twin. Neither Becky or Popo would have gotten involved in partisan politics. Eppie proudly remembers her father "knew a lot about politics, and he thought it was a good thing I would have the nerve to do that."

Eppie's singleness of purpose didn't go unnoticed by friends and neighbors. No matter what their political affiliation, Eau Claire residents recognized the good Eppie was doing. And because Eppie did things and got involved, she was talked about. Being the lone woman at some of the political meetings prompted idle chatter among her friends, who had little interest in partisan politics but admired Eppie's audacity. They recall she was completely unselfconscious about being a woman in an arena populated almost entirely by men.

Nor did Eppie mind being the only ardent Democrat among the coterie of GOP supporters who were wives of Presto executives. Through the Democratic party, Eppie was exposed to people from a range of social circumstances. If before she felt she had nothing in common with assembly-line workers and other blue-collar types, she now shared some of their biases and political opinions. Eppie discovered they weren't all bores, these members of the working class, and her understanding resulted in a new respect for them. But it was the more urbane contingent of party members who attracted Eppie's attention.

As she moved through the ranks of Democratic workers, Eppie acquired a new group of friends that included middle-class professionals, university professors, and owners of small businesses. It was the first time in her life she felt comfortable with a group of people who would be considered well educated.

Eppie learned much from her Democratic party work and the people she worked with. She developed new skills and learned the importance of being flexible, the art of compromise, and how to establish at least a partial consensus among the disparate elements of party membership. Most important of all, Eppie learned to function smoothly as part of a team. Her colleagues praised her efforts and her ability to adapt to almost any situation.

Frequent appearances at Democratic rallies and local fund raisers by the energetic and vivacious young Eppie attracted the attention of more seasoned politicians. Eppie articulated party positions with such fluency that party regulars soon recognized her potential as a major asset to the small, struggling local party. Soon she was the appointed head of Eau Claire's Democratic Party Speakers Bureau.

Short on funds, the party relied on donated office space for headquarters. Eppie spent nearly every day and night at the makeshift bureau arranging for speakers to canvass the county. Working shoulder to shoulder late into the evening, telephoning between bites of take-out sandwiches, the volunteers in Arthur Henning's campaign for the Ninth Congressional District seat developed strong ties and loyalties.

Eppie learned much about grass-roots campaigning from party pro Henning. Increasingly confident about her own abilities, and coaxed into it by Henning, she unabashedly assigned key speaking spots to herself. On behalf of local, state, and national candidates, and on behalf of Art Henning, she traveled on her own and convincingly presented their credentials and worked diligently to persuade the electorate. "She was a great vote-getter and a great speaker," Henning says admiringly.

But Henning lost the Congressional race. Eppie disguised her disappointment and valiantly held a "victory" party for him, a party more lavish than had originally been planned. She fiercely refused to admit defeat and postured that "just a little more work" would bring the Democrats the Senate seat that was up in 1952. Her enthusiasm was infectious. Party regulars maintain that Eppie was instrumental in keeping the local party together during the uncertain times of the early fifties.

In a special election two years later for her district's Congressional post, Eppie helped send Democrat Lester Johnson to Washington. His win after Henning's disappointing defeat for the same post two years earlier was sweet indeed. Eppie was thrilled. In four long years of dedicated party work, Lester was the first candidate she had worked for who actually got elected. Lawrence Wahlstrom, Johnson's campaign manager, remembers an exuberant Eppie, bussing every man at the victory party, oblivious to their embarrassment and their wives' discomfort.

Faced with enormous campaign debts, the party had to devote its efforts to raising money. Goaded by Wahlstrom, Eppie impulsively telephoned Hubert Humphrey, then U.S. Senator from Minnesota, at his Washington office. Would he come to Eau Claire to help out? Eppie hoped a visit from Humphrey would stir up local interest in the party. The senator gave his firm assent, knowing that it was a crucial time for the Democratic party in Wisconsin.

Probably Eppie dropped the Phillips family name into her conversation with the senator. She hadn't met him before, even though a few years earlier he had made an appearance at Jimmy Woo's restaurant in Eau Claire, at a fund raiser that had an embarrassing turnout of fewer than a dozen people. But Senator Humphrey was well aware of the Phillips family, one of his home state's richest and most giving, whose ties to him dated back to the days of his Minneapolis mayoralty. Wahlstrom and other Eau Claire Democratic loyalists applauded Eppie's cheek in tapping a senator she didn't know, much less one from another state.

In order to ensure a large audience for the senator, Eppie persuaded residents who weren't party members, but instead were Republicans and Independents, to attend the rally. She correctly reasoned that a widely known figure like Humphrey, who attained national notoriety at the 1948 Democratic Convention when he pushed through a revolutionary civil-rights plank, was well worth listening to regardless of party affiliation.

The tactic worked. Humphrey found a capacity crowd awaiting him in the Episcopal Cathedral Community House. The enthusiasm generated by the senator's appearance helped wipe out the Democratic party debt and stimulated optimism that perhaps in 1952 Wisconsin's Republican Senator Joseph McCarthy might be unseated. To be a Wisconsin Democrat in the early fifties automatically meant you were opposed to the alarmist Wisconsin senator. Democrats throughout the state had mobilized behind the slogan "Joe Must Go."

McCarthy, spouting his paranoid accusations of mistrust and communist influence in government, had, by 1952, offended many thoughtful people from all social levels and of most political persuasions. Frightened by his assault on civil liberties, Wisconsin Democrats were in the forefront of an incipient national backlash against his menacing presence in the United States Senate.

Eppie has repeatedly implied she was a leader in the anti-McCarthy movement. "I thought he was dangerous, a threat to our democratic way of life," Eppie states years later. Other concerned citizens in Wisconsin and throughout the country circulated petitions, wrote letters to newspaper editors, lost university jobs, and were even jailed in their ardent efforts to halt the spread of McCarthyism. By contrast, Eppie's efforts were mostly confined to organized party actions. Her insistence she was in the forefront of the effort to ensure his defeat irritates former union leaders active in the Democratic party. Democratic co-workers say that Eppie's part in the dump-McCarthy effort was negligible. Art Henning sums it up, saying, "She was definitely against McCarthy and his tactics, but not actively."

Despite growing sentiment against him, McCarthy retained his Senate seat. The Eisenhower landslide, as well as the many Republican victories across the nation because of the stalemated Korean war, government corruption, and rising prices and high taxes, had helped McCarthy. In Wisconsin, Democrats lost the governorship and all of the Wisconsin seats in the House of Representatives. Eppie realized the state and local Democratic party had a lot of hard work ahead.

Eleven

"Eppie's leadership was recognized, and she was proposed as Democratic party county chairman," Henning recalls. No one remembers who first suggested Eppie for the position, but as soon as she was proposed, the nominating committee was in unanimous agreement. Eppie's diligence, cleverness, and initiative in helping Lester Johnson win his Congressional race had contributed to the party's rejuvenation. She was the right person for the top spot.

In the fall of 1953, Henning approached Eppie concerning the chairmanship. It was a volunteer position appointed by the county Democratic committee. Though committee members felt Eppie would be perfect as chairman, they were concerned she might be unable to accept the job if it were offered because she'd have to pick up her own travel and hotel expenses during statewide canvasses, as was customary. There were not many people willing or able to incur these expenses. In addition, they at first were reluctant to force Eppie to make what they believed was a choice between a time-consuming job and her family. But finally, Eppie's suitability for the position outweighed all other factors.

≈ 87

The decision was a difficult one for Eppie. Finally, the recent death of Abe Friedman had to be taken into account. In late 1952 Abe was diagnosed as having cancer. At Mort and Popo's behest, he was moved to the Mayo Clinic in Rochester, Minnesota, for treatment. Just two hours south of Minneapolis and three hours southwest of Eau Claire, the Clinic was near enough to the twins so they could visit their father frequently. It was a tiring experience for his daughters, both emotionally and physically. Abe died there in July 1953 at the age of sixty-four.

Abe's death more likely would have induced Eppie to run for county chairmanship than to decline the nomination. Abe had long encouraged all his daughters, and especially Eppie, to act on their ambitions. Eppie understood that her becoming the Democratic county chairman from Eau Claire would have made Abe proud. But she initially rejected the nomination and cited her inexperience, not financial limitations or her home life, as the reason.

After careful thought, the nominating committee refused to accept Eppie's decision. Committee members called Eppie "a natural-born leader" and didn't want to waste her talent by assigning her a lesser role. Had they foreseen the shattering controversy that would result, it's likely they wouldn't have pressed her to reconsider. Flattered by their confidence in her, Eppie, with her best girl-next-door grin, graciously accepted the nomination.

Traditionally, the committee's choice for chairman went unopposed by the party regulars. Henning's twenty-odd years as chairman had been without opposition. He naturally surmised that Eppie's nomination would be supported by, or at least would pass by common consent of, the party members. But Henning's assumption proved woefully incorrect. Opposition to Eppie was loud and bitter.

Unknown to Eppie and her supporters, a significant faction of Democrats were becoming disgruntled with the local party organization. Leading the dissidents were union men, most of whom were also embroiled in a caustic dispute with Presto that threatened to disrupt production.

Tremendous disagreements between labor and management were taking place throughout the state and much of the country. The postwar refueling of the economy that generated renewed prosperity didn't always trickle down to semi-skilled workers. Labor demands and unemployment, salary disputes, and high prices contributed to the general unrest.

Despite the profits Presto reported in 1953, including an astounding 48 percent return on net worth the year before, Presto management shocked union employees with a proposal for wage cuts. President and owner Lewis Phillips was heard to remark that he wouldn't accede to the demands of the CIO Steelworkers Union. Only the summer before, President Truman had seized the steel industry to prevent a nationwide strike. The day after the Supreme Court ruled Truman's action unconstitutional, the union formed a picket line that stood its ground for three weeks. Labor clashes were brought uncomfortably close to home for Eppie because of her ties to Presto Industries.

Although Eppie's brother-in-law Mort maintained a conciliatory, live-and-let-live attitude toward Presto employees and was well liked by union members and thought of as a "decent guy," other high-placed managers were accused of harassing union members and undercutting their unionization attempts. Jules, as head of sales, was somewhat removed from unionized production-line workers, and the rank and file did not regard him as an enemy. Still, union leaders exploded when they heard that fellow Democrats were proposing Jules' wife, Mort's sister-in-law, a "Phillips girl," as county chairman, and charged an insensitivity to union members who worked loyally for the party's resurgence.

Worker hostility toward what they considered exploitation by a single family was more than faintly incited by blue-collar prejudice against Jews. The combination of a company management perceived to be callously anti-labor and a union with some anti-Semitic members led to a volatile situation.

The perception that the Phillips family had profited immensely from defense contracts during a war in which many union members had braved battlefront bullets also helped turn the local party election into an unprecedented fray. In the ordnance days of World War II, the same .50- and .30-caliber machine-gun bullets used by soldiers at the front were tested on a ballistics range snug below the row of hills to the southeast of the Presto plant.

Instead of being shot at, maimed, or killed on isolated islands in the Pacific or in trenches in France or Germany, it was implied the Phillips family members, including for a time draft-age Mort, were fulfilling their wartime obligations in the verdant valleys of west central Wisconsin, all the while reaping a fortune in greenbacks. Canny union leaders lost no time in turning Eppie's nomination into an opportunity to embarrass Presto management and the Phillips family. Eppie herself didn't know what hit her.

Homs Schwahn, an attorney for the Steelworkers Union, was persuaded by Kenneth Nispel, head of the union at Presto, to run for the county chairmanship against Eppie. Nispel, an outspoken ex-marine sergeant and World War II veteran, was one of Presto's long-time workers.

Schwahn and Nispel's depiction of Eppie as a dilettante Democrat, a "Phillips girl," was intended to turn the election into a union-versus-management battle as well as a political contest. Relying heavily upon the beer-hall camaraderie of fellow union members, Schwahn and Nispel talked up Eppie as a society candidate whose husband and brother-in-law were associated with a company that oppressed local workers. In pool rooms and corner taverns, at lunch time and on weekends, Eppie, because of her family and connections, was portrayed as a union buster.

Although Eppie was dismayed by the vehemence of the steelworkers, she didn't offer to step aside. Never one to quit, Eppie launched herself into the fracas with an even greater determination.

Nearly all of the Eau Claire party members who weren't part of the union believed that Eppie had been unfairly treated. "The workers attempted to take out their frustrations on her," Henning remembers. "She wanted no part of the fight. She wasn't tied to the company other than the fact her husband worked there."

Eppie's colleagues recall that she presented her qualifications convincingly through speeches, handouts, and radio and newspaper interviews. She stood by her constitutional rights as a private citizen to engage in the democratic process of an election. Throughout her campaign, Eppie told the press she was a housewife, and not part of Presto management. "She had the right, as a citizen, to participate in the activities she chose," explains one defender.

Because it was politically expedient, she sought to distance herself from the Phillips family and contrasted the modest top-floor apartment in a Jefferson Court duplex she and Jules rented with Popo and Mort's large house and terraced grounds. Eppie insisted she lived far more humbly than her twin. Once again she resorted to being that Sioux City, Iowa, girl who's small town at heart.

Eppie's public battle with her union opponent couldn't help but publicize the Steelworkers' skirmishes with Presto. Although she felt no pressure from Jules, Mort, or Popo, Presto management recognized that a defeat for Eppie would be a humiliation for the company as well. A win for Schwahn would be seen as vindicating the union.

The unique dilemma for Presto was admitted in some off-the-record conversation several company officials had with Henning at the Masonic Lodge. If Eppie were pressured to drop her candidacy, the company would appear to have been intimidated by the union. Since she was already involved, management conceded, it had no alternative but to remain silent, refuse to capitulate, and hope for Eppie's victory.

Popo, in her own way, sided with her sister. Although Popo had supported Eisenhower in 1952, probably on account of Mort's influence, she more and more was beginning to prefer the sentiments of the Democratic party. To get around town, Popo and Mort generally used either their Cadillac convertible or a Buick station wagon. They bought separate figurines for the hood. When Popo drove the Cadillac, she removed Mort's silver elephant and replaced it with her silver donkey. Mort made sure his elephant was in place when he drove.

Using the same tactic she employed to sell dinner tickets to the Humphrey fund raiser, Eppie eagerly enlisted people who were Eau Claire residents but happened to be Republican or Independent to pay the $2 Democratic party dues in order to be able to vote in the election. "She loaded up and bought Democratic memberships to gain control," charges a former Presto worker who characterized Eppie as a "fast worker."

Eppie's defenders, however, insist that her actions to add to the voter roster were good for the party. They say it helped put the county Democratic party back on a sound financial base. "She didn't want anything for herself," Henning asserts.

In a similar manner, Schwahn and Nispel went about signing up voters who would support their platform. They encouraged union members who worked in Eau Claire but didn't live there to register for the local party. Strictly speaking, signing up nonresident members violated the state party constitution. The Eau Claire Democratic party soon was composed of local Republicans and Independents and out-of-town Democrats, as well as the more typical local Democratic members. Regardless of the candidates' intent, the Democratic party treasury increased dramatically. Party membership expanded fourfold.

Rubber Workers Hall on the night of January 19, 1954, overflowed with people standing two and three deep in the aisles between the metal folding chairs. Democrats of many persuasions and from many geographic areas lined up on the narrow flight of steps leading to the street and the storefront one story below. Lawrence Wahlstrom, staunchly supportive of Eppie and witness to many prior elections, recalls that usually only a half-dozen citizens bothered to show up for a county chairman election.

Both Eppie and Nispel were alarmed by the unexpected number of voters who turned up for the election. Certain there were nonresidents in the crowd, Eppie demanded that IDs be checked. Nispel took one searching look at those assembled and began to rail about the presence of Presto managers, who were known to be Republicans. Eppie's supporters repeatedly raised the issue of nonresident voters. After much hollering back and forth, all persons holding Democratic party membership cards were allowed to vote.

In the final tally, Schwahn swamped Eppie by a two-to-one margin.

Disappointed and furious, Eppie wasted no time telling the local press how she felt. The next day's headlines in the *Leader-Telegram* screamed RIGGED, PACKED, AND STACKED—A PHONY. She telephoned her supporters and complained that the election was a sham. Not ready to admit defeat, Eppie convinced Henning to use his influence with state Democratic party bigwigs to order a new election.

Henning, himself a member of the state administrative committee, played a key role at their meeting to discuss the election. The administrative committee at first wasn't convinced that the nonresidency clause in the bylaws ought to be enforced. Some were union members who felt it made more sense to allow workers to vote where they worked rather than where they lived. But the committee decided to play by the rules, and a new election was scheduled for March 7.

"Clout and money. We got sold out," complained a union member about how the administrative committee decision didn't provide for disqualifying Republicans who were instant Democrats. And at the second election in March, Eppie made sure that her converts to the Democratic party were there in force.

"She got all her friends to come," Marshall Atkinson gleefully recalls. "I never knew so many mink coats existed in Eau Claire. Mink coats in a Democratic caucus?"

A last-minute ploy by Nispel backfired. Instead of running Schwahn for chairman, Nispel wanted Dale Milnes, another Presto employee, on the ballot. Nispel thought Milnes was more articulate than Schwahn and would make a stronger contender.

Eppie swiftly invoked parliamentary procedure and had Schwahn reinstated as the opposing candidate. Many union members, angry at how Eppie controlled the ballot, refused to vote. She won by a three-to-one margin.

A chorus of "Fraud, Cheat, Faker" rose from the assembly of union members when the results were announced. "We were out-monied by Eppie and her friends," Nispel bitterly contends. "I bet that not even 5 percent of those people Eppie dragged in, and there must have been several hundred, maintain any connection with the Democratic Party today."

Defeat for the union members carried ominous overtones. Hostility between Presto management and the steelworkers per-sisted. Although the strike was eventually settled, relations between the two groups grew increasingly difficult until, as a last resort, the production line was closed down.

Some of the machinery was shipped to plants in Jackson, Mississippi, and Abilene, Texas, where less costly, nonunion labor could be put to work. Nearly 400,000 square feet of floor space was mothballed and didn't tool up again until the mid-sixties when Presto once again got Defense Department contracts for 105mm and 8-inch shell projectiles destined for Vietnam. "When Presto pulled out for Mississippi, it broke the back of the union," says Henning. The company that by the early fifties had grown into one of the largest employers in Eau Claire had abruptly and in its own best interests put more than a thousand laborers out of work.

By the time Jules took a job in Chicago later in 1954, he had gotten much of what he wanted out of Presto. He had proved himself, increased the company's sales, and in the process added an im-pressive item to his résumé.

For Jules, Chicago and the presidency of a large company were just what he wanted. Accepting a job at Autopoint, a subsidiary of the Cory Corporation and a manufacturer of ballpoint pens, was a wise career move. Relations at Presto were becoming strained. Shoptalk hinted Jules was being forced out because he spent too much money and traveled too much. People he worked with say top management was bothered about his propensity for throwing money around and assuming that it would pay off in profits. Jules wasn't exactly fired from Presto, but he was perceptive enough to see he was out of favor.

Besides, there was no position for Jules to aspire to at Presto. Between Mel Cohen, Uncle Lewis's son-in-law and Mort's cousin by marriage, and Mort himself, few upper-level posts were available.

Popo has a different viewpoint on why Jules took the job in Chicago. She insinuates that Eau Claire wasn't big enough for both Friedman twins. "[Eppie] made Jules leave. She couldn't stand it."

Eppie sees it differently: "Jules makes his own decisions, and he had outgrown Presto. She's as wrong as when she says I wanted to marry a millionaire. I didn't have to. She's the one who needs the assurance of money."

The twins had and still have a lot of unresolved conflicts in their relationship. Confusing as it sounds, Eppie was important to Popo because she was her twin. Yet Popo couldn't help lording over her sister her loftier circumstances. Eppie wished her sister well but couldn't stand her patronizing air. Popo's marriage was important to Eppie because Mort had hired Jules for his first executive job. Without the Presto opportunity, Jules might not have been offered the Autopoint position.

Because of Jules's difficulties at Presto and the fragile relationship between the sisters, speculation in Eau Claire was that the Lederers moved from the Peanut Place to the Jefferson Court apartment as a prelude to leaving the area. When Jules accepted the job in Chicago, Eppie went along without complaining. She regretfully submitted her resignation as county Democratic chairman. The post she had worked so diligently to acquire was hers for just six months. Skeptical union adversaries who had called Eppie a dilettante felt vindicated.

Working relentlessly in the short time remaining, Eppie rescued the Democratic organization from debt by once again calling on Senator Humphrey. The rally held in the Elks Lodge was a success, both financially for the party and emotionally for Eppie. Photos of the event depict Eppie visibly delighted to be embraced by the senator in front of the assembled Democrats.

More public acclaim and recognition for Eppie came from fellow Democrats who hosted a farewell party in her honor. Repeated toasts commended her civic and party contributions. Speakers agreed Eppie Lederer was "one of those people you come across once in a lifetime." Eppie's departure from Eau Claire in late 1954 prompted an editorial in the *Leader-Telegram* cautioning Chicago to "watch out for Eppie Lederer—she'll make her mark on the city."

State party officials truly regretted Eppie's leaving the state. They believed she had the potential to become the state Democratic National Committeewoman, at that time the highest position allowed by custom to any woman.

Eppie's recollection of other offices offered her by the party is somewhat illusory. Years later she says, "I'm quite sure if I hadn't moved out of Wisconsin, where I was involved in politics, I would have become a senator because nothing could stop me." But even Eppie's more passionate supporters in Eau Claire reject the idea that she might have been able to run successfully for Congress. Party pal Art Henning seems to have had a more realistic view of Eppie's capabilities and didn't consider her Congressional material.

"I could have gone to Congress but didn't do it, because I felt my place was with a growing child," insists Eppie. In yet another interview she repeats her reason for not pursuing a political career: "I wouldn't leave my family for Washington." Though she perhaps overestimates her capabilities at the time, some Eau Claire residents believe that had Eppie somehow been elected, she would have been packed and at the train station well before Jules came home from work.

Twelve

I n Chicago, Eppie dedicated herself to transforming their stark, glass-walled, three-bedroom apartment at 1000 Lake Shore Drive into a showplace. The tall, modern apartment building leaning out over Oak Street Beach, on the site of a former Rockefeller mansion and just a block from the Magnificent Mile, was a fashionable lakefront address. Jules's salary at Autopoint was sufficient to permit the Lederers a modicum of extravagance. For the first time in her life, Eppie had an ample decorating budget.

Black and white tile was laid in a checkerboard pattern in the front hallway. Eppie liked a glossy and expensive circle-and-dot wallpaper so much that she repeated the bright and busy pattern throughout the entryway, living room, dining room, and kitchen. Taking her time, she gradually replaced serviceable department-store furniture with period pieces. Within a month, floor-length flowered draperies framed the dramatic fortieth-floor view of Lake Michigan.

Far below, many lanes of traffic moved noisily along the perimeter of the lake, hurtling over trestled roadway set above street level to provide beach access underneath. Forty stories above it was far more tranquil. "It's very quiet up there," Eppie said at the time. Before long, she found the quiet unbearable.

Winning the Democratic county chairmanship in Eau Claire had given Eppie a taste for public life. As a recent and enthusiastic convert to party politics, Eppie realized that Cook County provided a far wider range of possibility. Ever eager for center stage, she phoned her buddy Art Henning and persuaded him to introduce her to the head of the Illinois Democratic Party, Jacob Arvey. Eppie had no intention of starting out all over again in Chicago. She intended to shoot for the top. That meant one thing: Democratic National Committeewoman from Illinois.

Party power Arvey, the cigar-smoking Democratic bigwig of Cook County, politically weightier than Mayor Richard Daley, was somewhat amused by Henning's suggestion and Mrs. Lederer's presumptuousness. According to Henning, Arvey told him, "It's a pretty rough game in Chicago."

Arvey quickly chilled Eppie's aspirations. "National committeewoman? Ha. Forget it," he firmly responded. "Take up golf," Eppie was told. "There are hundreds of women more qualified."

The coveted post of committeewoman was earned with years of service to the local party. There was already a capable incumbent as well as many other women jostling for the spot. If Eppie Lederer was looking to bump the party faithful, she was looking in the wrong place. Liberal social causes in Eau Claire, Wisconsin, were far removed from Chicago's big-city political machinations. But Eppie's recollections have her alone making the choice to bypass Cook County Politics. "Chicago was run by the machine, and being part of that machine wasn't my personality. I am too independent and too scrupulous."

Eppie was restless. Chicago stimulated her. She craved more excitement than hard-working and frequently exhausted Jules could give her. Over dinner, Eppie confided to friends her indecision about a house they had seen on the ritzy North Shore. She returned several times by herself to look it over. Finally, she realized that life in suburbia would not be enough for her. She told Popo, "I want to use my brain and do something different."

Although she didn't know what she would eventually choose to do, Eppie was certain she didn't want to be numbered among the ranks of suburban matrons. Being only Mrs. Jules Lederer loomed appallingly bland to her. New Chicago acquaintances found it difficult to understand or sympathize with Eppie's indifference to being a wife and mother. And Eppie's restlessness began to tell in other ways. Friends began to notice that the Lederer marriage was not as blissful as it seemed.

Eppie's preoccupation with her personal ambitions and Jules's unrelenting work habits had begun to create a schism even before the couple left Eau Claire. The gap deepened in Chicago, friends say. It wasn't so much that Jules and Eppie were at odds with each other. It's just that they were heading in different directions. Jules was working twenty-four hours a day on his career at Autopoint, and Eppie was continually trying to find herself. They were beginning to lead separate lives, and the joy of shared accomplishment was missing.

"He was a compulsive workaholic," says a former Autopoint executive who finds it hard to forget Jules's commitment to his job. "Nothing you did that was not related to business was of any worth."

Unfortunately for Jules's colleagues, he expected them to share his singular devotion to Autopoint. "I worked on the Fourth of July. I worked on Christmas Day. I worked on Thanksgiving," remembers one now-retired executive. "He called me at two o'clock in the morning. He called the managers down to the office on Saturday and Sunday to meet around the conference table, drinking coffee until our eyelids were snapping like flytraps. If you worked for him, it was a real experience."

Impatient, aggressive, short-tempered and abrasive, but imaginative and somehow charming despite his willfulness, is how Jules's co-workers describe him. Jules's charm could be clicked on and off, depending on who he was talking with. Sensitive about being short and not being a high school graduate, he overcompensated and chose to play his disadvantages against his staff. All told, a lot of Autopoint employees didn't like Jules Lederer one bit.

Job applicants at Autopoint who were unusually tall were especially favored. Jules preferred to surround himself with taller men and, sometimes, extremely tall women. A female typist of over six feet in height may be uncommon, but Jules managed to hire one as his personal secretary.

Speculation in the ranks had it that Jules got special pleasure from chewing out the taller members of his work force. Emotional browbeating consisted of yelling up at a hapless salesman whose only recourse was to clench his fists and stare down at the company president. Jules let everyone know he was the boss. Because of his bellicose demeanor and not-so-pint-sized ego, it's no wonder the Autopoint staff called him "Little Napoleon" behind his back.

Since his lack of education was a sore point, Jules would bully executives who had the advantage of a university education. "One of Jules's greatest joys was to flay me around because I had a bachelor of arts and part of my master's," recalls former Autopoint executive Lewis Pollock. "Jules would taunt, 'I only have an eighth-grade education, and I'm your boss.' I sat there and ground my teeth and bit my nails."

In reading Jules's business correspondence, it's perhaps not surprising to find his written expression awkward and even crude. To get the sales force moving, for example, he resorted to questioning their manhood. A postscript in a letter to one salesman reads, "I'll bet you a new suit . . . that you aren't man enough to sell 100,000 3-X pens. One of the boys in Indianapolis called me on Sunday shortly before I dictated this note to you, and has got three deals cooking. . . . He can do it, but I don't think you can."

Autopoint employees also speculated that Jules's verbal abuse and constant intimidation stemmed in part from a tepid marriage. Co-workers discovered that despite his big ego, Jules had his match in Eppie. It became obvious that both felt compelled to dominate whatever situation they were in. Eppie had her own special way of putting Jules down to his associates. Over the telephone to the Foster Avenue office she'd ask, "Is the little man there?" Staff members felt themselves caught in the middle of the Lederer cross-fire. "Well, I wasn't going to say, 'Hey, Jules, little man, boss, your wife wants you,' " an employee admitted.

Eppie, ever conscious of her social rank, enjoyed the status her husband's new job conferred. Being the wife of the president of a company based in a city like Chicago was loads more important than being a sales director's wife in a town like Eau Claire. At Presto, even Mort didn't have the title of president of his own company. Popo's lifestyle back in Wisconsin, which Eppie had long envied, was now within her grasp.

In keeping with the family's elevated status, Eppie swiftly checked out the private day schools in the Chicago area. Despite her stated belief in instilling in children old-fashioned values, she soon enrolled Margo in the progressive and nontraditional Francis Parker school on Chicago's near Northside.

With Margo's education well taken care of, Eppie began to indulge in more frivolous pursuits, like a newly acquired hobby that filled the high-rise nest with a collection of carved, sculpted, and stuffed owls. Not lacking in discrimination, Eppie chose owls because her father's nickname for her had been "Owl Eyes." Eppie invited Popo to go shopping around the corner from her apartment, in the same Michigan Avenue shops where once she had only looked on while Popo did the buying. Eppie's expensive clothes were no longer hand-me-downs from her twin, and she made sure Jules was dressed in the finest masculine cuts and fabrics.

Eppie, a quick learner in the gracious arts, began to entertain lavishly. Her days of serving hot dogs by candlelight were over, and she must have wished her Eau Claire friends could see her luxurious household and her staff, which included a full-time cook/housekeeper.

On account of Jules's position, Eppie was obligated to entertain his business associates. The Lederers may have sometimes asked Autopoint clients to their home, but Autopoint subordinates were invariably taken out to dinner. Within a short time, Jules and Eppie became familiar figures at the choicest nightspots in Chicago, including Mr. Kelly's, the Pump Room at the posh Ambassador East, and the super-smart Gaslight Club, where couples squeezed through a phone booth to reach the former speakeasy's special back room.

Although Eppie was a cordial hostess, she had subtle ways of letting Autopoint executives and their wives sense that she considered herself their better. She made it clear that it was because she was obligated and not because she wanted to that she was sitting at dinner with them. Nor did she allow Jules to accept return invitations to their homes. "They never came to our house even though we asked them often," recalls the wife of an Autopoint executive. "They were too busy."

Not only did Eppie decline invitations, she often avoided eating while entertaining her husband's employees and their wives. Saying she was dieting, Eppie would order a pot of tea while her guests had their martinis, shrimp cocktails, steaks, and cherries jubilee. Throughout dinner Eppie wouldn't partake of any food, or, for that matter, conversation. Guests of the Lederers say she at times seemed vaguely preoccupied. "I'll never forget it," says Lewis Pollock's wife, Peg, who was particularly miffed by some of these episodes. "Eppie made it clear she didn't want to be bothered with us."

Labor Day 1955. Life was a bore. The apartment looked consummately upscale and Eppie was tired of shopping. Margo was starting a new year at Francis Parker. Jules had his career to occupy all his waking hours, and as much as she wanted to help her husband get ahead, Eppie couldn't stand being obligated to entertain people she thought were not up to her increasingly higher standards. "I only like the best, most interesting, most alive people," Eppie explains. "I like achievers, and I won't settle for mediocrity, in myself or in other people."

Eppie was having trouble finding her place in the spotlight. Her high-speed merge into party politics was slowed by the man behind the Cook County machine, Jake Arvey. In a big city like Chicago, the important charities were already monopolized by society women out to make a name for themselves. Besides, in Eau Claire Eppie had been involved in fund raising and hospital work and found it personally unfulfilling. "I had a lot of energy and knew it was time to try something else," says Eppie. "I wanted to serve, to do something for someone else." By the early fall of 1955 she'd been in Chicago nearly a year and felt she'd accomplished little since leaving Wisconsin.

Finishing breakfast one morning, having just sent Margo off to school and Jules to the office, with only the Chicago-based Don McNeill's Breakfast Club radio broadcast for company, Eppie found herself rereading the Ann Landers column in the *Sun-Times*. On impulse, she rang up family friend Wilbur Munnecke, the avuncular *Sun-Times* executive and business manager of the news division of Field Enterprises, who she had met on the train between Eau Claire and Chicago three years before. Did Ann Landers need any help with the mail, Eppie wanted to know.

"Funny you should ask," Munnecke responded. He explained that Ruth Crowley, the author of the Ann Landers feature and a veteran *Sun-Times* employee, had unexpectedly died July 19, and the newspaper was looking for someone to replace her.

Eppie didn't doubt for a moment that she could handle writing the Ann Landers feature. But she was concerned that others wouldn't think she was qualified. "I wanted to be in a helping profession but had neither the training nor the experience," she recalls. Answering letters in an advice column was one way of getting around her lack of training, even though that too seemed to demand a certain kind of professional training or job experience. Ruth Crowley had been both a journalist and a registered nurse.

Munnecke quickly informed Eppie that many women, most of whom were experienced journalists, were vying for the Ann Landers assignment. In addition, the column wasn't just a *Sun-Times* feature, it was syndicated to a couple of dozen other newspapers. Authoring an advice column was a plum assignment for newspaperwomen in the mid-fifties; it was a feature everyone could have fun with while doing some good, too. In fact, being a columnist was also a popular daydream for housewives. More than 10,000 people, mostly married women, wrote the King Features syndicate in the early fifties offering to write the Dorothy Dix feature, another popular advice column.

Eppie wanted in the competition. After hanging up with Munnecke she quickly thumbed through her phone directory searching for any and all connections who might help her. She had to convince the editors at the *Sun-Times* she ought to be given the opportunity to try out for the job despite her lack of credentials. Finally settling on Jake Arvey, she pressed him to influence Marshall Field IV, then publisher of the *Sun-Times*, to allow her to join the competition for the Ann Landers spot.

Chicago was mainly a two-newspaper town in 1955. The very righteous *Chicago Tribune* brandished Old Glory for the Republican party. The *Sun-Times*, the other morning paper and the *Trib*'s bitter competitor, defended Democratic party politics and politicians, among them Jake Arvey. Arvey and Field were good friends and party patriots. Since Eppie's move into Cook County politics was stalled by Arvey, it seemed that the least he could do was help her get a job at the *Sun-Times*. It was said that Arvey, along with his Democratic friends, convinced Field to intercede on Eppie's behalf, and got her in the running for the Ann Landers job.

Besides having influential friends, it turned out Eppie was fortunate in having dark, wavy hair and sharply defined facial features. Ruth Crowley's photograph had accompanied the Ann Landers column and it was preferable that the new Ann Landers resemble the late author. The *Sun-Times* was looking for a dark-haired, thirtyish woman to continue the feature, and no candidate looked like Ruth Crowley as much as Eppie Lederer.

Like the other contestants, Eppie met balding and owlish-looking Larry Fanning when she went to the newspaper office to pick up her contest package. Fanning, who smoked a pipe and squinted at the world through thick glasses, had just arrived from San Francisco to become editor of the *Sun-Times* syndicate. Until the paper hired a new Ann Landers, Fanning was writing the advice column. Needless to say, the experienced newsman, appearing crabbedly omniscient in his rolled-up sleeves and ever-present bow tie, wasn't impressed with Eppie's credentials.

"He stared in disbelief when I confessed I had never written a line for publication, had no previous record of employment and not a single professional reference," says Eppie. It was Eppie's maiden trip into a genuine newsroom. "I had no degree, despite four years at Morningside College in Sioux City, where I majored in boys." Eppie may have felt that she majored in boys, not journalism, but actually she spent only three years attending classes at Morningside.

"Finally," she says, recalling how little qualified she was, "the Iowa hay was still apparent, not only in my hair but in the way I put words together. The only thing I had going for me was that I had a teenage daughter. I could at least be described as 'a mother.' "

"You might as well try," Fanning told Eppie. "You have nothing to lose."

The contest package consisted of reader letters. Each of the twenty-eight job candidates got the same letters to answer. The contest was blind. Each applicant was assigned a letter code that served as a byline for her submission. Eppie was XYZ. "I was assured no one had an inside track and that my chances were as good as anyone else's," Eppie remembers. On her way home with the letters, Eppie realized she didn't have a typewriter. "To buy one would be presumptuous, so I phoned IBM and arranged for a rental." In three weeks, Eppie churned out forty sample columns.

Though versions differ, it was either Marshall Field, Will Munnecke, Larry Fanning, or some other *Sun-Times* executive who called Eppie early that October morning. Eppie picked up the telephone in her bedroom to be greeted by, "Good morning, Ann Landers. It's your column."

"I promptly went into shock," Eppie says. "When I recovered, I walked into Margo's room and uttered my first piece of advice. It was that old proverb: Be careful what you wish for; you might get it."

Thirteen

"The manner in which the column fell into my lap is enough to make a person believe in Santa Claus," Eppie later modestly admits. But that's only half the story. Sure, Eppie's timing was right when she called up Will Munnecke. It's true she was lucky to know the right people. But it's equally accurate that the Iowa challenger worked enough magic on her rented IBM typewriter to outshine the twenty-seven other contenders, most of whom were professional journalists. The other candidates? "I understand some of them have since been very sorry they didn't get the job," Eppie says.

Eppie claims because she called experts for advice her responses to the Landers queries were superior to the answers of the other contestants. Although earlier advice columnists had sought experts to bolster their own opinions, despite Eppie's claim she was the first to do so, not one of the other contenders for the Ann Landers column had thought to do so. Eppie's three responses that propelled her beyond the other hopefuls solicited expert opinions on a neighbor's property, interfaith marriage, and psychosomatic hives.

≈ 107

Recounted in various ways over the years, the first response had to do with ownership of produce from either an apple tree, a chestnut tree, or a walnut tree. In any case, apples, chestnuts, or walnuts fell on a neighbor's lawn. Who owned them? An expert on constitutional law was hardly the logical authority to call for a legal opinion, but that didn't stop Eppie from ringing up a U.S. Supreme Court justice.

Saying that her source was Justice William O. Douglas certainly gave Eppie's response the voice of authority. Not that she knew him very well, having been introduced to the famed Justice by Senator Hubert Humphrey only once in Eau Claire. "So I called Justice William O. Douglas, who was a friend of mine, and got his opinion," Eppie recounts. " 'And Bill, can I use your name?' 'Fin-n-e.' " Douglas himself, before his death, denied he was a source for Ann Landers, and neither his widow nor an ex-wife ever recall his mentioning the aid he supposedly provided Eppie.

"No, no, no, *no*," Douglas responded when asked whether he helped Eppie as Ann Landers. "She does not talk about those things. Just things that are happening in the world, her plans, her family, and so on. Just personal things."

On the question of psychosomatic hives, Eppie phoned the Washington, D.C., home of Dr. Robert Stolar, her dermatologist friend. Again, later, in order to impress an audience, she insisted that she had called upon the head of the dermatology department at the Mayo Clinic, a post Stolar never held.

The question about a Catholic/Protestant marriage merely meant a phone call to Father John Paul, a priest Eppie knew in Eau Claire. But once Eppie became famous as Ann Landers, saying she had consulted a Midwestern parish priest apparently lacked the necessary cachet. Changing her story not only about whom she consulted, but the content of the letter too, Eppie claimed to *Ladies' Home Journal* that she had called Father Theodore Hesburgh, president of the University of Notre Dame.

"A question about annulling a Catholic marriage? I called Father Hesburgh, president of Notre Dame University. 'Ted, can I use your name?' 'Fin-n-e.' " But Eppie still couldn't make up her mind. She later clouded matters further by bragging to a group of awestruck journalism students that she had called upon her friend Bishop Fulton J. Sheen, the flamboyant and by then very famous Roman Catholic TV celebrity, for her answer.

Granted, Eppie has called on a lot of people for their perspective since she became Ann Landers. If she mistakenly substitutes one person for another as the source for one of her column responses, it's perhaps only because she's answered so many reader letters over the years. What isn't so surprising though, is that the longer Eppie's been Ann Landers, the more renowned are the experts she consults.

Whoever Eppie consulted for their expertise, the *Sun-Times* editors were impressed with the housewife who considered the advice column a serious undertaking. What Eppie lacked in training and education, she made up for in earnestness. She acquired the Ann Landers feature much the same way she accomplished everything else in her life, with drive, energy, and nerve. Few women without newspaper experience would have dared compete for a column that already was nationally syndicated.

"Of course I was thrilled, and I'm still pinching myself," confessed Eppie a year after her debut as Ann Landers. Her starting pay at the *Sun-Times* hadn't been an issue. But when Eppie, turned out in a hand-tailored suit and a choker of pearls, told the hardworking newsroom staff that she needed to apply for a Social Security number, she was greeted with looks of disbelief. Her beginning salary was $87 a week. "They thought they were overpaying me, and so did I," says Eppie.

Upon her arrival at the newsroom for her first day of work in October 1955, she was appalled to discover that she had no office, no telephone, and no secretary. Her desk was buried under thousands of unopened letters emptied out of mailbags. "I felt like a sparrow that had been caught in a badminton game," she says. "The copy boy greeted me with, 'So you're the new Ann Landers. Well, here's your mail.' He then dumped about 5,000 letters on my desk. I didn't know whether to laugh or to cry."

Reporters with desks nearby, by now amused and somewhat unsympathetic because of her offhand remark about needing a Social Security number, were waiting to see how the housewife-turned-columnist would cope with the avalanche of mail. "The odds on the seventh floor were 12 to 5 that I'd fold within three months," Eppie says.

"No dame would work that hard unless she needed the money" was the sentiment expressed by newsroom colleagues, who actually placed bets on how long she'd last as Ann Landers.

Because *Sun-Times* executives were themselves unsure whether Eppie could handle the job, they decided to keep the identity of the new Ann Landers under wraps for six months. Eppie worked on a week-to-week basis. She was ordered to stay out of the limelight. She was to receive absolutely no publicity for the trial period.

Katherine Fanning, today the executive editor of the *Christian Science Monitor,* offers a unique perspective on Eppie's early days and first decade as Ann Landers. Kay is not only the widow of Larry Fanning, Eppie's editor for twelve years, but she was also married to Marshall Field IV, *Sun-Times* publisher and Eppie's top boss, until their divorce in 1963. Kay says that despite the lid on publicity, *Sun-Times* management "wanted her to succeed and thought she would." Marshall Field himself "felt Eppie was a very good choice for the job. I know he was aware of the choice," says Kay of her ex-husband.

Eppie, supermotivated, attacked the pile of mail with characteristic vigor and prepared her first column for an October 16, 1955, release. "It simply didn't occur to me that I didn't have the energy for the assignment," she truthfully explains. Eppie's reserves have always seemed infinite. And in a different frame of mind, she recalls, "When I started writing the column at thirty-seven, I thought I was worldly and sophisticated. I knew what life was about. Let me tell you, I didn't know anything."

Suddenly, and with only the vaguest of warning, that square, small-town, Midwestern lady was exposed to the troubles of a large and extremely diverse readership. She was astonished at what people would write to a stranger. Eppie was often shocked and sometimes downhearted reading about pregnant teenagers, abused wives, and alcoholic husbands. Larry Fanning presented Eppie with a copy of Nathanael West's *Miss Lonelyhearts* and cautioned his novice columnist not to let her readers' problems affect her as much as they had West's fictional character.

Eppie read the novel. "I never could become like the columnist in *Miss Lonelyhearts*. I'm too strong and confident," she says. Her desire to help others hadn't been a mere pipe dream. Later, she'd say, "I have learned how it is with the stumbling, tortured people in this world who have nobody to talk to. . . . I have learned that financial success, academic achievement, and social or political status open no doors to peace of mind or inner security."

From her first day as Ann Landers, Eppie had to steel herself against melancholy. Later, she'd look back and say, "No situation, I now realize, is too bizarre, too idiotic, or too risky to be real. Somebody, somewhere, will do anything if he or she is lonely enough, desperate enough, or pushed beyond the threshold of tolerance."

From her very informed perspective, Eppie was soon able to judge what was important and what was not. "The true measure of a human is how he or she treats his fellow man. Integrity and compassion cannot be learned in college, nor are these qualities inherited in the genes." In answering the more tortured souls who wrote for advice, Eppie had begun to learn the importance of kindness firsthand. But it's a lesson she perhaps learned years before, growing up in a loving family atmosphere in Sioux City, possessing a lot of "loving, happy family memories." Along with tireless energy, kindness and compassion would become the qualities she'd need in abundance to be a success as Ann Landers.

"Larry Fanning was my mentor. He taught me how to write," Eppie always says. She can't thank Fanning enough for all the help he gave her way back when. The experienced *Sun-Times* editor transformed a fledgling writer into a polished Ann Landers.

Without what one reporter called "considerable coaching and guidance," it's unlikely Eppie would have succeeded at the *Sun-*

Times. The newsroom contemporary of Eppie's recalls, "Fanning would literally shape that column. He taught her everything."

Fanning firmly believed, "You can deal with any human problem as long as you use the right language." He supported Eppie in her belief that the Ann Landers column should touch all facets of life. But most of all Fanning made it clear to Eppie that the Ann Landers column could not last without having credibility. "The column must have integrity or it will not survive," he constantly told her. And he supported his statement by insisting that Eppie call experts to document her opinions; he repeatedly told her not to sacrifice sound advice for a laugh.

William P. Steven, who held various executive positions at the *Chicago Daily News* and the *Minneapolis Star & Tribune,* was Fanning's long-time friend and contemporary. He agrees, "If you're accurate and careful with your language, you can say a great deal." It was one of Fanning's mottoes. When Steven met Eppie through Fanning, he commended him for having had the foresight to recognize her latent abilities. "Larry had an excellent nose for talent," says Steven. "Mike Royko was another one of Fanning's discoveries. Larry was a great editor."

When Eppie speaks of her takeover of the column, she says she broadened the range of topics discussed and enlivened the writing. "I thought I could give the column some spark," and she says she told Will Munnecke that the column had the potential to "cut through a wide area of human life." Fanning agreed. Or perhaps it was Fanning who helped Eppie form her ideas on what the column could become.

Kay Fanning remembers that even before Eppie took it over, "the Ann Landers column was very popular." She confirms that Larry "taught Eppie an enormous amount about the techniques involved and how to communicate. He taught her to be a journalist." She also says that Eppie was a talented pupil. "She showed a flair for it," says Kay, and she attributes the tenor of the column to Eppie, not to Larry. "The style is hers. That sort of slightly sassy, flippant style is definitely hers. It wasn't his."

Eppie implies that her predecessor, Ruth Crowley, considered herself an expert on child care and emphasized "bringing-up-baby" in the column. "I told Munnecke," says Eppie, "there were other problems besides mothers and their babies."

For whatever reason, Eppie blurs the distinction between another *Sun-Times* column, Ruth Crowley, R.N., which was primarily oriented at mothers of young children, with Crowley's authorship of Ann Landers. When Marshall Field asked Ruth Crowley to fill in as a lovelorn columnist for the *Chicago Sun* in 1942, she was already writing her child-care column under her own name, hosting a daily television show, "Women's Magazine of the Air," and raising three kids.

Journalists contend it was Crowley who initiated the irreverent, shoot-from-the-hip answers that characterize the Ann Landers feature. They charge that Eppie was just clever enough to imitate Crowley's approach. One woman insists that Eppie "continued the fresh, snappy style which had originated thirteen years earlier. The wit, originality, and freshness of Ann Landers began many years ago as a product of the creativity of Ruth Crowley."

San Francisco Chronicle columnist Patricia Holt, Ruth Holt Crowley's niece, questions whether Eppie's approach was totally new, or an extension of her aunt's technique. "My family still takes pride in the fact that Aunt Ruth was the first lovelorn columnist to burst the shackles of sob sister sappiness. She launched the no-nonsense style for which the Ann Landers column became so famous."

A veteran of the *Sun-Times* newsroom corroborates the memories of Crowley's niece and contradicts Eppie's version, which credits only herself with changing the look of advice columns. "What she's said is not true. Crowley didn't write a bland column. She put wit into it. She was a very sharp, very attractive, warm, and knowledgeable woman, certainly as knowledgeable as Eppie is."

A look at an Ann Landers column written by Crowley tends to confirm that Crowley was the pacesetter. For example, Crowley's November 24, 1954, column response as Ann Landers to a critic who reproved her for "glibly advising everyone on every possible subject" was "Look, Bub, why don't you read the comics, there's no law that requires you to read what I write." Over time, though Eppie's barbs and responses may have become bolder and more to the point than those of her predecessor, the style itself was Crowley's. Some people say Eppie was smart enough to imitate the former Ann Landers's approach.

By somehow getting a few names and dates wrong, Eppie, in a way, shortchanges Crowley even more. She told a *New York Times Magazine* writer that a *Sun-Times* editor in 1952 thought up the name Ann Landers. In truth, Crowley invented the name. Shortly before the column first appeared in an edition of the 1942 *Chicago Sun,* which some five years later merged with the *Chicago Times,* Crowley asked a family friend, Bill Landers, if she could borrow his surname.

The four-days-a-week Ann Landers column was, in fact, thirteen years old when Eppie took over in 1955, not three years old as Eppie so often claims. Records in the United States Patent Office indicate when the name Ann Landers became registered and by law the property of Field Enterprises, Inc. The registration records the first use of ANN LANDERS as a trademark by the *Sun-Times:* "First use Oct. 8, 1946; in commerce Oct. 8, 1946. The name 'Ann Landers' is fanciful."

It was far from typical in 1955 for the wife of a company president to pound a typewriter for a paycheck. But Eppie needed to assert herself. There was no way she'd sleepwalk her days forty floors above Lake Shore Drive, basking in the complacency of knowing how good she had it.

Margo, accustomed to seeing her father bring work home from the office, has implied that she found it acceptable to see her mother do likewise. On another level, Margo may have accepted her father's workaholism because she had no other choice. When she saw her mother begin to work at home too, her reaction may have masked her dismay. Margo may have found it difficult to see her mother act so differently from her friends' mothers. But at the age of fifteen, when her mother became Ann Landers, the impact may not have been that great.

Jules believed being an advice columnist suited his wife perfectly. In his opinion, she'd never been reluctant to express herself on any and all subjects. According to Margo, Jules began calling his wife "general manager of the world." If he had second thoughts about having a working wife, he kept them to himself. In any event, her starting earnings at the *Sun-Times* amounted to mere pin money. Jules told her to keep it for herself; he was in charge of supporting the family.

In talking about her marriage and how Jules reacted when she became Ann Landers, Eppie says, "I have been very supportive down through the years. I've been willing to do whatever he wanted, whatever was needed. Then, when I got my job as Ann Landers, he returned the compliment and was supportive of me. He didn't resent the time I spent on my column, and he didn't resent his wife having a fulfilling career."

Telling Popo about getting the job at the *Sun-Times* promised a heady triumph. For once, the news Eppie could impart was nearly equal to her twin's revealing her engagement to millionaire Mort Phillips years before. At long last, she had topped her twin. She had accomplished something on her own, and what was more important, she did it first.

In fact, Eppie shared more than her excitement with her twin. She realized that she needed help, and she needed it fast if she were to keep up with the quantity of mail that kept clogging her desk top. Eppie says she started the column "with the understanding that I would answer every letter." Since the twins had worked so well together on their college undergrad column, "Campus Rats," Eppie suggested they resume the old partnership. Unknown to Fanning and Eppie's syndicate bosses, Popo, who had recently moved to the west coast, flew back to the Midwest to assist her twin.

While Fanning would instruct Eppie in the mechanics of column preparation, "he wielded his pencil like a machete, hacking away at redundancies, clichés, inanities," she says, Eppie would relate the lessons to Popo. The sequence was precise: from Fanning to Eppie, from Eppie to Popo. Popo may have been the quicker to catch on, but Eppie was no less astute in recognizing that her twin's bright, breezy, and expressive style was effective. Popo soon returned to her new home in Hillsborough, California, but the collaboration continued.

As Popo explains it, "Sis got that job and shot those letters to me. I provided the sharp answers," she modestly admits. "I'd say, 'You're writing too long'—she still does—'and this is the way I'd say it.' My stuff was published and it looked awfully good in print." Obviously, Eppie's twin was fast becoming accustomed to seeing her answers in the papers. Popo remembers, "I loved what I was doing. I loved writing those letters." She adds, "I was ecstatically happy and having a ball!

"Then, suddenly the ball was over. Eppie called to say that her syndicate had put the kibosh on her sending mail 'outside the office,' so there would be no more letters coming my way."

When Fanning learned that some of the confidential reader letters were regularly being sent across the country to be read by Eppie's double, the new Ann Landers was given a stern lecture on journalistic ethics. Eppie was ordered to terminate the unauthorized twin act. What Fanning didn't realize was that without Popo's aid, the new Ann Landers might not have been so successful so quickly.

However, the extent of Popo's help is debatable. Kay Fanning says that she never heard the story about Popo helping Eppie with the letters, either at the time from her husband, Marshall Field, or later, from Larry. "I really doubt that," she says of Popo's version. "I never heard it."

At any rate, having had some encouragement, if not direct assistance, for a couple of months gave Eppie the confidence to go solo. Still, the enormous backlog of letters couldn't be easily cleared up by Eppie alone. Fanning didn't have the final say about additional staffing, but "he backed me to the hilt when I asked for secretarial help so that every letter with a name and address could be answered personally," Eppie recalls. The matter was taken before the syndicate bosses.

"If I'm going to write this column," Eppie told them, her integrity at stake, "we are going to answer every letter that has a name and address. . . . If we can't work it out, forget it, because I'm not going to run a phony operation here."

Because of the column's growing popularity, Eppie was granted her request. She got not one, but three assistants. She was armed to advise the world.

Fourteen

Within a year's time, Eau Clair had lost both Friedman twins. Shortly after the Presto production line closed down, Mort accepted the presidency of the family-owned liquor distributorship, M. Sellers & Company, and the family boarded a train west for San Francisco. Mort's career at Presto was stagnating. His cousin Mel, who was characterized by Presto employees as extremely competitive, had a law degree and Mort didn't. Despite being the president's nephew, Mort assumed that the gavel held by Lewis Phillips would likely pass to his son-in-law rather than to his nephew.

Lush Hillsborough, California, just thirty minutes from San Francisco, housed the estates of many monied individuals, including Bing Crosby and Randolph Hearst. By comparison to the neighboring properties, the Phillipses' pool-flanked, ranch-style home at 10 Summerholme Place was spacious yet far from grand. The rambling but roughly symmetrical one-level brick home was bounded on the street side by a carefully tended lawn and a row of identically pruned fruit trees.

Out back, intricate wrought-iron grillwork painted flat white framed the patio area where metal lawn chairs with cushions covered with a slippery, floral-patterned plastic were arranged for easy conversation. Inside, contemporary blond furniture upholstered in a nubby fabric popular during the fifties and walls of cabinets and bookshelves formed a backdrop for Popo's growing collection of ceramic monkeys.

The monkey motif was repeated throughout the house with wooden and painted monkeys grinning from every corner. Guests entering the living room were forced to duck around a life-size fabric monkey hanging in the doorway leading from the study where Popo displayed Mort's bronzed infantry boot. A wall of 8 × 10 black-and-white family photos in plain black wooden frames, including one of Mort in his World War II flight suit, covered an entire grasscloth wall of the study. In the living room, a glass-topped coffee table was placed before the large, comfortable plaid sofa. Popo, in bright pastels, smiled down from her three-quarter-length portrait over the slate fireplace.

Without much fuss, teenage daughter Jeannie was enrolled in a local private day school, and Eddie was packed off to San Rafael Military Academy, from which he was allowed to return home on weekends if his grades were B+ or better. Unwilling to succumb to the indolent haze of suburban life, Popo resumed much the same activity she had in Eau Claire. "After we were settled in our suburban Hillsborough home, I took stock of myself," says Popo. "I was a thirty-seven-year-old housewife with two teenagers, plenty of help in the house, and time on my hands. I was bursting with energy."

Popo volunteered in many of the same organizations she had worked for back in Wisconsin, including the Easter Seal Society and the county Mental Health Association. But much of what Popo was occupying herself with in Hillsborough was, for her, too similar to life in Eau Claire. As the wife of a very wealthy and influential businessman, she was expected to sit on charity boards, raise funds, and direct the tasks of others.

Popo quickly discovered that, compared with volunteerism in Hillsborough, volunteerism in Eau Claire was small potatoes. Because of the sometimes Machiavellian nature of the personalities on those charity boards, run by impassioned society women out to promote their own agendas, Popo, being new to the community, began to feel unfairly used and even underappreciated. Besides, Popo was already involved in philanthropy in a big way. Back in Minnesota, the Phillips Foundation, on whose board Popo still sits, was giving millions to worthy causes.

Later on, Popo hints why committee work was unfulfilling: It lacked the excitement of helping people directly. She says, "I have always gravitated toward people with problems." As Abby, "I still look forward to opening my mail every day. People are so grateful for any help you can give them." On a charity board, the element of hands-on involvement with the infirm, the needy, those who benefit the most, is missing. Too, Popo never much liked being taken for granted.

Had a perceptive artist accurately depicted Popo in caricature during her first few months in Hillsborough, he might have sketched an urgency where there could easily have been serenity. Surrounded by tangible evidence of success, the chauffeured car, the swimming pool, the hired help, Popo might easily have submitted to the nervous evasiveness or dreamy gesturing of a wealthy matron. If in Eau Claire Popo had been, as she says, bored out of her gourd, in suburban Hillsborough she risked becoming relaxed to the max.

Help came from her twin, just in time. Novice advice columnist Eppie got the assistance she needed from Popo. And Popo couldn't have been more pleased, being consulted about a stranger's personal problems. Each day's mail promised a diversion from the routine of Hillsborough housewife. Helping her twin convinced Popo that she, too, could write an advice column.

"I was sure I could," she says. "I've always been a compulsive letter writer." The co-author stint that Popo remembers so clearly lasted from October until December. For two months, Popo served as Eppie's shadow. Then, abruptly, the letters stopped coming.

Popo was crestfallen. For some reason she sounds more bitter than disappointed when talking about why Eppie ceased sending her the letters. Popo seems to imply that her responses were better than Eppie's. But whether they were or not is impossible to judge.

"I guess she felt threatened, because she said, 'I'm not sending any more letters; my editors don't want me to,' and she yanked them away," Popo complains.

Of course Eppie felt threatened; Fanning had ordered her in no uncertain terms to stop sharing the letters with her twin. Eppie's job was at stake. Popo, as brash and optimistic as her twin, was already hatching her next move. Popo looked at the last batch of letters she was returning to Chicago and thought, "I can do this." And just eighty-five days after the *Sun-Times* syndicate published Eppie's first column, she did.

Popo's first foray into the fourth estate was a bust. "Having acquired a taste for dispensing advice, and confident that I could do it well," she recalls, "I first called on the *San Mateo Times*." Popo shouldered her way into the newsroom, and, she says, "I asked to see the feature editor, whose name I have now forgotten, but (if he's still alive) I'm sure he hasn't forgotten mine."

Popo says she was made to wait for a half hour before telling the editor that she thought "his newspaper could use a readable, helpful advice column, which I would be happy to write."

"We can't afford another feature," he answered.

"But I'll write it for nothing, as a public service," she countered.

"Sorry, not interested," was his final response.

According to J. Hart Clinton, the blunt, serious-minded, and gravelly voiced publisher of the *Times,* Popo was "thrown out" of the newsroom. "Our editor had a feisty personality and was not foresighted," he says. In what can only be termed an extraordinary understatement, Clinton adds, "I think he made a mistake."

Popo was undaunted. She may have returned home with a bruised ego, but she wasn't cowed. Popo, a critical reader of the recently established Molly Mayfield lovelorn column in the *San Francisco Chronicle,* had begun to feel, "The answers weren't helpful. They lacked imagination. I could always come up with a better solution."

Shortly after the New Year 1956, Popo read a response that particularly irked her.

"I'll never forget that day," she says. "A woman had written into the paper with genuine despair. She had gone from man to man seeking real love, and that columnist had accused her of learning her morals in an alley. I was furious."

Popo, shocked into action, telephoned the *Chronicle* feature editor, Stanleigh "Auk" Arnold, about the insensitive response.

"That column is pretty grim," said Popo. "People with problems need sympathy and direction, not punishment. I could do better," she added.

"Fall in line," Arnold grunted amiably. "A lot of people tell me that."

"Then maybe it's time you listened," Popo shot back.

Popo persisted. Arnold invited her to drop by the next time she was in town. He promised to let her try answering some of the Molly Mayfield letters. What Arnold didn't tell Popo was that he was in charge of finding someone to write an advice column. The Mayfield column was a temporary substitute for a former advice column that had been plucked from the *Chronicle* by the Field syndicate and given to the newspaper's competitor, the *San Francisco Call-Bulletin*. The columnist Mayfield had replaced was none other than Ann Landers.

"I was charged with finding somebody to replace the Ann Landers column. We tried several writers but they just didn't have the zip of Landers," Arnold remembers.

Like Eppie's try for the *Sun-Times* spot, Popo had rivals for the *Chronicle* advice feature, although she doesn't admit to any.

"The word had gone out that we were interested in finding someone, and we had a number of people who wanted to submit copy. So we worked out a system," says Arnold. "I would give them last week's letters, send them home, and tell them to write their own responses."

The next day diminutive Popo was shaking hands with gangly 6'5" Auk Arnold and trying to keep her eyes off his prominent and busy Adam's apple. "I told him that although I had never written professionally, I had taken all the journalism and psychology courses my little college back in Sioux City had to offer. Then I recited the long list of volunteer organizations for which I had worked. He was visibly underwhelmed."

Popo was treated exactly the same as the other candidates, despite being Eppie's twin. Arnold says that when he met Popo, he had no idea she was Eppie's sister. The Lederer family, however, charges that Popo traded on Eppie's rising fame in her initial meeting with Arnold and that Popo sold herself on the basis of being the twin sister of Ann Landers.

"Definitely not true," says Arnold. "Mrs. Morton Phillips showed up. I didn't know her at all. Never heard of her. I just gave her these letters and sent her home, I thought. But she was back in a matter of hours with all the letters answered. Obviously, it was Eppie all over again. So naturally, right away, we signed her up."

Popo had walked the two blocks to Mort's office to type her submissions. She wrote what she now calls "humorous but sensible" and "tongue-in-cheek one-liners." Of course, the responses were just like the ones Ann Landers was becoming famous for, the ones Popo had initially helped write.

Perhaps Popo's favorite and her most famous, or at least most often repeated, one-liner is the answer to Blondie, who wrote, "Dear Abby: My boyfriend took me out on my twenty-first birthday and wanted to show me a special time. I usually don't go in much for drinking, but I had three martinis. During dinner we split a bottle of wine. After dinner we had two brandies. Did I do wrong?" Popo's reply: "Dear Blondie: Probably."

"Ironically," says Arnold, "I'd been instructed to look around for a column just like Ann Landers. There was not a question that she was exactly what we were looking for. I went in immediately to the managing editor and publisher and said, 'I think we have what we want.' " By the time Popo got back to her Hillsborough home, she had a phone message that the *Chronicle* was interested. "They told me, 'We like your style. You're serious and funny.' "

Popo claims she was careful to leave her chauffeured yellow Cadillac around the corner from the *Chronicle* building on her first visit. "I didn't want them thinking I was some rich society dame," she insists. "I wanted them to think I was a hard-working gal looking for a job."

In reality, Popo used her wealth as a shield when she glided through the messy newsroom, attentive to the animated and noisy hubbub but intent on seeking out Auk Arnold. Popo may have thought she looked like an unemployed journalist, but Arnold recalls otherwise. Popo's affluence was "obvious from the very beginning. The first day she showed up at the *Chronicle* she was wearing a leopardskin coat," Arnold chortles good-naturedly. "I didn't think she was exactly impoverished."

Salary was the first topic of discussion when Popo and Arnold met again the next day. "I asked how much the other girl made," says Popo, referring to the wife of an editor of the *Rocky Mountain News* who was then writing the Molly Mayfield column.

"Twenty dollars," was Arnold's answer.

"That'll do," replied Popo, who later says, "I didn't care about the money. I was willing to do it for nothing. But I definitely wanted to make up a pen name and copyright it. My husband told me I should do that for my own protection, and it was the smartest thing I could have done."

Popo has repeatedly stated that she alone selected the pseudonym Abigail Van Buren for her column. "I chose Abigail from the Old Testament. Abigail was a prophetess in the Book of Samuel, and it was said of her, 'Blessed are thou, and blessed is thy advice, O Abigail.' "

She chose the last name, Van Buren, "from our eighth president, Martin Van Buren, because I liked the aristocratic old-family ring." Van Buren had the right degree of class, thought the daughter of Russian-Jewish immigrants. "Abigail Van Buren. It sort of sings. And I could shorten it to Dear Abby; it sounded like someone somebody would write to," Popo recalls.

Selecting the name Abigail Van Buren was an extremely clever decision, and Popo justifiably takes pride in it. But she takes all the credit for it, too. Stanleigh Arnold was asked how the name came about, and whether he had a hand in it. "She has her whole story on that and I'm not saying whether we had any part in it or not," Arnold cautiously states. When pressed again with the same query, Arnold laughs and says, "Abby's story on exactly how her name was chosen is the one we're going by."

Popo's first Dear Abby column appeared January 9, 1956. "With my participles dangling and my infinitives splitting, I started my journalistic career," says Popo, later admitting it was a combination of talent and drive that got her the job, but "mainly it was just *chutzpah.*"

Unlike the significant alterations made to her twin's maiden efforts, Popo's submissions were hardly changed. Her editor remembers checking the columns before they went to press, but the editing "didn't take much. The copy spoke for itself. It wasn't a heavy editing process," Arnold says.

"She'd turn in her copy and we'd go over it. If I had any objection, I guess I prevailed, but it really wasn't an employer-employee relationship.

"Popo always said I was her boss, but it was a very relaxed kind of bossmanship," Arnold chuckles. In all, he remembers Popo with much affection and a great deal of professional respect. "I've always said her advice is fundamentally sound, and on the whole her influence has been beneficial."

Popo couldn't wait to tell Eppie about her successful venture into the world of journalism. "I immediately called my twin in Chicago to tell her I had been hired to write the advice column for the *San Francisco Chronicle.*"

"Congratulations!" was Eppie's automatic and heartfelt response. "That's marvelous. I'm so happy for you." Then after a moment's thought, she added, remembering it was twin sister Popo she was congratulating, "I guess it's all right, as long as you're not syndicated outside San Francisco."

"Don't worry," Popo replied. "Who'd want me?"

After

Fifteen

San Francisco Chronicle editorial offices. A weekday, late January 1956. A salesman from the New York City-based McNaught Syndicate was making a routine visit to the west coast hunting up new talent. One look at the newspaper's newest feature, the Dear Abby column, convinced him. He sensed instant success. While Eppie had yet to be offered a contract by the *Sun-Times,* sister Popo was offered a ten-year contract with McNaught, a syndicate with more marketing power.

It came fast, admits Popo. "In three weeks I was discovered by a New York syndicate."

Popo checked with Mort. Should she sign? His advice: "Go for the big spot, honey."

The Hillsborough housewife who less than a month before, in a little black dress by Dior and a leopardskin coat, had fast-talked her way into the *Chronicle* newsroom was being offered the marketing power of a nationally known syndicate. With Mort's blessing, Popo was as ecstatic as a bride. The note she appended to her signed contract read, "In anticipation of umpteen years of happy marriage."

Popo recalls that whirlwind first month as a syndicated columnist: "Before I could say Horatio Alger," Dear Abby was appearing in newspapers all over the country. "In a matter of thirty days," she crows, "I was in New York, Houston, Dallas, and New Orleans. The column took off like wildfire."

From a modest beginning as an innovative feature in one of San Francisco's leading newspapers, the Dear Abby column quickly saw ink on the pages of other metropolitan journals. The immediate success of Dear Abby surprised both Popo and her syndicate. Naughty, risqué, and flip, the column was a radical departure from previous lovelorn features. Because the column was humorous as well as helpful, the reader dividend made Dear Abby more popular faster than Ann Landers. During its first month of publication, Popo didn't hold back the one-liners.

One woman, for example, wrote saying her fiancé had run off to Alaska and left her pregnant. "How should I tell him?" she asked Abby. "In English," said Abby, "and fast." A twenty-four-year-old ex-soldier wrote that his landlady had asked him to marry her. She was a thirty-eight-year-old widow with five children; what should he do? Abby replied, "You need a thirty-eight-year-old widow with five kids like a moose needs a hat rack."

As Popo explains it, she instinctively knows what's appropriate and what's not. "I don't go off the deep end, but I'm not a marshmallow, neither am I tough. I just use my noodle." The humor, she says, makes the advice more palatable. "I don't write my column for entertainment. I write it primarily to inform, but I like to give advice with a chuckle whenever possible."

Still, some unsophisticated editors refused the column because they found it offensive. Other editors censored it. Popo recalls, "The *San Diego Union* refused to print the word *homosexual,* and I was told the first time they ever printed it was in my column in 1957. It was quite a breakthrough."

Others thought it was a put-on because it sounded like a parody of other advice columns, notably Ann Landers. "Initially, Dear Abby was a little brasher," says William Steven. "But then, the *San*

Francisco Chronicle was a little brasher than the *Chicago Sun-Times.* So what's new?"

Charles McAdam Jr., the hard-nosed and direct president of the McNaught syndicate, remembers that marketing the new feature "wasn't easy. Oh sure, the *New York Mirror* bought it, and the *Chronicle* thought it was okay. No way we could sell it to a typical small-city paper." In order to sell the Dear Abby column to small but important papers, McNaught used a standard pitch. If a newspaper bought a popular feature like the comic strip Joe Palooka, it got a discount on other new, untested ones like Dear Abby. Whether it was a comic strip or Popo's witty responses that made Dear Abby popular with subscribing papers, the column took off.

Sister Eppie, seeing the success Dear Abby was having, started getting bolder with her Ann Landers column. Proving the adage that old friends make the best friends, Marshall Atkinson back in Eau Claire was the first publisher to pick up the Ann Landers feature. He ran the daily feature in the *Leader-Telegram* primarily because Eppie had been a local girl. Atkinson says he was little prepared for the controversy that ensued over Eppie's forthright column.

"The uproar that followed, you wouldn't believe," Atkinson recalls. "Two advertisers threatened to pull out their advertising, and the Dean of Women at Eau Claire's University of Wisconsin campus raised Cain."

"Those columns were on the cutting edge of the change in the capacity of Americans to talk about sex and to talk about social relations," agrees Larry Fanning's friend Steven, the Minneapolis editor who bought the Ann Landers column early on. "The point is that the columns were with the mood of the country and not behind it. Before Ann and Abby, the columns had been behind it."

Another Wisconsin paper, the *Green Bay Press-Gazette,* bought the syndicated Ann Landers column. But something happened to the copy on the way to the pressroom. Editor John Torinus wryly recalls, "When I read the first installments to arrive, I was reluctant to print them because they were so frank and outspoken for those times. Some of them were downright shocking. I actually called and cancelled the order, proving how smart I was at buying syndicated columns."

Torinus, Steven, and Atkinson are referring to columns on subjects like French kissing. French kissing? And venereal disease. V.D.? And something akin to Eppie's answer about an unresponsive woman. "Many are cold, but few are frozen."

Popo lost some subscribers too, but she gained readers at a faster pace. Within a year, Dear Abby was subscribed to by eighty newspapers, only a handful fewer than Ann Landers—and Eppie had begun with the advantage of a couple of dozen already established outlets from Ruth Crowley's prior authorship.

Dear Abby's skyrocketing popularity rankled Eppie, who still lacked a signed contract with the *Sun-Times*. In what would begin *Time* magazine's earnest chronicling of the twin lovelorn columnists' climb to fame, an article that ran just three weeks after Dear Abby had been bought for syndication said, "In her brief tenure on the job, the new lovelorn writer, Mrs. Pauline Phillips, has proved herself just as snappy on the editorial draw as Ann Landers." Less than a year later *Time* once again gave "Abby Van Buren" a glowing write-up and called Popo, not Eppie, "the fastest rising lonelyheart columnist in the United States."

Management at the *Sun-Times* syndicate, under the umbrella name Publishers-Hall syndicate, then Field Enterprises and now News America, was slightly frosty toward Eppie after the appearance of the *Time* article. It was no secret that Eppie's former unpaid staffer was Popo; Eppie herself had given her sister the first taste of advice column writing. Now, the syndicate realized, the twins would have to share the pie. Management also considered that Ann Landers might be overpowered by Dear Abby.

Because of the commitment she thought she had from Popo, Eppie wasn't prepared for rival syndication from her twin. Popo, however, wasn't uneasy or ambivalent about her new venture. She reasoned that there were enough newspapers in the United States to support two advice columns. In addition, Popo hoped that Dear Abby would soon overtake Ann Landers.

"We started our columns within a few weeks of each other," says Popo, "but I became more quickly and more broadly syndicated before she." Needless to say, Popo saw the situation differently from the way Eppie did.

In order to lessen the competition, and perhaps to preserve their already-shaky relationship, the sisters made a new agreement, this time not to sell their columns in the same cities. Consequently, Chicago and Detroit were off limits to Popo. But when the important *New York Daily Mirror,* a tabloid that had one of the largest circulations in the country, stepped forth to buy Dear Abby, Eppie's bobbed nose was put out of joint.

"If Ann Landers can't appear in *The New York Times,*" Eppie announced, "then it's not going to appear in any New York paper."

"That'll be the day," retorted Popo.

The rapid success of Popo's column was difficult enough for Eppie to acknowledge, but Eppie was particularly galled that her twin had been foresighted enough to take ownership of the name of her column. The fact that Popo owned Dear Abby while Eppie initially was an employee of the *Sun-Times* meant that Eppie had to get approval before she appeared in public as Ann Landers, while Popo called her own shots.

Ann Landers was an established column, begun in 1942 and then owned by the *Sun-Times.* Eppie did no more than apply for a job with the Field newspaper in 1955. But Eppie's talent, business sense, and sharp insights quickly made publisher Marshall Field realize he'd inadvertently hired a diamond.

"She was a big success, and everyone was pleased," says Kay Fanning of Eppie's rapid rise. "Eppie was everywhere in Chicago. She did a lot of good publicity for the *Sun-Times.* From that point of view, Marshall and I were very interested. The *Sun-Times* was very much the second newspaper in Chicago at that time, although it was coming up very quickly. She contributed to the *Sun-Times's* success."

Kay, however, says that while she was married to Marshall Field, her and her husband's association with Eppie was strictly limited to Eppie's work at the newspaper. "We really didn't know her on a social basis," Kay states.

At the start of her newspaper career, Eppie was just another employee, the second Ann Landers. Popo's relationship with the *Chronicle* was altogether different. When she plotted her way into the *Chronicle* newsroom, Popo was canny enough to understand that she'd have a great advantage over her sister if she did not take over an already-established column. Clever Popo wanted to start a column that would be all her own. She realized she'd have greater control and a larger share of the profits if she alone owned the Dear Abby name.

Popo repeatedly says that Mort advised her to legally register the Dear Abby name. She says she wanted to copyright it for her own protection. Actually, Popo confuses copyright with a trademark. Names cannot be copyrighted, nor is Dear Abby copyrighted. Dear Abby is a registered trademark. Nonetheless, Popo registered Dear Abby as her own trademark, just as the *Sun-Times* registered Ann Landers as its trademark.

Acquiring property rights to her own creation was a brilliant move on Popo's part. McNaught chief executive Charles McAdam, however, disagrees with Popo's contention that it was Mort who first mentioned taking ownership of the column name. "She never thought of it until our naïve editor slipped and said we were going to get the title registered. 'Oh, I've already done that,' " McAdam remembers Popo quickly saying.

The syndicate took Popo at her word and didn't move to get the column name registered. Later, it had second thoughts about Popo's story and suspected that it had given Popo the registration idea. "We checked in Washington and found out it wasn't done until after our conversation with Popo. The application was never in." With more than a hint of anger in his voice, McAdam continues, "She never thought of it until we said McNaught wanted to register the title. We found out that she hadn't filed until months after that."

The U.S. Patent Office verifies McAdam's version of the story. Pauline Phillips filed for registration of Dear Abby six months after her first column appeared in the *Chronicle,* not immediately after as she repeatedly claims. McNaught officials are still resentful about what they see as Pauline Phillips' deception. But it works both ways. Had McNaught registered the name first, Popo would rightly have been incensed at their taking possession of something of her own making. Popo outsmarted the McNaught people, pure and simple.

Ownership of the Dear Abby name became a source of irritation between the twins. Eppie was envious that Popo owned her column name and resentful because Popo gloated about it. McAdam remembers, "Abby ran it into her all the time, 'I own the title, you don't.' "

Because only Popo can be Dear Abby, she delights in introducing herself, "Hi, I'm Dear Abby," while Eppie gives friends a cold stare when they call her Ann. For Popo, Dear Abby is a personal possession. Not so for Eppie. "Only strangers call me Ann," she says.

Not only doesn't Eppie like being called Ann Landers, she didn't like what readers called writers of advice features. Because virtually one and only one topic was addressed in the features, readers tagged the women who wrote them lovelorn columnists. Popo doesn't mind being called a lovelorn columnist. "I don't care what they call me. I know what I am and why I'm doing it, and that's enough for me." Eppie, however, hates it. "The word—I cringe when I hear it. It's an embarrassment."

If it hadn't been for the McNaught editor's gaffe, both Popo's career as Dear Abby and her relationship with Eppie might have been dramatically different. Popo incessantly says that Eppie has never gotten over her owning her own column, long before Eppie was able to gain control of the Ann Landers name. She relishes the fact Eppie hates to be called Ann Landers. However, Popo refuses to admit that her twin sister showed her how to become an advice columnist.

In March 1956, six months after she took over as Ann Landers, Eppie signed a one-year contract with the *Sun-Times.* Finally, two months after twin sister Popo became syndicated, Eppie officially became Ann Landers. Eppie thought a public announcement of sorts was in order. Propitiously, the television show "What's My Line?" called and asked her to be a guest. But her syndicate at first nixed the idea. They were concerned about their untrained columnist's ability to handle herself in front of a camera.

Eppie had no such reservations. She figured being on television couldn't be much different from speaking at political rallies. She had plenty of experience doing that. Eppie pleaded with the syndicate people to let her appear on television. Finally, they relented. With millions watching that Sunday night, Eppie Lederer, one of the Friedman twins from Sioux City, Iowa, was unequivocally and publicly identified as Ann Landers, the quick-witted advice columnist. When she got back to Chicago, Eppie heard from people she'd grown up with and gone to school with, people she hadn't spoken with in years.

Popo wasn't about to let Eppie be the only native daughter done good. She decided to scoop Eppie in their home town. Popo reportedly offered Dear Abby at a reduced rate, in perpetuity, to the *Sioux City Journal,* as long as the paper agreed not to run the Ann Landers feature. Eppie was irate. Popo's maneuver was unconscionably sly and underhanded.

In their competitive race, Eppie and Popo argued constantly over market share. By late summer 1956, reporters and editors attending an annual newspaper convention in New York saw that Eppie and Popo were avoiding each other. Then, by fall that year, all communication between the twins was on hold. No letters, no phone calls, no visits.

Their older sisters were aghast, but their attempts to intervene were met with silence. Jules and Mort decided to lie low and hope that the twins would solve their own problems. Instead of taking steps to reconcile, Eppie and Popo moved in opposite directions. Soon the "gentleman's agreement" the sisters had made over exclusive city markets was abandoned. Each woman viewed the nation's then forty-eight states as territory to conquer.

Sixteen

As Americans watched Ann Landers and Dear Abby join the pantheon of syndicated celebrities, a twinhood rivalry was festering that made Elizabeth I and Mary Queen of Scots' bid for the royal throne sound like sisterly cooing.

Popo would say that ten more newspapers had signed up for Dear Abby. Eppie would state that Ann Landers just got a dozen. Eppie would say she receives a thousand letters a week. Popo would declare she gets three thousand. The sisters' public bickering grew along with their column popularity. After a year's time, Eppie remained in the lead and nosed out Popo by only a few newspapers. "Things are going well," Eppie told a friend in a letter dated October 1956. "We've added more papers since I last saw you and now the count is eighty-six, tra la la la."

Apparently eager to take the spotlight off the twins' public acrimony, the two syndicates jumped into the fray and argued about marketing methods. The *Sun-Times* charged McNaught with requiring subscribers who wanted Dear Abby to take a package of less popular columnists as well. (McNaught evidently didn't have to use Joe Palooka to sell Dear Abby anymore.) McNaught executives countered that the *Sun-Times* was selling Ann Landers at well below market prices so that thrifty subscribers would chose that feature over Dear Abby.

In reality, the competing syndicates were delighted with Eppie and Popo's growing rivalry. They suspected that the twins' quarrel would titillate readers. Undoubtedly thinking that bad publicity is better than no publicity, Charles McAdam recalls that the sisterly venom "didn't bother us at all."

After years of being overshadowed by her sister, Eppie believed she had achieved something unique and very much her own when she took over the Ann Landers column. For once, Popo wasn't on the other side balancing the equation. Enter clever Popo, who with remarkable alacrity turned Eppie's singular accomplishment into another twin act. What could Eppie do but huff, "Very imitative"? Popo didn't want to hear that from her sister and got angry when Eppie refused to deny she'd said it.

Popo was partly motivated to start her own column because Eppie didn't publicly acknowledge her invaluable help during the first tremulous months of Eppie's takeover as Ann Landers. Popo claims that her responses were printed. But did she get any thanks? "Eppie should have given me credit, but she didn't, and I understand her wanting to forget," says Popo.

But you don't run out and hit up a newspaper to let you write an advice column just because your sister didn't publicly recognize your help with her own. There must've been other reasons for Popo's duplicate enterprise. Despite the distance of half a nation between them, Popo must have felt compelled to compete with her twin. And most of all, she wanted to best Eppie. "I can do a column better than Eppie," Charles McAdam, Popo's first syndicate boss, remembers her boasting.

Understandably, Eppie resented Popo's trespass. Yet the more bitter Eppie sounded, the more innocent Popo proclaimed herself to be. Popo insists that her becoming the country's top advice columnist occurred without planning or scheming. A wave of the wand and *poof*—Popo Phillips turned into Dear Abby.

"It was just like a dream," recites Popo, wide-eyed and all smiles. "I never dreamed of being syndicated. I never set out to

have any goals. It just happened to me. It just came naturally!"
She continues, "I didn't realize that I was going to be as successful
as I am."

Popo gives the impression she was disappointed when she
discovered that her new job was not going to enhance sisterly bonds
with her twin. "I had been so happy over her success that I assumed
she would be happy for me," relates Popo. If her naïveté is to be
believed, Popo was, of all things, surprised at the cool reception
Eppie accorded her at the news of her contract with the *San Francisco Chronicle*. Notes an astounded Popo, "She seemed disturbed."

Disturbed, yes. Angry, yes. Happy, no way. Eppie was cyni-
cally and realistically scrutinizing Popo's sudden transformation
into a top-selling columnist. Although a few "agony" columnists
like Dorothy Dix and Mary Haworth were still in print, they were
fast tumbling out of favor and being replaced with either Ann
Landers or Dear Abby.

Eppie had done the dirty work for Popo. Her initial success at
knocking off the competition made her all the more angry at her
twin's intrusion. "I had no competition," says Eppie, teeth clenched.
"There was nobody else around. I mean *nobody*." Eppie means not
even Popo. Eppie felt her sister betrayed her when she went ahead
and got syndicated.

Popo later, relying on some self-analysis, admitted, "Our
careers damaged our relationship." Many people, including the
columnists themselves, attribute the sisters' public hostilities to
professional competition. But the column rivalry perhaps only emphasized the unresolved problems of their twinship. It's even possible that the career rivalry, ostensibly the catalyst for the rift, served
as a convenient excuse for the twins to sever their relationship.

The twin act was played out for the moment. They both,
perhaps Eppie more so, needed a respite from its demands. It was
time for both sisters to collect themselves. A momentary chrysalis
might allow them to replenish their stores of equanimity. The sudden breach would give them time to transfer their energies to more
pressing matters, like inventing a newer and fresher identity for

themselves, one based on their column namesakes, Ann and Abby. "All this competition began a long, long time ago," says Popo. "A psychologist could have a field day with this."

Robert Stolar, who got to know Popo through Eppie, says that each Friedman twin wanted to "outdo the other." Eppie admits, "Being a twin was not easy, I must say, because we were each striving to be individuals. And it's hard to be an individual when you have someone who looks a lot like you who is by your side all you life. And this is the way it was with us."

"I think being a twin is marvelous," Popo has said. When told that Eppie remarked, "It's not easy being a twin," Popo, letting her voice drop off, said, "I don't know why. . . ."

Perhaps Stolar sees it clearly when he says, "Popo felt being a twin boosted her," while Eppie realized twinhood was damaging to her. Apparently Popo doesn't understand the depth of her sister's feelings.

But when giving advice to others, Popo realizes that it is usually best for parents not to raise twins identically. "I would encourage them to be individuals," she says. "We were not." Eppie echoes Popo, "Break up the vaudeville act. It may be good for the parents' ego, but for the kids it means trouble."

After breaking off relations with each other, Eppie and Popo were determined to upstage the other. Popo says, "Of course anyone who wants to do anything wants to be the best." Stolar characterizes her twin sister, saying, "Eppie likes to be better than other people." The competition was on, in earnest.

In April 1958, *Life* magazine made public what newspaper scuttlebutt was mongering all along. The sisters who advised readers on human relations have "an enormous, mutual lovelorn problem of their own." The unflattering commentary on the "unsisterly sisters" documented for the first time the twins' mutual animosity. Buried hostilities that seemed to go back as far as childhood surfaced in the interview with the *Twin Lovelorn Advisers Torn Asunder by Success*. The article afforded the twins one last public gasp about each other before the silence set in.

A few months before the article appeared, the *Life* writer and photographer virtually camped out in each sister's home. Jules faced the photographer at breakfast, over a bowl of cornflakes, and Mort, on his way to work, found him at the door, waiting to be let in. Spending four days with Popo and family in Hillsborough, then another four days with Eppie and the family in Chicago, provided the reporter with ample material for an eyewitness account that exposed the twins' private life and thoughts to public scrutiny.

Among the more biting revelations of twinhood stresses revealed to *Life* readers were Popo's statements that ran roughly chronological: From their early years, "Eppie wanted to be the first violin in the school orchestra, but I was"; to adolescence, "She swore she'd marry a millionaire, but I did"; and to adulthood, "In Eau Claire she was always known as Popo's sister."

Popo felt it necessary to comment on Eppie's nose job and to "speculate aloud that Ann revealed certain Freudian flaws of character by going through with the operation." She also revealed that she keeps "a tome entitled *The Hostile Mind* on her bedside table and occasionally consults it for clues to what she considers Ann's inexplicable behavior."

Eppie, for her part, didn't come off quite as spiteful as Popo, buzzing forth with quotable stings more or less in response to her sister's insinuations. "She's as wrong as when she says I wanted to marry a millionaire. I didn't have to. She's the one who needs the assurance of money." Slyly casting her twin as the instigator, Eppie briefly appraises Popo's character. "She's just like a kid who beats a dog until somebody looks, and then starts petting it."

And so on. Not too astonishingly, the sisterly carping by identical twins gave the columnists a rush of publicity that boosted their careers as advice givers. Shortly after their cover billing in *Life,* double the number of newspapers from two years before, or around 175 each, were subscribing to Ann Landers and Dear Abby.

One inadvertent outcome of the article Eppie hadn't bargained for was that it queered her friendship with Bishop Fulton Sheen. Not only was Sheen annoyed that the sisters' spat extended to a row over gold religious medals he had given them—" 'Abby's,' says

Ann, 'was silver, but she had it gold plated' "—but the priest of celebrities, who took pride in his ability to bring around to Catholicism even the most doubting Thomas, found out that one of the sisters had been leading him on. When Eppie, on a verbal roll, announced, "He's one of the greatest men I ever met . . . but he'll be a Jew before I'm a Catholic," the original, square Jewish lady from Sioux City, Iowa, hit a sore spot with Sheen. When he discovered he wasn't making progress with her and found out not from Eppie herself but through an article sure to be read by all of America, that ended it. Even the good bishop had a reputation to maintain, and he didn't like being cast as the court jester in their little drama.

Popo blames the *Life* article and the news media for playing up the angle of the high-voltage advice columnists who couldn't sort out their own relationship. "People were just pouring a lot of fuel on that flame. It just, it kept us apart, really." Press reports, and especially the profile in *Life,* both women say, were chock full of what they now call "misquotes."

But undoubtedly the columnists were aware the seemingly adverse publicity could only help their careers. Syndicate sources concede that the *Life* article and the subsequent ten-year feud heightened curiosity and interest in the Ann Landers and Dear Abby columns.

Whether it helped their careers or not, friends and even acquaintances knew that the twins weren't speaking. Kay Fanning, for example, says, "My impression was that there was a very real feud. It was not a publicity stunt or anything."

Recalls William Steven, then a Minneapolis editor, "We ran Ann on Sunday, and not Abby, and there was a lot of brouhaha about it. Popo didn't like that because she wanted to be in the Sunday paper too, and Eppie and she, at that time, of course, were not speaking, and one . . . did . . . not . . . cross . . . those . . . babes. We went right on with what we were doing and avoided conversation."

Taking advantage of their rising popularity and a cue from earlier columnists, both women began hawking at the end of each day's column twenty-five-cent pamphlets on subjects ranging from teen problems to wedding etiquette. Popo was able to copyright the Dear Abby pamphlets because she owned the name, and she got to keep the profits. Eppie's booklets were copyrighted by her syndicate, and she received only a share of the profits on each one sold.

Like all syndicated writers, Eppie and Popo receive a fixed percentage of the fee charged each subscribing newspaper. The columnists are free to negotiate the fixed percentage they receive. The typical columnist receives no more than 50 percent of the subscribers' fees. Initially, because she hadn't proved herself, Eppie received a smaller percentage. What riled Eppie was that Popo immediately received a 50 percent cut from McNaught. In addition, McNaught picked up the cost of Popo's support staff, publicity tours, and other expenses.

Popo, eager to cash in some more, compiled a book of columns. *Dear Abby,* which Popo dedicated "Dear Mort," appeared on the best-seller list for six months. Although the book was a rehash of previously printed columns, Popo's syndicate didn't share in the royalties. When Edward R. Murrow called and asked for an interview not only to help publicize *Dear Abby* but because Popo, by this time, was an honest-to-goodness celebrity, Popo felt mondo marvelous.

Since the 1958 telecast would follow Murrow's visits to the Duke and Duchess of Windsor and the home of Elizabeth Taylor and Mike Todd, it was clear that Popo's nationwide television debut would be a coup. She regarded the request as full-flush confirmation of her new status: "When Edward R. Murrow, the famous radio-television commentator, asked if he could televise me and my family from our home in Hillsborough on 'Person to Person,' I felt that I had really arrived."

Murrow, disarmingly debonair, talked to Popo through a speaker phone, and she was beamed back through a one-sided transmission to his New York studio. The telecast is vintage fifties hokum, aimed at candidly showing the ideal suburban family, just like any suburban family, except with lots more money. Murrow asks Popo why she puts her typewriter away at six o'clock each night.

Perched on the edge of a metal swivel chair, knees pressed primly together, Popo demurely replies, "Are you kidding? I never work in the evenings, Ed. I never work on my family's time."

"You mean you don't let being Dear Abby interfere with being Mrs. Morton Phillips, wife and mother?" Murrow asks in mock wonder.

"No, Ed," says Popo, repeating in singsong cadences her well-rehearsed credo. "What you might call my career is actually my hobby. My number-one career is my family, and I never let my hobby interfere with my career. That's how I keep my career and hobby apart, and both successful."

From her "mailroom," which looks more Warsaw Pact make-shift than Hillsborough contemporary, Popo, seductively straining the seams of a tight-fitting, flowered-print cocktail sheath with a double row of ruffles at the hem, reads a few letters, making certain to mention each of the subscribing newspapers that forwarded them. The cameras then hubba hubba the rear of her shapely figure to the patio, where she stands protectively behind Mort and her two children. She smiles relentlessly at the camera, holding her husband's hand and her other hand draped around Jeannie's shoulder.

Murrow asks Mort, who's wearing a business suit and seems unperturbed about the intrusion by CBS News, how it feels, after eighteen years of marriage, to suddenly discover his wife is a celebrity. "Ed," Mort sedately replies, "my wife had been a celebrity to me for twenty years. Nothing has changed." Nothing, Mort might have added, except for *Life* staffers hanging out in the kitchen at 7:00 A.M. and camera crews setting up in the living room.

Less comfortable, however, are Jeannie and Eddie. Shy and self-conscious but innocent-looking and pretty, teenage Jeannie stares down at the patio table, speaking in barely audible mono-tones. Eddie, thirteen, who bears a close resemblance to his father, sits ramrod straight in his military-school uniform, gulping and shouting "Sir!" in response to Murrow's questioning.

It quickly becomes evident that for Popo, the interview is a triumph. Popo's ease and self-assurance on live television was quite a feat for a woman only two years removed from being a stay-at-home wife. She looks and sounds totally relaxed and confident under the bright lights. So much energy. Popo's clearly delighted to be the center of attention, just as she was at Central High, Morningside College, and as a "Phillips girl" in Eau Claire.

Mort and Popo move to the living room, where Mort shows off his "best father" trophy and Murrow asks Popo how she comes up with the answers for her column. Mugging for the camera, tilting her head from side to side and arching the eyebrows she's plucked and reapplied dark and thick, Popo answers, "Well, Ed, it's just horse sense," wink-wink, "and as my good friend Dr. Franz Alexander says," yuk-yuk, "horse sense . . . can be found . . . in a stable mind."

In her office, which is "a veritable beehive during the daytime," but where everything gets put away before Mort gets home, Popo makes certain to drag out her husband's fossilized infantry boot. She shoves it at the camera, saying, "This is my baby's bootie," and then carries it back to the living room and ceremoniously hands it to Mort.

Murrow wants to know if Abby's career has changed their way of living. Mort tells him, "No, Ed, I'm teased a little bit for having a wife who's a successful working woman, and there are those who refer to me as Morton Van Buren. But," he quickly adds, shaking his head, "it hasn't changed our way of living." Gentle-gentle Mort appears truly devoted to Popo; despite the mawkish sentiment, he sounds sincere. The two of them, sitting close together on the sofa near the end of the telecast, purring, patting, and touching each other, appear blissful, loving, and content.

Getting serious, Murrow tells Popo he can't leave her until he's asked her what's a good formula for life. Without hesitating, Popo replies, "*Giving,* I think, is the key word to real happiness. Because, Ed," she explains, just before tossing him a good-bye kiss, "if you aren't giving, you aren't living."

Seventeen

After Popo's "Person to Person" appearance, Eppie began pressing her *Sun-Times* bosses for permission to publicize the Ann Landers column. Realizing she was ready, the executives encouraged her to travel and give speeches. Eppie promoted not only her column but also the newspapers that subscribed to it.

At first Eppie stayed close to home, talking to student assemblies at Chicago-area high schools on teen topics like petting and necking, and more worldly matters like smoking and drinking. Soon Eppie was more than willing to appear before college audiences, church groups, and civic organizations in places like Louisville, Wichita, Detroit, Pittsburgh, Evansville, and Washington, D.C. When her one-year contract expired, Eppie's success on the road settled the matter. She was asked to stay on as Ann Landers.

In Chicago, Eppie reveled in the heady atmosphere of the *Sun-Times* newsroom. She was discovering what seasoned journalists already knew, that newspaper work was exciting. But her demanding schedule forced her to limit her hours there and rely on her staff to get much of the Ann Landers work done.

Up as early as six-thirty to get Jules breakfast and see him off to work and Margo off to Francis Parker, Eppie, in her plaid bathrobe, began to establish her own daily routine. Mornings involved sifting through the letters her staff earmarked for her to see, looking for possible column material or happily coming across a congratulatory letter or thank-you note. After many cups of coffee and pages of copy, at around noon, Eppie would get dressed and go downtown.

Office garb for Eppie usually consisted of a St. John knit suit. She sometimes buys the signature cardigan jacket, pleated skirt, and coordinated blouse in every color the manufacturer makes, as many as five different colors of the same design. Cramming her letters, speeches, and other promotional materials into a cotton net shopping bag, Eppie would order her black Jaguar sedan brought round and drive to the office. A few short months after she became Ann Landers, Jules happened to take notice of his wife's facility behind the wheel in city traffic. From then on she had a car and driver.

A brief conference with her "girls," as she used to call them, in her seventh-floor office apprised Eppie of any problems that had come up, like scheduling conflicts or knotty travel arrangements. "Everything I do goes on the schedule," Eppie admits. "And that means everything. Even a visit with a close, close friend has to be penciled in." Eppie swears she's totally disorganized. "I'm not organized, it's my staff. They save me from myself a dozen times a day." If Eppie remembers, she'll scribble a note to herself, stash it somewhere, and forget about it. It's "one of my problems. Notes in my pockets, notes in my purses. Notes, notes, notes."

Getting organized to handle the ever-increasing volume of correspondence coming in was the first task facing Eppie during her early years as Ann Landers. She did it by hiring staffers, all women, who were accurate and fast typists and who cared "about the troubled people who write us." Eppie says, "I have the world's best staff," and, she adds, "I pay them damned well."

Although Eppie herself writes every response that appears in the Ann Landers column, it's her staff that answers the bulk of the

148 ≈

mail by filling pamphlet requests, scouting out local social service agency referrals, and sending off replies that adhere strictly to the prevailing Ann Landers philosophy. Defending the way she operates, Eppie asks, "How many new responses can you give to the thousands of teenage girls who write in each month asking how old they should be before they start shaving their legs?"

Next stop for Eppie was Larry Fanning's office. At the start, Eppie would spend most of her afternoon sequestered in Fanning's glass-walled office. He reviewed and edited her work and helped write the speeches she'd be giving. "Better check that one out" and "That's not helpful" were the kind of criticisms he would offer. Sometimes Eppie and Fanning couldn't finish all the work at the office, and he'd go home with her to the Lake Shore Drive apartment. Soon Fanning became a frequent visitor to the Lederer household. Jules called him "the Fan" and would fix him drinks while he worked with Eppie, while Margo, who grew to like the big-hearted newsman, called him Uncle Lare.

On occasion, when his schedule permitted it, Fanning accompanied Eppie to meet editors in other cities or to some of her public appearances in order to critique them afterward. Eppie and Fanning in the back of her chauffeured car, smoke circling up from his constantly lighted pipe, Eppie with a pencil gripped between her teeth, briefcase on lap, the two of them constantly motioning and talking, must have exuded VIP vibes cruising crosstown or on their way to the airport.

Confronted so often at public appearances with the question "How do you know what advice to give?" Eppie, like her twin, explains that she relies on common sense and the opinions of experts. "I'm not an authority on anything," Eppie admits, "but I tap the best brains in the country." Laughing, she'll often add, "My phone bill looks like the defense budget."

When Eppie began the Ann Landers column, it was natural for her to turn to her good friend Robert Stolar for his opinion. The dermatologist counseled Eppie on her personal life, so why not extend that aid to her column? "She would be on the phone three, four, five times a day," remembers Stolar of the early Ann Landers days. Eppie asked Stolar questions on "everything that came across the column." Stolar says he was the sole source of expert authority for the column well into the early sixties. "The additional people only came on the scene after that," he says, contradicting Eppie's claim of always having called on top authorities for help with her column.

Stolar says he had to urge Eppie to seek out other authorities for assistance. Although Stolar enjoyed helping Eppie, he knew that his opinion was often not the most well-informed one to use. Oddly, Stolar says that Eppie, for some reason, was uncomfortable telephoning well-known professionals who were strangers to her. Once again, Stolar offered his services. "Say that I suggested you call them," he proposed.

As Eppie received recognition as Ann Landers, she became more secure about contacting specialists around the country. Now she boasts, "No one is too important or too busy for me to call." When quizzed about her qualifications to advise people, she'll defend herself by saying she calls on top authorities. "I am qualified not because of what I know, but because of who I know."

"Eppie is a very smart, shrewd girl," says managing editor Steven, explaining why he felt good about running Ann Landers. "One of the elements that Eppie had, that I think was her insurance policy, was her use of able people as a resource. She used these sage people as her checklist, to keep herself in balance."

The last authority, however, is always that stolid and impassive voice that Eppie and her sister call common sense. "Common sense is better than any theory," says Eppie. But for both of them, especially Eppie, it's quite different from that ordinary type of understanding without bias or emotion that's generally referred to as common sense. "I see things through the prism of my prejudices," says Eppie, conceding that her advice, to some degree, is formed from personal experience.

She's perceptive enough to see that "for every authority there's a counterauthority." To illustrate her point, she says, "I have three psychiatrist friends who don't agree on anything. I can pick my psychiatrist, or my judge." Eppie knows it isn't that one has com-

150 ≈

mon sense and the other one doesn't. Instead, she sees that in confronting the more puzzling questions in human relationships, there's no one rule that applies in every situation.

Since her contract barred her from giving prescriptive advice, advice specific to a particular problem, for fear of a lawsuit, her answers are sometimes of a more general nature. She also knows she's not infallible, so she feels comfortable changing her mind. "Of course I have second thoughts," she says, "and third thoughts and fourth thoughts too. Sometimes even fifth thoughts. Sometimes I realize that the advice I printed wasn't so good, that maybe I could even have been wrong." Acknowledging that her errors end up displayed on the pages of the daily newspaper, Eppie candidly says, "If I make a mistake, it's a doozy."

What Eppie's implying is that there's another kind of authority operating, one that's more elusive and isn't so final or well defined as what so easily gets labeled common sense. Whatever enduring element of inspiration—or, better yet, imagination—it is that Eppie summons, it's a gift. Even Larry Fanning, who worked so closely with Eppie for more than ten years, had a difficult time defining the kind of insight she possesses. "This girl has something beyond mere shrewdness," he says, "a quality close to genuine wisdom, and I'm sure her sister has it, too. Where do they get it? Not by reading and not really by experience. It's some kind of inherited thing."

Only three years on the job as Ann Landers, Eppie was hankering to be recognized outside of Chicago. She wanted to be known for her concern with issues of national and international importance, and topics more spellbinding than teen dating and thoughtless spouses. To break out of the advice columnist mode, she figured she needed to do some factual reporting. With Fanning's help, who thought she was capable of doing a series on foreign life and "could find out what the hell people are up to over there," and the backing of good friend Will Munnecke, her syndicate was easily persuaded that its star columnist should be sent to the Soviet Union.

Eppie was fascinated by the Soviet Union because she believed that reports on how the Soviets lived were clouded with misunderstanding and veiled in political propaganda. Also, since her parents had emigrated from Russia a half century before, she had a personal longing to see the country and people they'd left behind. She also was curious about the extent of anti-Semitism in the Soviet Union.

Jules was busy at Autopoint, leaving Eppie free to prepare Ann Landers for a peek behind the Iron Curtain. To gear up for the trip, tireless Eppie says she worked sixteen hours a day for a month to build up a backlog of columns and took Russian language instruction from a Berlitz tutor.

The three-week jaunt in late summer 1959 was a public relations triumph. Happily, Eppie's visit to Russia coincided with the Soviet *Luna 2* satellite's landing on the moon and Premier Nikita Khrushchev's tour of the United States and meeting with President Eisenhower. The series of twelve articles that ran in ninety-three newspapers across the country, depicting Eppie delivering the western message to this "Godless society," is a homey and informative narrative of daily life behind the Iron Curtain.

Handing out her husband's ballpoint pens in Gorky Park, a crinoline-skirted and high-heeled Eppie interviews everyone she sees, from an eleven-year-old boy who wants to be an engineer to Moscow University students, whom she asks some "tough questions, which they dodged." Because of her persistence, foreign correspondent Eppie manages to plow through the levels of Intourist bureaucracy and reveal the underbelly of Soviet life. And in her articles she demonstrates a reporter's eye for details.

Three times denied permission to visit a Soviet courtroom, Eppie calls up UPI's Moscow correspondent and discovers anyone can attend a session of the People's Court. Once there, she's amazed at the number of platinum blondes awaiting divorce proceedings— "There's a lot of peroxide action in Russia"—and sets out to confirm that it's hogwash what her Intourist chaperone's been telling her: "We are too busy and hard-working to have problems."

Eppie sees many "shabbily dressed" and "tense and troubled" people and discovers that "the problems of people are the same the world over." As she suspected, "Ivan is worried about Irena's supervisor at the factory. . . . Trina is concerned about Alexander's excessive drinking. . . . Elina has a lecherous boss. . . . Igor hates his mother-in-law." Eppie shops at GUM, where "almost every salesperson who smiled needed dental work," goes to a café—"eat something first," she advises—and attends a Roman Catholic mass in a TV showroom where she learns to her surprise, that "there is only one synagogue in Moscow."

Resourceful and determined, Eppie convinces a doctor who's traveling in her group to join her in knocking on an apartment door, so she can glimpse how the people really live. In "one of the most heartwarming experiences" of her life, Eppie and her companion, happily having knocked on the right strangers' door, discover the "Russian people" to be friendly and generous. Showing pictures of Jules and Margo, Eppie gets the chance to lecture about the merits of capitalism. She tells them her husband's president of a factory that makes pens.

"Oh, big money," the family agrees, nodding heads all around.

"No, just big responsibility," Eppie answers.

"His father owned the factory," they guess.

"No. He started sweeping the floors in a store," Eppie tells them, waiting for the big question.

"How did he get to be the boss?" they ask, bewildered.

"Under capitalism," Eppie begins, slowly building suspense, "anybody who has 'tah-lont' and is willing to work hard can be a boss. There are no limits in America." She adds that Jules has several hundred people working for him.

"They are happy?" asks the family.

"They ought to be," says Eppie, perhaps sensing that some of Jules' employees will read her articles and not wanting to speak for them directly. "They have good wages, profit-sharing, insurance, and vacations with pay."

Eppie must have felt that she had, at last, imparted something of importance to the family who lived around the corner from her hotel. Her mission was almost complete. She had only to tell America about the Soviet people, and write about her experiences when she got home. Downing a tumbler of vodka, "no small task for a teetotaler," Eppie's told to "take the message home to America that the Russians are your friends."

If the Cold War had begun to thaw some, it wasn't readily apparent from all of Eppie's reporting. Her approach sometimes resulted in misdirected zeal, like when she skewered an elderly Jewish man with her sharp queries about Soviet anti-Semitism in the presence of her Intourist guide, an interpreter, and the press. "He looked at me with the most frightened eyes I ever saw and whispered, 'Please don't ask me these questions with that girl [guide] standing there.'"

A few times the reporting sounded, how you say, off a beat or two. Describing the dial on the telephone in her room at The Ukraine, a "swanky firetrap," Eppie says, "The dial looks like this: A, B, an upside-down L, a mah-jongg tile, E, two K's back to back, an N backward, K, and a Hebrew gimmel." Other times, Eppie's right on target, like when she asks an Intourist guide whether she enjoys her work and reports with no comment the woman's answer, "Americans are very agreeable but I am getting entirely too many New York Jews."

The timely Moscow trip garnered Eppie the wide press coverage she coveted. It helped establish Ann Landers as no mere lightweight, but rather as a contemporary figure involved with serious international concerns. Unlike Popo, who shunned international expeditions as Dear Abby and was more content speaking to the local PTA or before high school students, Eppie desired to be "out in front, on some real issues."

Although Eppie as Ann Landers gradually got more active politically than Dear Abby, the twins' repeated claims of great dissimilarities in their column material simply don't hold up. Not only did they adopt almost identical work habits, but the topics addressed in their columns were much the same. Stanleigh Arnold, Popo's first boss, says, "Popo and Eppie hated to admit that their columns sounded the same, but they did."

William Steven agrees. "There wasn't really a difference between the two columns. They had a very good formula and they both used it."

In print and in public, the women then and now look and behave very much alike. Neither twin likes to be photographed wearing slacks. The clothes they wear accentuate their trim, shapely figures. Scooped or plunging necklines and black afternoon dresses set off with a strand or two of pearls to complement their creamy complexions became a favorite of the sisters.

Once the twins discovered that they had bought identical dresses, Popo having bought hers in San Francisco and Eppie, in Chicago. Both women are conscious of the image they project and devote considerable time and effort to their appearance before they go out in public. Popo says, "I feel I owe it to my public to pull myself together when I leave my home." Eppie agrees. A *Look* photographer who accompanied her on a lecture trip to Evansville, Indiana, counted seven changes of smart-shop gowns in two days. Eppie explains, "I owe it to the audiences."

The sisters each rely on several top hair stylists to attend to them. And both women claim they first adopted the well-known starched side flip that identifies them as either Ann Landers or Dear Abby. Cloyd Koop started doing Popo's hair in 1958. It's Koop, Popo says, "who first introduced my Dear Abby hairdo. Some say its dated, but it suits me."

Koop willingly takes credit for the Dear Abby "do." "It's almost a logo. She's comfortable with it. When she walks through an airport, you know that's somebody. She clicks. The hair is the confirmation."

The hairdo is also the confirmation of how much the twins were working on the same public image. The more revealing dissimilarity had nothing to do with their public profile. The difference was in their home lives. Both were preaching the fundamental importance of home and hearth. But only Popo lived it. Eppie's marriage was starting to crumble.

Eighteen

With Eppie winging her way all over the United States, spreading the Ann Landers gospel, and Jules engrossed in his job at Autopoint, Margo was left to fend for herself. "They both pursued their careers so aggressively that someone had to suffer, and it was Margo," says Sol Shulman, who worked with Jules and later succeeded him as president of Autopoint. Lew Pollock confirms Shulman's opinion that Margo lost out at home. "They were too busy to bother with this kid. She just grew up. Very fancy neighborhood, very fancy apartment."

But even before the Lederers moved to Chicago, during the time Eppie was so involved in Democratic party politics, Margo was described by family friends as "headstrong" and "spoiled." One teacher at the Campus School in Eau Claire describes how she would seductively climb onto a male teacher's lap in an attempt to embarrass him. Since the Campus School was on state university grounds, Margo was able to flirt with college boys. "At home on campus at age fourteen," was how her school principal in Eau Claire describes her.

The deliberately provocative behavior continued when she got to Chicago. At sixteen, she had a good figure, like her mother's.

Jules and Eppie had some friends over for the evening and Margo walked out of her bedroom into the party wearing what was described as sheer, shorty pajamas. Jules was livid. "You walk in front of company like that?" he yelled. "Why not?" was Margo's curt response.

During the summer Jules got Margo a job working for the advertising agency used by Autopoint. Staff at Autopoint dreaded her marching into the firm with a bunch of what they called "snot-nosed brats" whom she referred to as "my team." One Autopoint executive says she was "totally obnoxious and treated other people in the office like they were peasants."

As much as friends of Jules and Eppie's, and Jules's business associates, disliked Margo, they felt sorry for her. They placed the blame on her parents for not giving priority to raising their daughter. It was Margo, and not Jules or Eppie, who was pressured into fending for herself and making the compromises necessary when both her parents were working double time on their careers. It was as though "Margo just . . . she just came along," says Shulman. Another acquaintance says, "Margo grew up all by herself."

Like any teenager, Margo could play mother and father off each other. Eppie herself remembers, "When my daughter went to high school, Jules gave her permission to drive the Cadillac to school. Now, I didn't know about this. . . . She outsmarted me and got to him first. So he said yes, whereas I would have said no, I don't believe kids should be driving Cadillacs to school, they can walk."

But Eppie let Jules's decision stand. The overriding rationale was her husband's authority, not her daughter's upbringing. Margo was second runner-up, first to her mother's career, and then to Eppie's concern with Jules's status in the family. "Once he said yes, I wouldn't change the decision," Eppie says, "for this would emasculate him. I wouldn't contradict him and then have Margo say, 'But Daddy said.' So I didn't. I just let it go."

It was Jules, not Margo, who Eppie thought needed her attention more. So she assigned Robert Stolar the task of talking sense to her daughter, who she felt was becoming entirely too self-centered and uncontrollable. Stolar had helped Margo before, when she had severe asthma attacks that he suspected were related to emotional problems. So again, Eppie turned to the Washington doctor to help find out what was bothering her daughter. While Stolar counseled Margo over the phone for an hour a few evenings a week, Eppie, time permitting, attempted to concentrate on Jules. But it wasn't easy. They rarely saw each other long enough to work together on their marriage.

A visit to Will Munnecke's northern Michigan summer place convinced Jules and Eppie that they needed to escape their busy Chicago workdays and devote more time to being together as a family. But soon after they bought a secluded A-frame in a birch forest outside of Traverse City, Jules began lugging out his briefcase full of papers, while Eppie clacked away at a typewriter in the spare bedroom. They passed their time much as they did forty floors above Lake Michigan, only the amenities were more rustic and the air was much healthier. Weekend visits became increasingly infrequent, and they gave up going there altogether and sold the vacation home.

Jules's compulsive work habits, his colleagues suspected, were damaging his marital relations. "Jules would never leave the office unless he was loaded down with briefcases full of work," says Sol Shulman. "I'm positive that affected his home life." He became even more involved in his work when he realized he was faltering as Autopoint's chief executive. "He almost busted the company," says another co-worker. "It wasn't possible to manipulate Autopoint the way he wanted to. Jules's conception was brilliant, but his implementation was weak."

His deteriorating management coincided with the end of Eppie's first year as Ann Landers. During Jules's first few years as Autopoint president, he embarked on an aggressive sales campaign that didn't produce immediate enough results. Executives at the Cory Corporation, the owners of Autopoint, withholding their concern with Jules's management techniques, resented his bellicose manner. Board members were dismayed by Jules's quick temper, and his status at the parent company slumped.

Because of her rising notoriety as Ann Landers, Eppie occasionally stepped forth to bail Jules out of uncomfortable situations. Buoyed by her skyrocketing success, she didn't hesitate to call up Cory higher-ups and smooth over ill will created by Jules's arrogance and churlishness.

If Eppie insinuated herself into Jules's career, so did Jules willingly embroil himself in the fracas between his wife and her twin. A colleague at Autopoint overheard what he says was Jules's loud and rancorous telephone conversation with his sister-in-law. "Popo, don't give me that," Jules exploded over his work phone. "It wasn't Eppie's fault that you two had the falling out. She was first and you were second."

Back at Autopoint, morale declined. Not only was the big guy out of favor with the Cory board, but Jules was asking his sales staff to drop in on local editors while they were on out-of-town business to promote his wife's newspaper column. A favor for the boss couldn't be refused, so a stop at the local newspaper and a chat with the editor about the Ann Landers column became a requisite sales call before the Autopoint salesman returned to headquarters.

Jules did the asking, but Eppie wrote the thank-you note. To a salesman who had called on the *Seattle Times* about the Ann Landers column, reporting "Reception good, results nothing," Eppie wrote, "You're a livin' doll. . . . It was darned good of you to give them a pitch." Then, employing the Jules Lederer tactic of appealing to his subordinate's social status to get him moving, Eppie adds, "My editor . . . was very pleased. He said: 'Eppie, just to have a guy with some class walk in and mention our syndicate is good.' Whenever you want to do it, we are grateful."

Aware of his faltering corporate image, Jules began to investigate other money-making ventures. A possible tie-in to Autopoint that at first seemed like a smart move resulted in a large investment of Eppie and Jules's money in a ball-bearing factory in Puerto Rico. Jules hoped to build up a supplier for Autopoint's line of ballpoint pens. But the factory deal fell through. What's worse, it wiped out the Lederers's savings.

Losing their hard-earned nest egg was a blow for the frugal and economy-conscious Eppie. "Jules took all of our savings and invested them in a factory in Puerto Rico. And he lost all of our money in that factory. *All of it.* Boy!" Eppie recalls, "That was a lot of money. . . . But I didn't nag him or reproach him and say 'What have you done?' "

Encouraged by Eppie's positive attitude and undeterred by the large financial loss, Jules continued to look around for other business opportunities. Calling her husband "tremendously gutsy," Eppie says, "After he got more money in the bank, on a hunch he thought of the idea of Budget Rent-A-Car." In 1958 Jules visited the fledgling car rental business that Eppie's cousin Morrie Mirkin had started in Los Angeles. Mirkin had purchased four dozen used cars for his enterprise. The discount rates appealed to sailors stationed at nearby San Pedro and Long Beach. But the Budget fleet needed upgrading if affluent Angelenos were to be customers.

Mirkin sought Jules's advice. "Morrie, it's a great name, it's a great concept," Jules told him. "But used cars? These Jews aren't going to want to take used cars to Palm Springs!"

In exchange for bankrolling Budget's purchase of a fleet of new Chevrolets, Jules took a stock option. "I financed the purchase of Budget's first one hundred new automobiles," Jules explains. "I decided to charge $5 a day and five cents a mile when Hertz and Avis were charging $10 a day and ten cents per mile." And Budget took off. "Blessed with a wealth of ignorance and inexperience in the car rental field, I had the advantage of not knowing what couldn't be done," says Jules.

Soon, Autopoint salesmen were performing another errand for their boss while on Autopoint business. It was no secret around the company that Jules was spending his business hours setting up franchises for Budget. And he requested the same of his staff, asking them to scout out locations to further his new venture. One of Autopoint's salesmen, in Hawaii on company business, was asked to make side trips to check out car rentals on the islands. The extra expenses were picked up by Jules.

But Jules's prevailing concern was finding backers for Budget. Despite Eppie's claim that her husband began Budget solo with only a $5,000 bank loan, Jules had to seek investors having access to large sums of money. Eppie herself was unable to provide the hefty infusion of funds. Her salary as Ann Landers at the time was paltry in comparison to the amount of money needed.

In any case, even if Eppie had been able to bankroll Budget's expansion, it's unlikely Jules would have accepted his wife's money. Still smarting from the loss of a year before, Jules rebuffed Eppie's unimpressive paychecks and because he found even the idea of it emasculating, insisted that no portion of the family's living costs be paid for by his wife. "I want to make one thing clear," he told her. "I support you. I'm the financial head of the house." Without argument, Eppie began to invest her checks.

There was only one truly wealthy person Jules knew well enough to hit for big bucks: Mort. The sisterly squabble may have been in high gear, but Jules talked Budget over with Mort Phillips anyway. "He's a very bright guy," as Jules later described his brother-in-law, "but when I started Budget his attitude was, 'If it's such a great idea, why hasn't anyone else done it?' "

Jules was forced to look elsewhere. Potential investors who asked him about his educational background were informed that he had dropped out of Northwestern after two years. "I did," says Jules. "Only it was Northwestern High School in Detroit." Enthusiastic and optimistic, Jules was able to convince some high rollers to gamble on Budget. In 1959 he bought out Morrie Mirkin and left Autopoint, taking a few co-workers with him.

Budget's success depended on establishing an effective franchising system. Jules didn't know much about setting up that kind of operation, but in 1959 no one else did either. When he became Autopoint president, Jules joined the Young Presidents Organization, an organization that sponsored seminars and annual meetings of interest to top business executives. At a convention in Miami, Jules met the then chief officer of National Car Rental, Earl Smalley, as well as Warren Avis. He also met Kemmons Wilson, who founded the Holiday Inn system of franchises and was generous in sharing his knowledge and experience with Jules.

Although he greatly benefited from Wilson's advice and picked up some tips from Smalley and Avis, Jules and Budget had some shaky times. "I still made a lot of mistakes, naturally," says Jules, "and some of them cost me plenty. But on the whole, I did rather well." In a few years Budget expanded to Europe, and then to Mexico and South Africa. Jules had clearly made it big. He attributed his growing fortune to "hard work and good timing." His friends agreed, "Jules worked his tail off for Budget."

Though Eppie wasn't unaware of or completely insensitive to Jules's needs, especially during her early years as Ann Landers, she was as devoted to her career as Jules was to his. Eppie claims that her husband "didn't resent the time I spent on my column." But Jules was complaining loudly and bitterly to his colleagues, "I have no home life." One friend remembers, "Jules told us that he would sit at his desk and work and she sat at her desk and worked and that was their whole life." But that's not surprising. After all, Eppie admits, "I learned my work habits from Jules."

Eppie's many trips to hype Ann Landers were beginning to tell on Jules. In 1959 alone, Eppie received 1,004 speaking invitations and actually made 101 appearances in 39 cities as Ann Landers, not counting her three-week trip to the Soviet Union. The following year was no different; Eppie's career landed her in 41 cities. In Chicago, Eppie was a frequent guest on local talk shows, often broadcast live. Her few quiet moments were spent reading up on psychology and religion. Earnest for self-improvement, she subscribed to the Great Book series, a middlebrow curriculum that spread across America from Chicago.

Frequent trips to Washington enabled Eppie to maintain friendships with some politically powerful men. In the company of Senator Hubert Humphrey, she continually met many preeminent national figures, like Senators William Proxmire and Charles Percy, and even Lyndon Johnson. Eppie also continued her friendship with Senator Eugene McCarthy, who had first met her in the early fifties in Wisconsin, when he was a congressman from Minnesota.

Washington was a lot more interesting than Chicago for Eppie. Spending time at the Statler Hilton's bar in the nation's capital with Justice Bill Douglas was headier than sitting home on Lake Shore Drive waiting for Jules to arrive with a briefcase full of work.

Justice Douglas's soon-to-be second wife Mercedes, now Mrs. Robert Eicholtz, wasn't pleased with the way Eppie monopolized her husband's time. She remembers that Eppie was "rather a thorn in my side" during the time she and Bill were courting. "I'm not so sure she wasn't after him," Mercedes says, indicating that Eppie always seemed to be flirting with Bill Douglas and that Mercedes herself often "had to wait around for Bill because Eppie was playing footsie with him." After Bill and Mercedes were married, Eppie stopped calling him at home and limited her talks with him to the office.

Jules took pride in his wife's initiative, yet he would have preferred that she be less driven by her column. Vocal dissatisfaction with Eppie's behavior, however, was reserved for colleagues. Once when he and an associate arrived home at O'Hare Airport from a business trip, Jules spotted his colleague's wife waiting for him at the gate. "Eppie is meeting me too," Jules wryly joked. "She's going to wave to me as she walks through the terminal on her way to her own flight."

Eppie seemingly did not need or seek a closer relationship with her husband, who sought and wanted approval from her but rarely got it. Jules began to feel adrift from his wife and his daughter. To traveling companions he'd remark again and again, "You're going home to a family. I don't know why the hell I'm going home."

Another salesman vividly remembers returning to Chicago from a four-week sales trip, astonished to find Jules waiting for him at the Midway terminal. Jules explained that he had the company plane standing by to whisk the two of them to a weekend sales conference in a Wisconsin cabin. When the man complained that he hadn't seen his wife or family for a month, Jules barked, "Oh, what's the difference."

The picture of an empty home was hidden from public view. Eppie carefully sustained the façade of a devoted wife dedicated to a good marriage. Early-morning publicity photos show Eppie in a tight black dress and high heels, sending Jules off to work with a loving hug and kiss. She took pride in repeating that she had "Jules's wife" rather than her own name embroidered on the linings of her mink coats.

On occasion, Eppie accompanied Jules to meetings of the Young Presidents Organization, not only to be with Jules but also conveniently because she could meet influential people there. Despite these public appearances, Eppie and Jules together still seemed apart. At YPO meetings they'd go their separate ways, advancing their own interests. In each other's company, Eppie tended to upstage Jules, and there seemed to be an emotional distance between them. In a sense, they were together only because they stood side by side.

At a convention in Phoenix just before she became Ann Landers, Eppie met the president of the University of Notre Dame, Father Theodore Hesburgh, who after her falling out with Bishop Fulton Sheen made a dandy clerical substitute for maintaining a Catholic connection. Eppie immediately liked Hesburgh, whom *Time* once called "the most powerful priest in America." She was drawn to him because he was a young man of high achievement with a moral commitment to liberal social values. Also, like Senator Humphrey, Hesburgh was an outspoken champion of civil rights, an issue of national importance soon to be dear to Eppie.

Hesburgh recalls that Eppie wasn't ill at ease or self-conscious introducing herself to a famous university president. "Eppie was never bashful about anybody," he says. "She's not awed by presidents, college presidents or presidents of countries. She was always very quick at making friends. From the very beginning she was very open, very friendly, and very uninhibited. I think it's just part of her personality." Meeting Hesburgh was a fortunate moment for

Eppie. She'd later depend on him to help her through some troubled times.

Despite her interest in other religions, mostly from an educational and not a spiritual basis, Eppie still looked askance at interfaith dating and marriage. When Margo was accepted at Brandeis University, through the help of Senator Humphrey and Justice Douglas, Eppie made her promise to date only Jews. It wasn't much of a promise, though, given that Brandeis is the only Jewish-affiliated secular university in the country. Calling home during her freshman year, Margo asked if it was okay to date the son of His Highness the Aga Khan, then a student at Harvard. "You say his name is Kahn?" Eppie joked. "Go ahead, doll."

Eppie was proud of Margo at Brandeis. In the company of other bright students at that liberal Boston-area school in the very early sixties, her daughter shed her teenage apathy and became involved in social and political issues. Eppie remembers Margo "at Brandeis University, nineteen years old, doing a sit-in in a dime store. Full of causes, full of purpose. And I think that was sort of swell. Sort of neat."

Margo wanted to go to Alabama and participate in one of the civil-rights marches there. After it had taken place, it turned out to be the kind of demonstration that Eppie herself would like to have taken part in. Eppie recalls, "One of the regrets of my life is that I didn't go to Selma." She says, "Something was happening at the time that seemed more important. It can't have been more important because I don't even remember what it was. I should have been there."

Margo was well aware that being Ann Landers governed where her mother went and when. Margo tried out for and got a singing and dancing part in a Brandeis production. Eppie recalls, "She had a great part, she sang and danced, and I didn't even know the kid could sing and dance." But when showtime came, Eppie told her daughter that an Ann Landers engagement meant that Mom had to send regrets. "I didn't go see her," Eppie admits, indicating that her priorities then were perhaps mixed up. "That's been one of the big regrets of my life. At the time it didn't seem like such a big deal. But now that I look back I'm sorry I didn't go."

To let her daughter know that out of her sight didn't mean out of her thoughts, Eppie dedicated *Since You Ask Me,* her first book, published in 1961, not to Jules but "For Margo." The few times Eppie did visit her daughter at school, she got all dressed up like Ann Landers, wearing big sunglasses and her benevolent celebrity smile. On her way to Margo's dorm room, she shook hands with the students and introduced herself to everyone, much to Margo's chagrin. Eppie recalls Margo telling her that the girls in the dorm "thought it was terribly square, the epitome of high camp, that she'd come to college and put a picture of Ann Landers on her mirror." Margo says she was teased a lot before she admitted, "Well, it just so happens she's my mother."

Like her mother, Margo never got to finish college. Early in her senior year she started dating John Coleman, a slight, freckled, red-haired, and beady-eyed investment consultant with Tucker, Anthony & R. L. Day in Boston. Coleman, twenty-six, was just five years older than Margo. He grew up in Chestnut Hill, a Boston suburb home to many well-to-do families, where his father ran a successful plumbing supply business. After getting a history degree from Rutgers University, Coleman attended and then dropped out of Harvard Business School to join the investment firm.

By December 1961, Margo and Coleman decided on a May wedding, much to the consternation of Eppie and Jules. They took an immediate dislike to their daughter's fiancé and tried to talk Margo out of marrying him. But Margo wouldn't listen. She was determined to marry him.

Eppie had little basis for argument. Coleman met the one criterion Eppie had established for Margo's boyfriends: He was Jewish. Still, she was uneasy. Eppie didn't know Coleman all that well, but what she knew of him she didn't like. What probably bothered Eppie was that Coleman went out of his way to qualify his Jewishness.

Since Coleman was adopted by an affluent Jewish couple at the age of two and raised as a Jew, by strict interpretation of Jewish law he wasn't a Jew unless his biological mother was, a technicality that he was determined to investigate. The court records on his adoption were revealing. "I found that I was English, and Irish, and Protestant," he says. "It was my identity."

Whether Coleman told Margo or her parents that he'd been married before is questionable. Neither Eppie nor Margo will discuss it. But if the Colemans' oldest daughter didn't learn about her father's first marriage until she was eighteen, it seems likely that Margo herself didn't know about her husband's brief prior marriage until her honeymoon, or later.

Regardless of how ill conceived they regarded their daughter's impending marriage, Eppie and Jules made plans to give Margo the type of wedding that the only child of a famous celebrity columnist and hugely successful businessman deserved. They consoled themselves with the knowledge that at least their soon-to-be son-in-law had some money and knew how to make more.

Not wanting more twin feud publicity on her daughter's wedding day, Eppie invited Margo's Aunt Popo to the May ceremony and reception held afterward in the Guildhall of the Ambassador East. However, the twins were still not speaking to each other, and their frosty behavior embarrassed big sisters Kenny and Dubbie and most of their other relatives.

William Steven, who was at the "very spectacular and lush Jewish wedding," remembers that Senator Humphrey also seemed annoyed by the twins' behavior toward each other, especially at such a joyous affair. In the presence of all Eppie's well-known and some not-so-famous friends, many of whom knew Popo too, Humphrey attempted to get the twins together. "He danced with both of them at the same time," recalls Steven, amused by his own recollection of the three of them, Eppie, Popo and Senator Hubert Humphrey, dancing together.

Eppie's exhaustive list of the most important people she knew included, among many others, Father Hesburgh, Chicago Democratic big shots Jake Arvey and Ben Heineman, and Ohio Governor Mike DiSalle. Eppie's fame was helping her and her husband acquire the right sort of friends. Though Jules later rebelled and found

Eppie's need to surround herself with celebrities offensive, he too was enjoying a first-name relationship with Chicago leaders and national figures. It was becoming increasingly obvious to many of their acquaintances that Jules and Eppie's social life was structured around the people who could do them the most good.

Nineteen

he west coast lifestyle was good for the Phillipses, and especially for Popo. Shaking off her early Iowan rigidity, she began to relax with friends and enjoy good liquor at her many parties, champagne being her spirit of choice. Popo and Mort in Hillsborough and later Los Angeles, like Eppie and Jules in Chicago, were enjoying the company of a diverse assortment of well-known people.

Popo counted among her friends Senator Eugene McCarthy and his wife, Abigail—who calls Popo "Dear Abby," while Popo calls her, "Abby dear"—Gordon and Sheila MacRae, Jane Russell, Dinah Shore, June Allyson, Dr. Abraham Stone of Planned Parenthood, and Dr. Franz Alexander. She also kept up her friendship with Jerry Lewis and Dean Martin, whom she had met in Palm Springs and in 1951 had gotten her a bit part in the movie *At War with the Army.*

Shortly after she became Dear Abby, Popo wrote Dr. Rose Franzblau, a psychologist who took a different approach with her advice column, which was published in the New York *Post* and syndicated nationally. Popo asked if she could meet her because she felt that Franzblau was a "fearless pioneer in her profession."

Franzblau would select a single letter as a springboard for an in-depth discussion in her daily column, often continuing the intense psychoanalytic monologue for as many days as necessary.

The two women became good friends. Popo found Rose Franzblau warm and vibrant, and she respected the quality and depth of her work. Rose, in turn, enjoyed Popo's quick sense of humor and her engaging lack of pretension. Whenever Popo, who made it her custom to accompany Mort on business trips, was in New York, or Rose and her husband, Dr. Abraham Franzblau, a psychoanalyst, were on the west coast, the couples made certain to get together.

Through the Franzblaus, Popo got to know recognized authorities in the medical and psychiatric fields, and she oftentimes went out of her way to establish a friendship with them. Once, at a gathering in Franzblau's Manhattan home, Popo amused guests by sitting on the lap of Abraham Stone, author of a best-selling marriage and sex guide. Wearing a filmy and seductive blue gown, Popo reached for a pair of manicure scissors and carefully trimmed Stone's moustache. "Popo, act like an adult," she was admonished by Rose Franzblau. Only then did Popo coyly slip off Stone's lap.

For Jeannie and Eddie, the California scene was equally salutary. Both Phillips children were well mannered and seemed not to be unduly affected by their mother's notoriety and their father's wealth. Though the teens were teased about the Dear Abby philosophy, and their friends called it "square and old-fashioned," they took the ribbing in stride. After all, not many of their friends had a mother as famous as theirs.

Teenaged Eddie, perhaps more so than Jeannie at that time, had a slightly more difficult time coping with having famous and wealthy parents. Being packed off to San Rafael Military Academy, not a terribly unusual choice in the late fifties for the son of wealthy parents but evidence of a couple's strict child-rearing philosophy, probably helped insulate him from his parents' lifestyle. While not enthusiastic about attending a military school, Eddie nonetheless achieved good grades. When he was at home, during the summer, though, Eddie had a harder time of it. Because he disliked being driven in the family limousine, especially to Little League games, Eddie would instruct the driver to stop a few blocks short of the playing field. When asked as an adult how he felt growing up in a privileged atmosphere, Eddie says, "Wealth is sometimes an embarrassment."

Like her sister, Popo was taking trips to further her career, but she scheduled them less frequently and limited them to within the States. Wherever Popo went as Dear Abby, she made her presence known. In Washington, D.C., at the behest of President Eisenhower for a 1960 White House Conference on Children and Youth, Popo, decked out in a leopardskin coat, a bright red hat, a red scarf, and black leather gloves, was met at National Airport by a pack of press hounds who recorded her every move.

With Jacqueline Kennedy, the elegant new First Lady, spending extravagant sums on art and clothes, the fascination was reflected in the daily press. In the early sixties, the press corps that followed Popo mostly consisted of "society" reporters, and as a result, her wardrobe often got more play than her opinions on social issues. Popo obliged by talking about one of the subjects she thought she knew best.

In a tight, slinky, raw silk dress: "Oh boy! I like form-fitting clothes. I think a girl shouldn't hide her assets. What a war I waged against the sack dress." Popo explained her passion for flamboyant outfits and gave out a fashion tip that could have been learned from Eppie: Have several duplicates of the same dress. "I have eight in all! Three blacks and others in navy, beige, charcoal, powder blue, and cocoa."

But despite her penchant for passionate contrasts and clashing color schemes, when it comes to jewelry, said the woman who only a few years before was seen sporting clunky gold bracelets and dangly gold monkey earrings, "If you have to wonder whether you should wear it, leave it off." Simplicity is important, Popo advised. "When in doubt, don't. After all, the most important jewelry in the world is your wedding ring."

In three days, Popo got interviewed on NBC's "Monitor," appeared on Milton Q. Ford's TV show, attended a National Symphony Orchestra luncheon at the Willard Hotel, and completed a segment for a Voice of America broadcast. What interested Popo in coming to the Conference on Children and Youth was the problem of pornography.

"It's vicious to peddle this sort of garbage to youngsters under any disguise. I don't know how anyone would confuse that stuff with art," she said after a tour of the Post Office's collection of confiscated mail. "I'm going to tell my readers when this revolting garbage comes in the mails to send it promptly to the Post Office Department so action can be taken immediately against the persons who mailed it."

But like her twin, Popo still had no self-help answer for their unsisterly estrangement. For all her traveling, Popo didn't call on Eppie when in Chicago. Few people were able to be friendly with both sisters. Robert Stolar, along with Henry Ginsburg, the Sioux City friend who had introduced Popo to Mort, were among the few exceptions. Downplaying the rivalry to the press, Popo would dismiss it by saying, "Blood is thicker than water, and it boils quicker." But the head of Popo's syndicate saw it otherwise. "Abby was at McNaught ten years," Charles McAdam says. "They fought through the whole decade. And Popo bragged about it."

"Wherever my husband goes, I go," said Popo about her move to Los Angeles in the spring of 1960. Business interests required that Mort be there for an indeterminate amount of time. Settling into a luxurious hotel suite in Beverly Hills, for what at first appeared to be only a temporary stay, Popo declared, "I'm married to a man, not a city."

Popo soon discovered she liked Los Angeles a lot better than Hillsborough. Sure, she lived among the rich and famous in northern California, but she lived in a suburb; San Francisco was thirty minutes away. Los Angeles was Popo's first introduction to living in a big city, where issues took flame and things really happened. It suited her flashiness.

Always striving to keep her private life separate from her public one, Popo found it easier to manage there. Popo also found out it wasn't considered cool to go looking for recognition in Los Angeles. Celebrities were a common sight. That was fine with her. She'd act famous when and if she wanted to.

Daughter Jeannie, by the time of the family's move, was a student at UCLA, conveniently close by. Eddie, still boarding at military school, came home on weekends. To welcome her to L.A., an organization of 1,700 women called the Helping Hand named Popo "Mother of the Year" and held a Mother's Day luncheon in her honor at the Beverly Hilton Hotel. The publication that same year of her second book, *Dear Teen-ager,* prompted Popo to wise-crack, "They call me the matron saint of teenagers."

For the next few years Popo successfully juggled public appearances with family life. In spurts, she'd visit a city to address an advertisers' convention at a "Sweetheart Day" luncheon and in quick succession do a radio talk show, appear on TV's "Inga's Angles" the next morning, then an interview with Milt Grant on another network that afternoon. In early 1962 Popo flew to Washington, D.C., to be named National Chairman of the Easter Seal Society. A photo session of Popo in the Oval Office with President John Kennedy handing the first sheet of seals to that year's special handicapped child kicked off the campaign.

Later that same year, Popo packed up once again and moved to Portland, Oregon. Home was the Benson Hotel downtown. While Mort investigated business opportunities in the northwest, Popo continued with her column and commuted to Los Angeles as often as possible.

She began a daily feature for the CBS radio network called "Dear Abby," which she termed "more fun than work." A radio version of her advice column, the five-minute spot not only garnered Popo extra income, but also increased exposure. When a year later Popo and Mort again had to move, this time back to Minnesota, where they had lived as newlyweds, Jeannie, having just graduated from UCLA, stayed behind to script her mother's show.

Popo, reluctant to leave, fearing a move back to the Midwest would distance her from the rapid social change beginning to occur on both the east and west coasts, decided to keep her Dear Abby office in Los Angeles and visit it as often as possible. Aside from her fears about misreading the pulse of America, Popo didn't like the idea of perhaps becoming known as the Midwest's "second" advice columnist.

Resigned to the 1964 move to St. Paul, where Mort would succeed his father, Jay, as president of Ed Phillips and Sons, Popo packed up her husband's bronzed infantry boot and chose a new home for it. The penthouse atop the prestigious twenty-four-story highrise at 740 River Drive commanded a panoramic view of the Mississippi River and the Minneapolis skyline. Missing the excitement of California living, Popo consoled herself by peppering the penthouse with familiar keepsakes and doodads.

The boot, sprouting fresh flowers, was stationed on a table in the ivory-carpeted living room, near a large and curving blue and purple couch below a seascape of the Pacific coast by Robert Watson. Family photographs along with Popo's vast monkey collection were scattered throughout, and next to a portrait of her father wearing glasses and squinting at a newspaper sat a carved wooden monkey wearing wire glasses and squinting at a newspaper. Popo, the visual punster, explained, "My father would have loved that monkey as much as I do."

A paneled and book-shelved, red-carpeted study served Popo as her home office, furnished with the latest in stereo equipment, tape recorders, and three typewriters, including one for speeches. In the gilt-mirrored dining room, a large crystal chandelier floated over potted ferns and red plush chairs where Popo preferred to entertain no more than eight or ten guests at a time because, she says, "More than eight and the conversation, the good conversation, suffers." Paintings by Picasso and Chagall hung in the gallery that led to the two seldom-used bedrooms for Jeannie and Eddie, Eddie having just finished his first year at Stanford University in Palo Alto by the time of his parents' move to Minnesota.

Popo had the master bedroom painted royal blue and allowed Mort to design the closets for her wardrobe. Shelves of shoes, eight to a row, were stacked floor to ceiling and stood alongside shelves of hats, handbags, and some dozen wigs in blonde and dark brown and nearly every shade in between. She wanted to maintain the anonymity she enjoyed in Los Angeles. "I do like to travel incognito once in a while" is how she talks about the disguises that allow her to leave home without being instantly recognized as Dear Abby. Racks of furs, necessary for the snowbound Minnesota winters, according to Popo, included a long dark mink and a short gray chinchilla.

Cozy in their deep red study, Popo and Mort enjoyed their evenings alone together, talking about drafts of her latest column or planning their busy schedules for the next few months. Popo made sure Mort saw everything she wrote. "He's my editor, he's the M," Popo would say, using early-sixties lingo for "the most." In addition to being her editor and chief counsel, "He's the only man I know who's never been wrong," Popo unabashedly gushes. Mort's business acumen made sure that her substantial earnings from Dear Abby were invested wisely. "I've never had a press agent or a business manager," she says. "With Mort, I don't need one."

Aside from Popo's promotional trips as Dear Abby, she and Mort took many trips together, for pleasure and for business, many times on Mort's company plane to board meetings of companies like North Central Airlines or various charities. Another trip Popo took in early 1964 was back to Sioux City to accept an honorary degree from Morningside College, the school she had left for marriage exactly twenty-five years before. Sister Eppie received an honorary Doctorate of Humane Letters too, but because of the friction between the twins, they chose to accept their awards at different ceremonies.

With Eddie away at Stanford and Jeannie in Los Angeles, Popo and Mort made time for themselves. The Phillipses were seen together at opening nights of the Minnesota Opera Company at the Ordway, at benefactors' performances at the Guthrie Theater, which had just opened, and with other culture buffs at special performances at Northrup Auditorium at the University of Minnesota. Southern California living must have acted favorably on Mort too, because an intimate recalls him as an "animated and entertaining conversationalist," while Popo, moving through the ranks of the

Twin Cities' social echelon, exhibited a certain "folksiness, with no sense of being a super celebrity."

Those halcyon days passed mostly uneventfully, with Popo working in her tailor-made office producing her column, sharing with Rose Phillips, her mother-in-law, an interest in the Sholom Home and the Jewish National Fund and attending fund-raising teas, and dividing her time between California and Minnesota, "the best of two worlds," according to Popo. Away from home, the Phillips children seemed safe from the burgeoning drug culture of the sixties and the turmoil of protest activities resulting from the nation's increased involvement in Vietnam.

"I'm very lucky," Popo was modestly saying. "I am a doggone good wife. Morton is the biggest thing in my life. So are my two children. Thank heaven they are independent of us, which makes us, I think, successful parents.

"They are," Popo adds, "beautiful on the inside and on the outside. They live their lives exclusive of mama and daddy. They don't lean."

Daughter Jeannie, however, was finding independence a difficult experience. Even Popo was beginning to worry that all was not well with her only daughter. In Los Angeles, Jeannie was drifting along, lacking her mother's ambition and beginning to show frequent signs of lassitude and ambivalence.

As Jeannie explains it, "I think for me there was great difficulty in looking at something and recognizing what I saw, and that carried over into what I saw when I looked into a mirror."

Working as script girl on the Dear Abby radio show wasn't completely satisfying, and Jeannie was questioning her own self-worth. The program was successful, and Jeannie's contributions may have kept it so, but Jeannie would say, "But it isn't mine. It's hers." The radio program "Dear Abby" was inextricably tied to Dear Abby the public figure and advice columnist.

But Jeannie didn't blame Popo for being overbearing or for her own lack of adjustment. "Mother always thought she had only so much time to nag about the important things. She tried to impart to me the important values of life, like honesty and integrity. She's never been one on table manners and pick-up-your-room."

Seeing that Jeannie was troubled during this period, Popo encouraged her to see a psychotherapist who had been recommended by family friend and analyst Dr. Judd Marmor. After five years of intensive psychotherapy, Jeannie felt secure enough to end the counseling. She also felt secure enough to leave the show.

"I wanted something that would permit me to be more expressive for myself," she explains. With no hard feelings or regret, Jeannie says, speaking of her tenure as script girl on "Dear Abby," "I enjoyed it. It was very interesting and kind of fun."

Relieved that Jeannie was under gifted care, regaining the insight into herself she needed, Popo concentrated on her work on her column. Like Eppie's on Ann Landers, the work rolled so smoothly that writing the material became nearly automatic. Occasional twinges of doubt over the relevance of her advice sometimes crept up, and she consulted with Mort or her children. Jeannie and Eddie shared liberal beliefs, and Popo recognized that their convictions were typical of their generation.

Penetrating critiques from both her children, who were aware of the changing sentiments on college campuses, prompted Popo to reevaluate her professional advice. "I've gone through a gradual process of loosening my views as my children became adults, and they and their friends taught me that maybe I was a little out of step," says Popo.

Birth-control pills, popularized in the sixties, had started changing sexual behavior, and the nation's birth rate began to level off. Divorce was on the rise. By the sixties, 90 percent of all homes had televisions, and the U.S. policy of global intervention and the visual reality of what was happening in Southeast Asia was beamed into the nation's living rooms.

Popo turned to her friend Dr. Franz Alexander to help her keep up with the changing times. He drew up reading lists for her and became her trusted advisor on problematic social issues. Sticky, controversial subjects relating to rape, incest, or homosexuality were referred to Dr. Judd Marmor, whose practice in Los Angeles confronted these matters head on.

Like her twin, Popo was relying on her staff of eight to handle reader mail while she was away from the office. Her goal was to have every letter answered within ten days of its arrival.

Aside from the letters that Popo sets aside for her column, Popo maintains that the ones which give her the most satisfaction in answering are those she marks "Not for Publication" and answers herself. "So many have urgent personal problems. And that's what makes me feel best about my column, when I can feel I've helped them," she says.

Critics in the sixties were beginning to be alarmed by Popo's brand of "mail-order psychology," which criticism inspired her all the more to stay on top of what was happening during those turbulent times. Dr. Rose Franzblau, as much as she liked and respected Popo, was a bit wary of Popo's advice giving, which sometimes didn't fit the psychoanalyst's stricter and more proscriptive outlook. "Such criticism doesn't bother me," Popo responds. "If you want a place in the sun, you have to put up with a few blisters." Besides, Popo, like her twin sister, felt that in most cases a little encouragement from a professional columnist went a long way. They shared the opinion that many people, once they were sufficiently able to articulate their troubles and were offered a minimum of guidance, were capable of working their problems out.

Eppie too, barred from offering prescriptive advice on account of her contract with the *Sun-Times,* referred readers to their priests or ministers, or social service agencies more able to deal with reader problems. Her staff maintains such a complete list of these organizations that she says the former U.S. Department of Health, Education and Welfare occasionally asked her for referrals. But again, Dr. Rose Franzblau, with her sometimes arch and Freudian-based gospel of human development, had occasion to fume over what Eppie printed: "Who does Ann Landers think she is, discussing complex problems with no background to bolster her opinions?"

"Cute and peppy" Popo (Abby), at left, and "Peppy and cute" Eppie (Ann), juniors in high school.

The Friedman home at 1722 Jackson Street, Sioux City, Iowa.

(Bob Davis)

Even at age eighteen, the Friedman twins "always knew everything first." Popo is at left.

(Dickinson College Archives)

Of course the twins double-dated. The "robust but choice" Morningside College coeds (Eppie at left) were a familiar sight on other campuses.

The radiant twin brides in identical gowns of "medieval inspiration" reigned over Shaare Zion synagogue's first double wedding.

With the men in their lives at a 1949 Presto convention in Florida. From left, Jules and Eppie Lederer, Popo Phillips, Abe Friedman, the twins' father, and Mort Phillips.

Peanut Place, Eppie and Jules's home in Eau Claire, Wisconsin, near the outskirts of Altoona.

Popo's place, the Phillips home in Eau Claire.

"Larry Fanning was my mentor. He taught me how to write," says Eppie, thankful that her *Chicago Sun-Times* editor helped transform her into a polished Ann Landers.

The first Ann Landers, Ruth Crowley, with her children. Daughter Diane, now the new *Sun-Times* advice columnist replacing Ann Landers, is at right.

"Popo always said I was her boss, but it was a very relaxed kind of bossmanship," declares *San Francisco Chronicle* editor Stanleigh "Auk" Arnold, conferring with a confident Dear Abby.

Suddenly an honest-to-goodness celebrity, Dear Abby blows a goodbye kiss to Edward R. Murrow at the conclusion of her 1958 television debut on "Person to Person." Husband Mort is seated next to her.

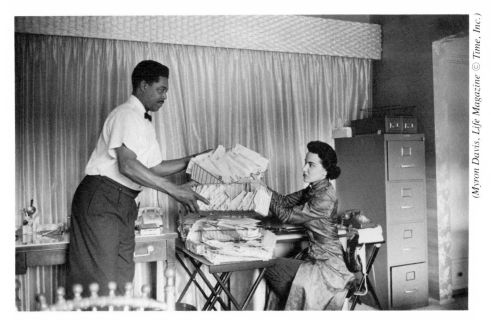

Dear Abby, in the "mailroom" of her Hillsborough, California, home, wrestles with the morning batch of reader letters delivered by her houseboy.

Up as early as six-thirty to pose as an ideal wife for the camera, the newly minted Ann Landers makes sure to see her husband off properly.

"My number one career is my family, and I never let my hobby interfere with my career," affirms Popo. Daughter Jeannie is at the piano with, from left, son Eddie, Popo, and Mort looking on.

(Frederick Lyon, Life Magazine © Time, Inc.)

Eppie, at the age of forty-four, was already a grandmother. From left, Jules, Eppie, John Coleman, the first of Margo's three husbands, and Margo, with newborn Abra.

(Vatican Archives)

"When we stepped forward, he knew all about us," remembers Popo of Pope Paul. Reconciled after years of silence, the twins with their husbands traveled to Italy on their 30th wedding anniversaries.

"We just want to go home as the Friedman twins," the sisters proclaimed at the 40th reunion of Central High's class of '36. But the Friedman twins, Popo (left) and Eppie (right), couldn't escape the spotlight even as they compared yearbook photos.

(Bob Davis)

Ann Landers consults her friend, adviser, and confidant of nearly fifty years, Dr. Robert Stolar.

"She knows where the power is and she's got her finger on it," says Father Theodore Hesburgh, former president of the University of Notre Dame, with Ann Landers at an anti-nuclear rally in Chicago.

In 1980, after twenty-five years as Ann Landers and the publication of her 1,212-page *Encyclopedia*, Eppie Lederer and the *Sun-Times* were ready to celebrate.

Ann Landers, keeping her nails extra long for the occasion, cements her handprints in Chicago's version of Hollywood's Walk of Fame.

(Photoreporters)

Dear Abby joins the celebrity ranks of ERA supporters. Marching at the Los Angeles rally are, from left, Abby, unknown, Ira Bernstein, Florence Henderson, Marsha Mason, Neil Simon, and Joan Hackett.

Abby's residence in the hills of Bel Air, just west of Los Angeles.

(Michael LeRoy)

Abby makes no secret of her extravagant wardrobe and shoe collection.

(Colin Dangaard)

Ann Landers awash in letters, reading, writing, and phoning.

(Colin Dangaard)

(Elliott Erwitt/Magnum)

In one of her many publicity photos, Abby poses in her glamorous bathroom.

"We've been anonymous and we've been famous," says Abby (left) at their 50th class reunion at Central High in 1986. "And it's more fun famous."

Like Popo, to stay up to date on social change, Eppie constantly reevaluates her positions on social issues. "I will change my mind," she says. "I don't think that damages my credibility."

Both twins in their early advice columns, for instance, incessantly spoke of the need for a girl to hold onto her virginity until she married. Eppie called virgins "white-flowered girls." A decade later, in 1968's *Truth Is Stranger,* she would still write "Premarital sex is dumb. It is dumb because it violates the moral and ethical rules of our society." She then listed the penalties of premarital sex: "guilt, self-deprecation, worry, and a sullied reputation." But by 1981, Eppie was stating that her perspective on certain subjects had changed, but not her values. "I think I changed my *point of view* on virginity. When I first got into this work I thought a woman should remain a virgin until she married or died, whichever came first. This was the way I looked at it. Nothing was going to change that. Well, I changed my mind about that. Because I realized if you're gonna live in the real world you'd better get with it. You'd better be realistic."

Eppie's coterie of close and influential friends provides a network of expert counsel. When they deplore her skimpy credentials or sometimes-flimsy oversimplifications, Eppie naysays her detractors by throwing their expertise back at them.

At a Harvard seminar, Eppie was invited to speak to fifty or so psychiatrists, lawyers, welfare workers, and sociologists. Eppie let them have it, and speaks about the experience without malice, sweetly, and charitably. Eppie predicted, "They are going to put me on the hot seat. They will want to know who I think I am. These are the authentic, the credentialed boys who are having a tough time finding the answers. How many of the doctors at Menninger's say to me, 'You know, I wish you would teach us how you do it. How you get to the point. How do you separate the wheat from the chaff? How do you get it right in two, three, or four lines?' "

Both sisters were realizing that their responsibilities were awesome. Eppie calls it "staggering, yes, but not frightening." Someone has to do it. She continues, "The responsibility is there for the taking. There is an enormous need for such a column, and I view it as one of journalism's great challenges, a unique opportunity to spotlight ignorance, fear, and stupidity. I pray only that I am equal to the task."

Twenty

*E*ppie, mustering the wherewithal to take slim note of her harshest critics, persisted in her campaign to witness first-hand the ills befalling people less fortunate than she. Shortly after her daughter's marriage in 1961, Eppie accompanied Robert Stolar to a leper colony in Nassau. She recalls that Jules and Stolar's wife refused to go along, fearing contamination, but their concerns were unfounded.

"The doctor and I went without them. Dr. Stolar, a dermatologist, knew that leprosy is very difficult to get, but the irrational fear of the disease kept these people isolated. Our visit with the patients and staff lasted several hours. We ate with them, visited at length, and shook hands when we said goodbye. It was one of the most rewarding and uplifting experiences of my life."

Her spunk, her bravery intact, by the early sixties Eppie's view of herself, her family, and her career was changing. Though in her column she still maintained a hard line on interfaith and interracial dating and marriage, and still disapproved of premarital sex and divorce, her personal views on other matters of human relations were slowly beginning to alter. "When I was younger," she says, "I was a very hard-line moralist. Right was right. Wrong was wrong."

Part of her changing philosophy came from lessons culled from her readers. "I am much more compassionate. . . . I guess I always had a victory syndrome. I was a winner. . . . If I could do it, why couldn't they? It never occurred to me that I had many things going for me other people didn't have, things I wasn't even responsible for . . . tremendous energy . . . good health."

And that's naming only a few. Aside from the energy and health, Eppie was enjoying a life in which everyday needs were amply provided for. In addition, as her Ann Landers wages escalated to serious money, she slowly acquired a portfolio of healthy investments. "Good stocks, real estate, a little here and there," she recites. "You know, money is not important, because I don't have to think about it, I guess. . . ."

As she became aware of her growing fortune, exposure to how less-privileged people lived fell heavily on Eppie. The drab levels of existence discovered through her readers' mail, where husbands couldn't afford surprise gifts of $1,200 alligator attaché cases and sable coats, constantly awakened her to the duties she felt obligated to perform. "I know I've got it awfully good," Eppie says, and through her column she dedicated herself to caring about people who didn't.

Her home life, financially secure but far from ideal, was making Eppie rethink her priorities. Because of Jules's business dealings and Eppie's devotion to her career, they didn't see that much of each other. Margo was married and starting a family. Abra, named after Margo's grandparents Abraham and Rebecca, would be the first in a line of three. Eppie, at the age of forty-four, was traveling hither and yon to promote her column, acting as national chairman of the 1963 Christmas Seal Campaign, active in the National Council on Alcoholism and the Epilepsy League, guest speaking for the Family Service Association, and phoning home to Jules and visiting Margo and her granddaughter when she could manage it. She was leading a very full and productive life, but niggling doubts about the completeness of her family relations kept cropping up. As Eppie tells it, "I have learned that financial success, academic achievement, and social or political status open no doors to peace of mind or inner security."

It was perhaps reflection on her own understanding of what constitutes peace of mind, or perhaps the geographic closeness of her twin, now in St. Paul, that inspired Eppie to attempt to reestablish their sisterly bond. Popo herself, for the few years previously, claims she sent letters to Eppie, begging her twin to resume their friendship. Popo says she even sent an olive branch. Eppie, she says, ignored the overtures. "Stony silence," Popo recalls. "Stony, stony, stony."

Finally, Eppie telephoned Popo.

"Suddenly, 1964, the fourth of May, I picked up my telephone and I heard that husky voice, so like my own," says Popo.

"Hello, Popo, this is Eppie."

"My heart started to pound and my throat closed up. I just couldn't, I couldn't talk," remembers Popo.

"What do you and Mort plan on doing for your twenty-fifth anniversary?" Eppie asked.

Popo, stunned, quickly and happily answered, "We plan to go to Bermuda for a few weeks."

"Do you want to make it a foursome?" asked Eppie.

"Yes!" said Popo, and it took a mere second to say it.

The feud had made great copy. But friends and relatives were vastly relieved when it ended. It was difficult to understand how identical twins, once so close, could become so antagonistic. Everyone concerned had pressured the twins to stop bickering. That they did. Yet they were still unable to resolve their deeper, lifelong hostilities.

America's two premier advice columnists agreed never to discuss their column work with each other, work that consumed much of their waking lives. At all costs they avoided confronting the paralyzing misunderstandings that would continue to haunt their flawed relationship. By Eppie telephoning Popo, the sisterly feud may have been buried, but events fewer than twenty years later would show that it was not dead.

* * *

At the end of the twins' first decade as advice columnists, Popo topped Eppie with some 700 subscribing newspapers. Eppie ran second with 638 newspapers. Though the disparity may have irked Eppie, who still felt that her twin was the newcomer to the advice business, what disturbed Eppie more was that her long-time friend and trusted editor, Larry Fanning, was moving to Anchorage with his new wife, Kay.

Two years after Kay's 1963 divorce from Marshall Field, she went to Alaska as a reporter for the *Anchorage Daily News*. When Larry and Kay were married the following year, they decided to settle in Anchorage. Larry moved into the newsroom at the Anchorage paper and Kay recalls his attempting to edit the Ann Landers column long distance. He "was still editing Eppie's column some after we moved. He tried to edit it from Alaska and it really didn't work, so he told her he just couldn't do it."

In 1967, when the Anchorage paper was up for sale, Kay and Larry bought it. Kay fondly remembers the courtesy Eppie extended to them as they labored to keep the newspaper financially sound. "When I was editor of the *Anchorage Daily News* we ran the column," Kay says. "A very sweet thing Eppie did, because we were very, very short on money, was that she always let us run her column free of charge." As a tribute to her friend and mentor, Eppie continued the favor even after Larry's death. "Long after he died, in memory of Larry," says Kay, "she let us have it free of charge."

Eppie says Fanning was always telling her, "If I get hit by a bread truck, Trez is your man." A protegé of Fanning's, Dick Trezevant, whom Eppie characterizes as a "tough but tender guy," in 1967 took over editing Eppie, who by then needed little more than a pat on the back or some minor alterations to tidy up her column for publication.

William Steven concurs that Trez was the right choice as Eppie's editor. "She never let anyone edit her column who wasn't damn good," he says.

The *Sun-Times* syndicate had much in store for Eppie on the occasion of her tenth anniversary as Ann Landers. For the first ten years of her column writing, Eppie's syndicate owned the name under which she wrote. Like any other employee, Eppie could have been fired under the conditions of her contract, her job given to anybody else. But after ten years, Eppie certainly had proved herself, and as a gesture of thanks the syndicate, she says, presented her with the name Ann Landers and an Illinois vanity license plate bearing AL1955 for her chauffeured Fleetwood.

Star treatment also was deemed in order, and *Editor & Publisher,* the trade journal of the newspaper industry, carried on its cover an oversized Bodoni Bold advertisement headed A LOVE LETTER TO ANN LANDERS. Inside, the letter cites the syndicate's devotion to Eppie Lederer, who "made a gloomy, old thing in newspapering named the 'Agony Column' perk up and smile." The accolade continues, "We love Eppie so much, we all want to tell her we hope she'll stick around for at least 100 more years." The love letter is handsomely signed, the *Chicago Sun-Times.*

The well-deserved public recognition to Eppie's hard work and earnest dedication pleased everyone but Popo. Determined to confront her syndicate, Popo began with the front office at McNaught. With her ten-year contract up for renegotiation, Popo was in fighting form. First off, she wanted a bigger cut of the profits from her feature. More significantly, she wanted McNaught to pay the taxes on her income.

"She resented the high taxes she was paying," says Charles McAdam. "Abby bothered us. She kept fighting us to see if there was some way to block the income tax."

Popo's desire to avoid taxes may sound mercenary, but it's perhaps only indicative of the last resort of someone strapped to a financial relationship she no longer finds palatable. Increasingly, people earning large incomes, like sports stars, were looking for contracts that would reduce their personal tax burden. McNaught could do little about Popo's somewhat enviable tax problem. "You've got to come up with a solution to my taxes or I'm going to leave you," McAdam recalls Popo insisting.

≈ 187

While emphasizing that the impending break would be due to the tax issue, Popo meanwhile "was shopping around" for a $140,000-a-year package, an account of her demands published in *Newsweek* that she denies. The McNaught president says that the syndicate couldn't meet Popo's proposals, and Popo wouldn't even consider its counteroffer. Husband Mort, as hard-nosed on contract negotiations as his wife, actively took part in the discussions.

There were other factors too. Popo felt that McNaught wasn't doing all it could to promote Dear Abby. "She was always fighting with us for more publicity," admits McAdam. "We said get all the publicity you want, send us the bills. But that was just an excuse. She wanted the whole feature for herself. That's all it was. She's money crazy."

On top of that, Popo objected to the syndicate's practice that newspapers take less popular features before they could have Dear Abby. "Sure we did it," Charles McAdam says. "But when she started out we used Joe Palooka to promote her."

Vexed particularly because the syndicate had devoted a great deal of effort in marketing Popo's impish column, McNaught executives are convinced that it was their efforts that launched an unknown housewife into a celebrity columnist. Charged Peter Bogg, a McNaught salesman, "When you take them from nothing and make them big, they're unappreciative."

"Let's just call it a legal separation" was Popo's coy response to the breakup.

"One of the spectacular snatches in syndicate annals," heralded *Time* in late 1965, three months before Popo moved to the Chicago Tribune–New York News Syndicate based in New York City and today the Tribune Company Syndicate. Equaling Eppie's exposure some months before, the *Tribune*'s new star was announced via a glossy three-page color advertisement in *Editor & Publisher*. The words *Dear Abby* were splayed across a dramatic centerfold mountain range.

Among the top columnists in the United States, Popo was able to set her own price tag at her hand-picked syndicate. Popo's contract called for escalators in her take, which by the end of her second decade would top 90 percent, with the Tribune Company paying some of the income taxes on her Dear Abby earnings. Syndication expert Richard Weiner calls Popo's second contract, which guaranteed her several million dollars over the next decade, "one of the most unusual in the journalism field or, for that matter, any business."

Arthur Laro, Tribune Company president, who met Popo's dollar figures, expressed his hopes for a long and happy relationship with their newest star. "Miss Van Buren wanted to change syndicates, and we are honored and pleased she chose us to handle her column for newspapers at home and abroad." In addition, Laro announced his intention to increase Popo's subscribing newspapers by 200. But Charles McAdam, still smarting from "losing the biggest-selling column in the country at the time, no question," doubted that the number of subscribing papers could be increased. "There weren't any left," McAdam insists, talking about the daily newspapers that ran either Ann Landers or Dear Abby. "They had saturated the market when Abby left McNaught."

Oddly, the Tribune Company was placed in a difficult situation by acquiring Dear Abby. Because of its affiliation with the *New York Daily News,* which ran the Ann Landers column, and the *Chicago Tribune,* which ran Dear Abby, the twins became ever watchful of whose feature was getting the most play. "My sister is getting more space," Don Michaels, the Tribune Company syndicate's senior editor, remembers Popo complaining. "Couldn't we even it out?"

Although Popo didn't gain the 200 new subscribers Laro had hoped for, she profited from an increase of about twenty or thirty, enough to maintain a lead of a hundred more subscribers than her twin. But by all accounts, the monetary gain from this comfortable margin doesn't seem all that dramatic.

Why two women with luxurious home lives would want to work so industriously for another million dollars is hard to understand. Popo says, "I have nothing now materially that I didn't have before. I lived well before, and I still live well." Eppie echoes her twin, saying, "I don't need the money, I'd do it for nothing. I live well, but I think that I deserve to." Maybe it wasn't the money that led the sisters to keep score. It was the gnawing fear that their advice giving was becoming passé.

As the sisters were complacent with their position as the two top-ranked advice columnists in the United States, the petty squabbling over who was ahead in the syndication race perhaps was an odd source of amusement for them, as well as a barometer of how well they were serving their readers. Ann Landers and Dear Abby had scooped the field and eliminated all national competitors. A loss in subscribership could mean only one thing, that they were falling behind the times.

The press had virtually exhausted the saga of the feuding love-lorn columnists. When in the spring of 1965 Eppie was asked once again whether she and her twin were on speaking terms, her answer was, "That's nonsense. Ours is not the chummiest sister relationship . . . because the natural rivalry between twins is far greater than in ordinary siblings. But we are not feuding, and it is not true we do not speak." Contradicting nearly every friend and colleague of theirs at the time, Popo too, chimes in, "There was never a time we weren't speaking to each other."

With no feud to concentrate on, critics of Ann Landers and Dear Abby turned to their relevance, a sensitive issue for both sisters. The twins felt obligated to get back to business, the real business of keeping up with the grayer areas of human relationships, without forsaking conventional values.

Says Eppie, "The world has gotten racier and I feel I must respond to what is going on out there. If I'm going to be useful, I'm going to have to deal with all kinds of human problems." But the twins' transition from embracing middle American viewpoints to taking up social causes was a gradual one.

It would be false to say that the twins lacked the virtue of compassion or didn't possess an almost uncanny understanding of human behavior. Still, despite their intent to keep up with the new morality, it would take a few more years before either sister would feel secure enough to stand back from her square, middle western, small-town Jewish upbringing and seek a less inflexible view of the human condition. And it would take even a few more years after that for small-town newspaper editors, ever standing in judgment of what is fit for local consumption, to accept the more enlightened cultural views of two women starting to move freely amid the urbane world of progressive thinkers and decision makers.

It didn't take too many angry readers like the one who chided Eppie, saying, "How come your column isn't dated Vatican City?" to make her realize that times were changing.

Twenty-One

Fame for both sisters didn't come without a price. One night in 1967, Popo lost $40,000 worth of jewelry when the Phillipses' River Drive penthouse was burglarized. The items taken included a diamond bracelet valued at $11,000 and a $5,000 platinum, pearl, and diamond ring. At the specific request of the influential Phillips family, St. Paul authorities at first withheld the police report from the press. And Eppie, having just consented to a six-page photo spread in *Look* a few months before, decided there'd be no more publicity photos in her lavishly appointed Lake Shore Drive apartment.

Popo's physical well-being was also threatened in a bizarre encounter with a troubled Dear Abby fan. Love letters and floral arrangements kept arriving at her home, sent there by a strange woman. Jay Phillips, Popo's father-in-law, began to receive anonymous and frequently harassing long-distance phone calls from the same woman. Popo, scheduled to lecture the next week, appeared at the lectern despite her apprehension. In the audience sat the persistent fan. She had flown to Minneapolis to hear Popo speak.

"She was an enormous woman with a man's haircut. She hugged and kissed me," recounts an embarrassed Popo. "I felt trapped. She was harmless, but obsequious and obsessive."

The incident convinced Popo to instruct her staff never to divulge the location of her public appearances to inquiring readers or curious fans. Innately cautious on account of her family money, Popo became increasingly reluctant to discuss her children, her friends, or her private life with the press. But the strictures Popo set on her life as Dear Abby didn't apply to social life in the Twin Cities. After just two years in St. Paul, Popo and Mort had entered the ranks of the social elite and were seen together at all the "most wonderful, marvelous parties in town," many of which they hosted themselves.

Popo, wading through crowded gatherings at the Sheraton Ritz or the Oak Ridge Country Club in one of her Norman Norell sequinned sheaths that eventually became her signature outfit, charmed guests with her quick wit and effervescence. As the night proceeded and the revelers danced and chatted quietly, it wouldn't be unusual to see Popo persuade good friend Ted Mann, the California theater owner and husband of Hollywood actress Rhonda Fleming, to play the piano with her and sing hit tunes to the delight of those present.

Mort, elegantly attired and ever the gentleman, was considered quite different from Popo, but "very bright and very supportive" of his vivacious wife. "He was quite an enigma," says one acquaintance of theirs in the Twin Cities. "He was on the board of the Minneapolis Institute of Art, and was more interested in the arts than in commerce." In a way, says the same friend, "they were levelers for each other." An intimate of the Phillipses concurs. "Clearly there was a robust marital bond. Mort took his wife's success in stride. He has a secure psyche."

With their sisterly squabble buried, husbands Mort and Jules made sure that the twins saw enough of each other to cement their rapprochement and prevent any past animosities from cropping up. Eppie and Jules attended many of the parties Mort and Popo gave. Jay Phillips, too, was a firm believer in harmonious relations and family solidarity, and he and his wife, Rose, would use any excuse to convince Eppie and Jules to come to Minneapolis for the weekend to dine with them at the Oak Ridge Country Club or celebrate one family event or another.

Amid the partygoing, vacation and business travel, helping, as a board member, to chart the direction of the Phillips Foundation, and her attentiveness to her children, Popo established many close friendships in Minneapolis/St. Paul. She befriended former Bishop James Shannon, who at the time was president of St. Thomas College in St. Paul but later made headlines as one of the highest-ranking Roman Catholic clergymen to give up his vows.

"I met Abby through Ann," recalls Jim Shannon. "I was a priest in the archdiocese of St. Paul at the time, and each of them after that would send me a letter and say they'd appreciate my telling them how I would answer it. I don't mean to imply I was one of their steady references, but I did get queries from them. And that led to a very warm friendship between each of them and me." The kinds of letters both Eppie and Popo sent to Shannon covered a "wide range of issues. Theological, moral, ecclesiastical."

Mrs. Ralph Green, the former Grace MacDonald, who in her earlier days was a Broadway dancer, first met Popo in Palm Springs and later, when she moved to Minneapolis, found in her a "close and devoted friend. A friend in the truest sense of the word who would go to hell and back for you."

Attesting to Popo's loyalty, Grace continues, "There were two occasions in my life I needed help and clout, and she helped me. I don't know who else I could have turned to."

It was Popo, Grace maintains, who discovered Erma Bombeck and launched her on her syndicated career. "Popo gave a marvelous, fun party for Erma Bombeck," says Grace. It was 1965, about the time Popo herself was searching for a new syndicate to replace McNaught. Popo had read Bombeck's column on *hausfrau* humor in a local paper and thought it was hilarious. She invited her as well as reps from a number of different syndicates to the party. In a short time Popo had picked her own new syndicate, while the

Newsday syndicate, in addition to the *Minneapolis Star,* had signed up Bombeck.

As the sixties' counterculture values became integrated with American standards, Popo was evaluating Dear Abby to ensure that it was in no danger of becoming outmoded. Against the backdrop of war protests, the sexual revolution, and the women's movement, there was the possibility that both Dear Abby and Ann Landers were beginning to appear staid and conventional.

Popo chose her speaking engagements carefully and geared her subject matter to her audience. Before the members of St. Peter's Church Altar Society at the Edina Country Club, Popo delighted the women with her generic recitation of her duties, portraying Dear Abby as the one person people can talk to because they "may be too ashamed to face people with their problem and find it easier to write a letter."

Other times, however, Popo as Dear Abby wasn't quite so reticent, like when she told the *Washington Star* that Pope Paul's encyclical banning contraceptives "set the Roman Catholic church back fifty years." Calling it "a pity, a real shame," that the Pope could be blind to the "most critical problem facing mankind today, the population explosion," Popo admitted she was not endorsing the Pill as the panacea for controlling world population, nor did she desire to position herself as preacher, judge, or jury. Instead, Popo says, she was advising people to make up their own minds. Perhaps inadvertently quoting Jiminy Cricket, Popo was repeatedly chirping, "If there is a question in your mind, I always say, 'Let your conscience be your guide.' "

Popo, through her column, was confronting the sometimes confusing state of the sixties culture. "Today, the moral issues seem to be obscure," she was saying, but like her sister, Popo continued to espouse virginity for unmarried women of any age and to warn readers of the dangers of divorce and interfaith marriage.

Perhaps because Eppie had permitted it a little more than a year before, Popo allowed *Look* readers an insider glimpse of the "Salty Oracle on the Agony Beat." Heavy on family and fashion photos and slim on cerebral content, the four pages depicted Popo at work and at play, dressed in cocktail chic and in mischievous mod. The only surprising revelation in the accompanying text occurs in the last paragraph, in which Popo gives short answers to a few standard queries.

On drinking and smoking and sex before marriage, the answer is "No." On hippies, Popo answers, "They disgust me." But on abortion, Popo says, "I don't think any woman should be forced to have a child she doesn't want."

Eppie too, shared her twin's pro-choice sentiments, but it wasn't until years later that she felt secure enough to discuss in her column a woman's right to an abortion. At that time, nontherapeutic abortion wasn't only controversial, it was an illegal act. The 1973 Supreme Court decision *Roe* v. *Wade,* which effectively legalized abortion, was six years off.

Once again, unlike Popo, who owns Dear Abby, Eppie was constrained by her syndicate on what views she was allowed to articulate, however vague the restraints might be. Even in interviews, Eppie didn't allow her more liberal thoughts to be ascribed to Ann Landers. Strong opinions on an issue as fraught with emotional debate as a woman's right to an abortion might not at that time have passed muster with her syndicate.

"She's always been careful," agrees William Steven about Eppie. "She's been careful in two directions. She's careful to have the approval of the ownership and editors of her paper, and she's careful that she gets the benefit of expert advice."

Throughout the sixties, Robert Stolar was counseling Eppie to take a stand on important issues, but at the same time Dick Trezevant, her editor at the *Sun-Times,* was telling her to steer clear of political things.

Despite Trezevant's advice, in May 1967, Eppie, as Ann Landers, by way of Travis Air Force, Honolulu, Wake Island, Guam, and Manila, landed at Tan Son Nhut Air Base just outside of Saigon. Her ten-day USO tour of hospitals in the war zone followed that of Bob Hope and a swell of other celebrities. Ann Landers readers were prepared for the trip by a release issued by her syndicate and picked up by most of the papers Eppie's column appeared in. "Have your questions ready," the USO is said to have alerted wounded GIs. "If anyone can answer them, she can."

Eppie Lederer was not just anyone. Not knowing whom she'd meet, Eppie set out her first day in a black-and-white silk shift and pearl earrings. "Hey, I know you," said a suddenly alert but puzzled Army sergeant. "You're Ann Landers. But what are you doing in Vietnam?"

After an exhausting day of joking with GIs, working jigsaw puzzles, and autographing foot casts, "That woman has an incredible gift for saying exactly the right things to everybody," said a doctor who accompanied her. Eppie spent the night at the house of the commanding general of the Qui Nhon support unit. To ensure her safety, several MPs were stationed on the balcony to her bedroom.

Eppie understood the dangers involved. Before her trip, she stated, "Whatever the risk, the trip is worth it."

Coptering to field hospitals, a phalanx of armed escorts shadowing her, Eppie roamed the wards the next few days in more sensible duds: dark stretch pants, high-heeled ankle boots, and a light tunic top.

"How long has it been since you've smelled perfume, fella?" the middle-age Eppie asked, leaning over the bed of a corporal from Wyoming.

"Ten and a half months," the corporal replied.

"That's all for you, brother," joked Eppie. "You could be dangerous."

Her unceasing optimism was directed at soldier and officer alike. Praising the military and its "excellent medical facilities and treatment" of the wounded, Eppie unwittingly patronized a surgeon to whom she said, "When you get back to the States and think back on this, you'll realize what a wonderful job you've all been doing."

"When I get back to the States, I'll try to forget everything that has happened" was the reply she received. The doctor's rebuke left even the upbeat Eppie speechless.

"What can you say to men like that?" Eppie later said. "They're simply magnificent."

According to the coverage by Eppie's flagship paper, the *Sun-Times,* most of the men who accompanied Eppie thought she was pretty magnificent too. "Most celebrities who come here walk through a couple of wards, get their pictures taken, and leave. This woman has visited every single patient," said an Army officer. "It's almost eleven at night and I know she's been on her feet since this morning. Where in the world does that little woman get all her energy?"

"I keep going the same way you keep going," explained Eppie, truly believing she was getting back a lot more than she was giving. "When you are around people who are giving as much as these fellows are giving, how on earth could you do less?"

Press coverage of Eppie's trip to Vietnam was mostly naïve and uncritical. "Miracle worker" is what the *Sun-Times* chose to call her. Eppie must've come back from Vietnam feeling mighty good about her trip. She had taken her earlier international trip as Ann Landers, to the Soviet Union, to prove herself. In Vietnam, already a name-brand celebrity, she got a lot of positive free publicity. There were indeed trade-offs, but in this case the bargain was equitable. She acquitted herself with considerable aplomb and succeeded in rousing wounded and homesick GIs, who managed to summon the requisite soldierly enthusiasm in the presence of a caring and attentive female from way back home.

The only sour media note to the Ann Landers trek was sounded in a *New York Times* article that criticized what it called self-serving celebrities who gained prestige and publicity through tours of Vietnam. Citing Eppie's ninety-minute visit with General William Westmoreland as a prime example, the article stated, "Periodic pleas from Saigon to Washington to slow the stream of visitors have so far gone unanswered." *The Times* also cited military statistics showing that almost all the time of the top military brass in one area of Vietnam was taken up with briefing and escorting celebrity visitors.

As public attitudes shifted against the war, the columnist could look back in 1974 and confidently claim, "I was one of the early doves." Eppie later says she "had felt for years that Vietnam was an immoral, impossible, unwinnable war. Hubert Humphrey asked me to go because he thought if I just talked on a one-to-one basis with [Ambassador] Ellsworth Bunker and General Westmoreland I'd come back convinced. Well, not in a million years could they have changed my mind."

Traveling as an "Angel of the Battlefield," administering counsel to the wounded, may have considerably lessened the political implications of Eppie's trip to Vietnam. But Eppie says she was opposed to the war even then, in the spring of 1967, when vocal opposition was still confined to distinct minorities of students and some clergy. She says she "made no explanation of my feelings about the war to the boys, I was just there to cheer them up and offer to call their moms and dads or their wives for them when I got back."

She told reporters she had lectured Vice President Humphrey many times in the sixties, telling him to help bring an end to the war. She claimed to have in her possession an apologetic note from him saying, "I should have listened, Eppie, you were right about Vietnam." But when a *New York Times* reporter asked to see that letter, Eppie refused to show it to her.

If Eppie was speaking out against the war, she was doing it privately. In Washington, Eppie recalls, "Whenever I had an opportunity to see him, say at a small social function, I would try to get him off to one side. I'd say, 'Now look! We've got to get rid of this war!' And then he'd say, 'I know, but how do you do it?' " Sighing, she continues, "I never could do a thing with Lyndon Johnson."

Antiwar leader and Vietnam expert Richard Barnet, when asked about Eppie's activities to put an end to United States involvement, said, "There were none." The former White House fellow and co-founder of the Institute for Policy Studies, an organization that had taken a firm stand against U.S. military involvement in Southeast Asia, added, "I certainly don't remember Ann

Landers taking any public stand against the war at any moment when it would have made any difference."

"I was extremely anti-Vietnam, long before it became popular to be against the war," Eppie repeatedly states. But Senator Eugene McCarthy, the leading political spokesman for the antiwar movement, doesn't remember either Eppie or, for that matter, Popo, coming out publicly against the Vietnam war early on.

"They came in late, a lot of people did," he says. "I don't recall that either one of them was doing anything on Vietnam in '68. They weren't aggressively or actively opposing Vietnam at the time of my '68 campaign."

What McCarthy does remember is that later, years after he failed to win the Democratic presidential nod on a platform that called for the complete withdrawal of U.S. troops from Vietnam, many influential Democrats like Eppie and Popo were supporting the antiwar movement.

"Their opposition to Vietnam seems to have come well after '68," he says. "That's true with a lot of people," he chuckles. "A lot of Democrats. . . . I'm very tough on that," he continues wryly. "If you weren't involved in '68, it doesn't even count."

Clearly there's a discrepancy between Eppie's recollection and the extent of her "early dove" activities. Eppie's financial contributions to Johnson's presidential campaign, entitling her to membership in the controversial LBJ President's Club during the war's intensity, also seem to contradict her view of herself as an outspoken Vietnam pacifist.

Eppie wrote her first tactful but hollow public criticism of the Vietnam war in 1972 but cloaked it within an obliging discussion of America's youth. "There is no rational defense for personal neglect, dirt, bad manners, or foul language," she stated in her column. "And there's no denying it—it's more prevalent both off and on campuses than it used to be. But there is also less hypocrisy, and a stronger commitment to higher ideals. A generation that is against the Vietnam war, outspoken in behalf of equal opportunities for minority groups, dedicated to fighting pollution and saving the environment, can't be all bad."

In 1972, public opinion polls showed that the majority of Americans wanted United States participation in the war to end. Far from being in the vanguard of public opinion, as Ann Landers, Eppie instead reflected prevailing sentiments of the day. She was doing her job by keeping in sync with her readers' views.

Twenty-Two

At the thirty-fifth quadrennial Democratic National Convention held at Chicago's downtown Convention and International Amphitheater in August 1968, two issues were pre-eminent: the poverty and rioting in black-populated central cities, and the cost of the Vietnam war in dollars and lives. Racial unrest had scarred urban ghettos beginning in Watts in the summer of 1965 and later spread to Newark and Detroit and other large urban areas.

By year's end 1967 there were nearly half a million American troops in Vietnam. The killings of Martin Luther King Jr. and Robert F. Kennedy earlier in 1968 only served to ignite further the growing unrest that culminated in clashes between youths and police, tear-gassed demonstrators, and finally, federal agents as well as the National Guard at the Democratic Convention. The big issue was Vietnam.

Intellectually, Eppie may have had reservations as early as 1968 about military involvement in Vietnam, but she wasn't about to allow her political views to obstruct her social aspirations. She willingly sought the company of influential Americans who staunchly supported U.S. involvement there.

Circumventing the ragtag and bobtail during Convention week, Eppie and Jules attended party after party, from the cocktail buffet given by Marshall Field and Bailey K. Howard at the Chicago Armory to the preprandial millings with the likes of Clare Boothe Luce, Katharine Graham, John Glenn, and the Arthur Ochs Sulzbergers, first at the Prudential Building and then the Mid-America Club. After greeting masses of VIP friends from New York, Washington, and other cities, Eppie changed out of her black chiffon party dress into a full-length black sequin and marabou-trimmed gown and awaited the Sunday-night arrival of guests at her Lake Shore Drive apartment.

"It's for about 200 friends, people we know and like," said Eppie. Invitations to the Lederer "do" included the three primary candidates, Humphrey, McCarthy, and George McGovern, all personal friends of Eppie's. Chicago Mayor Richard Daley, by no means a close friend of the Lederers', was hosting a party late that same Sunday night. But it was a mammoth reception for Illinois delegates and 2,000 others at the Sherman House, hardly competition for the more intimate and soigné gathering of knows and likes at Eppie and Jules's place.

As for Popo, she'd already decided which candidate to back. At the party, which conveniently coincided with Mort's fiftieth birthday, Popo sported the upper-income equivalent of a peace button. The gold lapel pin replicated the vice-presidential seal mounted on a diamond-and-ruby frame and signaled a giant-sized donation to HHH. After Humphrey's primary win, but before the Humphrey/Muskie loss to Richard Nixon in 1968—which disappointed sister Eppie too, who called it a "half-assed election"— Popo started venting her political views in her column, much to the dismay of many Republican newspaper editors.

A few years later, at about the same time Eppie as Ann Landers was offering lukewarm public commentary against the war, Popo, apparently, had had enough. She began urging her readers to write their senators and congressmen to "bring an end to this senseless war in Vietnam." Dear Abby's joining the ranks of those opposing the war prompted William Loeb, the arch-conservative publisher of the Manchester (New Hampshire) *Union Leader,* to write, "I am a great admirer of yours, but you are on the wrong track here."

Other newspaper editors were angered by the intrusion of politics into Popo's advice column. "You are not qualified to comment on foreign policy," editorialized an Oklahoma paper. Some Abby readers criticized her pacifist stand. A felt-tip pen in hand, Popo unhesitatingly marked the envelopes holding the critical letters: "IDIOT." The few GIs who wrote Abby wondering why they were in Vietnam got their letters forwarded to President Nixon with the question "What can I tell this young man?"

Although both Eppie and Popo tested prevailing sentiment on the Vietnam conflict before letting Ann or Abby state an opinion, it is astonishing that Popo ever ventured to publicize her convictions. During the same period Dear Abby was advocating that readers write their elected officials, the Phillips family was reaping profits from the manufacture of 105mm and 8-inch projectile tips for use in Southeast Asia. National Presto Industries, the former kettle works, received defense contracts totaling more than $100 million while Mort was a director there.

Soon after it received the defense contracts in 1967, Presto's stock split. Profits were large. After the war's end, the Department of Justice's National Renegotiation Board charged Presto with making more than $11 million in excess profits from the shell-making contracts awarded the company between 1967 and 1972.

Presto responded by saying the government action, brought during the Carter administration, was "purely politically motivated," and defended its profits. After Ronald Reagan became president, the Department of Justice settled out of court with Presto, allowing the company to keep the $11 million it had withheld and paying Presto partial interest of $1.4 million. Today, Presto continues an "in-place standby" contract with the Department of the Army for projectiles.

The year 1968 was a financially rewarding one for Jules Lederer. Transamerica Corporation, the San Francisco–based conglomerate, bought Budget Rent-a-Car for $10 million in stock. Jules was offered a five-year contract as Budget's president. For a few years, life looked terrific to Jules.

Feeling rich, the Lederers followed the lead of Popo's in-laws and established a charitable organization they called the A.B. Foundation, named after Eppie's dad. The stated purpose encompassed "religious, charitable, scientific, literary, or education purposes and . . . the prevention of cruelty to children or animals." But the A.B. Foundation was destined to be short-lived. Although they were required by law, numerous annual reports weren't filed, and the Foundation's charter was revoked. The Illinois attorney general sued to enjoin the Foundation from further activity.

"We didn't file the state reports because we weren't certain what the income was," Jules explained to reporters. "There was no withholding of information. We merely didn't want to file an inaccurate report."

Dismissing the failure of the A.B. Foundation, flush with money and feeling successful, the Lederers willingly joined the Phillipses in celebrating their double wedding anniversaries and the twins' birthday. The quartet traveled all over the western world, to places like Budapest and Zagreb, Montreux, Bermuda, and Buenos Aires. On their thirtieth anniversary in July 1969, the couples' trip to Italy was highlighted by an audience with Pope Paul.

"Haven't I seen you before?" the pope kidded Mort as he shook his hand.

Popo was flabbergasted. For years she'd been telling close friends she thought that Mort, on account of his beard and Semitic features, "looks like he stepped out of the Old Testament, or more like the Pope than the Pope himself."

Pope Paul read Dear Abby in the Rome *Daily American.* "When we stepped forward, he knew all about us," remembers Popo.

The sisters intentionally avoided discussing the pope's controversial stand on birth control. "That would have been outrageous," says Eppie.

Instead, Eppie offered the Pope greetings from Cardinal John P. Cody, archbishop of Chicago, who arranged the twins' reception with the pontiff. She told Pope Paul that Cardinal Cody, upon her advice and direction, had shed thirty-nine pounds.

"Ah, so the good cardinal has diminished in size, but increased in stature," joked the Pope.

Typical of the twins' take-charge personalities, after fifteen minutes of conversation with the pontiff, Eppie and Popo decided it was time to leave. Glancing at each other, the sisters stood up to say good-bye. Later, Popo learned they'd violated protocol. "The Pope looked a little startled," she confessed. "You're supposed to wait until you're dismissed."

Once again comfortably compatible, the twins repeatedly declared their renewed amiability. The patched sisterly bond was displayed for their readers. If their feud had been public knowledge, Eppie and Popo were determined that America be equally aware of their regained harmony. But every now and then, small matters popped up that repeatedly tested the extent of their resolve.

"Piccadilly Circles!" exclaimed Popo, attired in apron and oven mitt and hovering over a pan of English muffins. "You're solving a lot of problems for Dear Abby!"

Dear Abby was doing television commercials.

Popo declared that her earnings from the English muffin commercials were being donated to the Franz Alexander chair of psychiatry at the University of Southern California. No matter. Eppie's view of Popo's enterprise was one of disgust.

"She does *not* need the money. Believe me, she does *not* need the money," Eppie emphasized.

"I don't know what she thought," Eppie was saying. "The work that we are doing is hard enough to keep at a decent level and keep it respectable. Then, something like this happens!"

Because the public often confuses Ann Landers with Dear Abby, and vice versa, Eppie was particularly sensitive that her readers would believe it was Ann who was endorsing the English muffins. She was right to worry. Shortly after the first appearance of the Dear Abby commercial, Eppie heard from an irate reader.

"You've always batted a hundred in my book, but now, since I've seen you selling food, you're down to zero."

Popo's Dear Abby milk endorsement elicited criticism from a source more threatening than her twin. "I very seldom have a cold," a healthy Popo was boasting on television. "I think I probably can attribute that to the fact that I have been a milk drinker all my life." Is that so? the Federal Trade Commission responded, filing a complaint against the California Milk Advertising Board, terming Popo's statement "false and misleading," since no evidence exists linking milk consumption with fewer colds.

Eppie sanctimoniously proclaimed to her readers, "I have never endorsed a product in my life—and I never will. Ann Landers is not for sale at any price!"

But Eppie's statement may just be sour grapes over her sister's freedom to endorse products. While pointing to herself as a model of ethical behavior, Eppie neglects to tell the whole story. Her contract with the *Chicago Sun-Times* syndicate forbade her to appear in commercials.

Despite their disagreement over endorsements, both sisters spoke emphatically about their friendly relationship. Eppie told a *Washington Post* reporter, "We get along fine." To make sure the reporter understood the message, Eppie firmly repeated, "We get along *fine.*"

Eppie and Popo readily admitted their recovered bond had its boundaries. They made a pact not to discuss their jobs. "We don't talk about each other's work," Eppie said.

The twins easily passed off their mutually forbidden shop talk. They had reconciled, yet in order for them to avoid a confrontation, they had to agree not to discuss a part of their lives vital to each of them. Their future relationship would have to remain superficial. The omission also meant they would be unable to work out the cause of their deeply embedded hostilities.

By the late sixties, Eppie was a grandmother three times over. Margo's third child by John Coleman, called Andrea Ted after Father Theodore Hesburgh, was born the day Eppie landed in Vietnam, May 17, 1967. A year and a half before, Margo had given birth to Adam Stolar Coleman, named, of course, for Dr. Robert Stolar.

Eppie enjoyed being a grandmother, time permitting. She brought the children educational puzzles and toys and loved holding them in her lap. "She's pretty businesslike with my kids," Margo says of her mother then. "She wants to teach, instill values. They go to her house for a coloring contest. She's not an impartial judge; whoever needs the lift most, wins."

Eppie made it clear to Margo that she wasn't at her beck and call. "When my daughter had a child," Eppie says, "I told her, 'I'm no babysitter. If something is very important, call the hospital and get a nurse.'" It was nurse Grandpa Jules who could be called upon when the babysitter cancelled at the last minute. Margo recalls him arriving with his briefcase full of papers and toys for the kids.

Despite the children, eight years of marriage, and John Coleman's growing successes in real estate investing, the Coleman–Lederer alliance was a mess. Though they had plenty of money, and Margo acquired Aunt Popo's habit of consuming conspicuously, bills still went unpaid. In particular, an incident in 1967 where the driver of the school bus taking two of the children to a private nursery school refused to let them get on unless the overdue bill was paid not only submitted the young children to an unpleasant scene but underscored Coleman's curious behavior at the time. It wasn't soon after that Margo and her husband separated.

Both Margo and Coleman were undergoing psychoanalysis, Margo in Chicago with a doctor recommended by Robert Stolar and Coleman in Topeka at the Menninger Foundation. Coleman says, "I was insecure, and I lied about my background. I always set myself up for rejection, and consequently I was afraid to give love." Today, Coleman says he tries to be a good father to his three grown children.

"He didn't do this while he was married to my daughter," says Eppie. To this day, Eppie is said to despise John Coleman. A Washington hostess has said, "Ann Landers really hates John Coleman. She's vociferous on the subject."

At the end of Margo's analysis in late 1970, she divorced Coleman. Eppie was worried about Margo's three young children, and the effect of the divorce on them. She also had to admit that she had raised a daughter who was only too human. Eppie, however, refrained from telling her daughter what to do. "I stayed completely out of it," Eppie told a reporter. "I had absolutely no advice to give. I felt she was a very solid girl. . . . I knew she'd land on her feet, and she did."

Her daughter's experience "made her rethink her position on divorce," recalls former Bishop James Shannon, Eppie's friend in St. Paul. Other friends agree that the end of Margo's marriage prompted Eppie to modify the formerly rigid stance on divorce taken by Ann Landers. Eppie also feared losing credibility when her readers discovered that the Chicago columnist who preached the insolubility of marriage had a divorced daughter.

But Margo didn't remain single long. In no time she was out dating celebrity eligibles like Erich Segal, the author of *Love Story,* and Sam Brown, the peace advocate. As a between-marriage hobby, Margo began writing a once-a-week newspaper column in late May 1970 for the *Chicago Tribune.* By the date of her divorce decree from John Coleman, January 12, 1971, the column had turned into a thrice-weekly feature of social commentary appearing in sixty newspapers. Margo's feature, which perhaps reached its zenith when she was sued by David Reuben for calling his book *Everything You Ever Wanted to Know About Sex* *But Were Afraid to Ask* "absolute garbage," had been picked up by her mother's syndicate.

Just five months after receiving her divorce decree, Margo married Jules Furth, a good-looking and athletically built Chicago undertaker. Margo told reporters she "picked him up in a bar," but the "bar" was really the Standard Club, a Chicago Jewish club she belonged to. The ceremony took place June 24, 1971, at the Sinai Temple on South Shore Drive. Only family members attended the wedding and the dinner at her parents' apartment following the service.

After Margo and her new husband took off on their honeymoon, Eppie, who liked Furth a lot better than she had liked Coleman, told her readers, "Apparently some people must live through one unsuccessful marriage to know how to make a second marriage work." Commented one Eau Claire friend on Margo and Eppie's view of her divorce, "I think Eppie has had to make an about-face on a lot of things."

Twenty-Three

Two marriages within two years for her two children led Popo to remark two days before her daughter's wedding in 1973, "I hope this marriage takes, because I can't go through this again."

Eddie's August 1971 marriage to Deanna (Dee-Dee) Pfafer, who was "descended from a grand old liquor family from St. Paul," according to a Minneapolis socialite, was solemnized in an offbeat ceremony that included a flutist and guitarist playing Beatles music. The couple wrote their own vows and walked down the aisle together at Mount Zion Temple. It was Dee-Dee's second marriage, and she chose a Victorian-style beige lace dress.

Popo bustled about the reception afterward in the Flame Room at the Radisson emitting brief but blinding coruscations each time a flashbulb caught her contrasting gold metallic and purple *peau de soie* Lamendolo just so. Not to be outdone, Aunt Eppie wore an aqua-and-blue floral print and a white mink wrap that framed the outfit's plunging neckline.

"I'm praying for snow," Eppie laughed.

"There's no way, kiddo," riposted sister Popo.

Eddie adopted Dee-Dee's son, Dean, from her first marriage, and within a year's time, the couple had another son they named Tyler. As a mother-in-law, Popo was somewhat difficult. The columnist who advised women on how to behave toward their in-laws didn't follow her own advice. Dee-Dee, however, was forewarned. It started during her engagement to Eddie, she says. "I was told by my mother-in-law that I had to have my teeth capped. We were married in August and she sent over a fur, a fox stole, saying it was important for the family to present a good image."

It was back to the University of Minnesota for Eddie, where he had just earned an M.A. in clinical psychology, before he joined the family business, Ed Phillips & Sons. Alco Standard, the Pennsylvania conglomerate, had bought the company in 1971, a month after his marriage to Dee-Dee. Returning to Ed Phillips & Sons in 1973, law degree in hand, Eddie was the anointed heir to the former family business. Two years later, holding Alco stock then valued at a couple million, he took his father's place as president and CEO at an annual salary in excess of $200,000 and a seat on the Alco board of directors.

According to a Minneapolis insider, "When time came for Jay to choose who'd take the reins, he really chose Eddie, not Mort. Mort's interests were definitely not in the liquor business." Eddie, however, knew that his promotion was based on the decision of the parent company, Alco Standard, and not his grandfather Jay. "Alco had every justification in the world to choose somebody else to run the company," he says. "But they chose me anyway."

Sister Jeannie, at about the same time Eddie joined the family business, married Luke McKissack, a top-rated civil liberties lawyer whose clients included black radical Huey Newton, Eldridge Cleaver, and RFK assassin Sirhan Sirhan. Jeannie, described by a friend of Popo's as a "lovely, warm, nice gal, a distillate of all her mother's good qualities," met Luke on a blind date arranged by a girlfriend who worked at the American Civil Liberties Union. The two-year courtship begat a wedding in September 1973 called "the wildest affair in the history of the Beverly Wilshire Hotel."

Popo didn't seem to mind that her daughter was marrying out of her faith. "He's a beautiful man," said Popo. Jeannie "waited thirty years to get married, but when she did she picked a good one."

Jeannie wore sister-in-law Dee-Dee's beige lace dress for the civil ceremony performed by a California Supreme Court justice in the hotel's Burgundy Room. At the luncheon reception, Mort toasted the newlyweds with Taittinger champagne and called his new son-in-law "a man with a cause," and Jeannie, "a girl with stars in her eyes." Music for the occasion was provided by Luke's friend Herb Alpert, and Ronee Blakeley sang folk songs. Popo, in a turquoise-and-white chiffon dress from La Mendola and a triple strand of pearls, delighted in the trendy west coast ambience scented radical chic. Guests ranged from "Black Panther types to the mayor and elite of Beverly Hills, all mixed together," recalls one of the wedding guests. "The best man had a foot-wide Afro."

Soon after the wedding, Popo and Mort departed heartland America and joined their daughter and son-in-law in Beverly Hills. In 1975, when Mort retired from the presidency of the wine and spirits group of Alco, the Phillipses kept their St. Paul penthouse and bought a large and airy salmon-colored brick house in Bel Air, a neighborhood of Beverly Hills that has the toniest Los Angeles ZIP code, where they still reside. The sprawling single-story residence atop a winding drive forms a complete square, with a swimming pool set in the center courtyard glowing like a brilliant aquamarine. Popo's mauve-toned bedroom opens from a wall of glass into the pool area.

High arching doors frame the entrance to the house. Off the front hallway is Popo's yellow velvet office. Another wide hallway, lined with a rogue's gallery of family photos, leads to the cathedral-ceilinged public rooms, holding large, sturdy furniture, some modern, some of earlier vintage, under mammoth chandeliers. Still partial to monkeys, stuffed, ceramic, or in paintings, Popo has them throughout the house; one specimen in the butler's pantry wears a red motorcycle helmet inscribed with the trademark "Dear Abby."

"Popo's taste is California moderne," says a visitor to the Phillips residence. "It's not only California kitsch, but pretentious. Nothing unusual about that in Beverly Hills."

Neither Popo nor Mort moved back to Beverly Hills to retire. Mort founded Westland Capital Corporation, a company that makes conservative investments in industries like health care and cable television and provides advice to small businesses. Headquartered in Reno, Nevada, son Eddie as well as many family friends serve on the board of directors. Together the Phillips family owns more than 80 percent of the stock in the closely held corporation.

Gregarious and outgoing, Popo was overjoyed to return to California. There was no doubt in her mind that Los Angeles was more exhilarating than the Twin Cities. Her ten-year stay in the Midwest had made Popo apprehensive that she was missing out on new trends or changing contemporary mores that appeared first on either coast. A year before, CBS radio had dropped her daily five-minute feature, "Dear Abby," for a new series called "The American Woman."

Popo's radio spot had run for twelve years. The new feature on American women would report on "the changing living and working patterns of women and the resulting changes in family structure." Weren't these some of the same concerns Dear Abby attempted to address? Was the Dear Abby column growing stale? Popo recognized that the lead she had taken twenty years earlier over an established Ann Landers column was largely due to Dear Abby's wit and oftentimes outrageous quips. In the mid-seventies, competition from radio call-in and television talk and news shows threatened the appeal of a newspaper advice column. One-liners were going the way of vaudeville. Happily stationed back on the west coast, Popo was determined not to lose her advantage.

Eppie, ever mindful of maintaining the façade of a happy marriage, was presenting her readers with the image of a devoted wife and loving husband. In 1970 she was telling interviewers, "Jules is my best friend. . . . He's always buying me presents. He loves to." In late 1971 Jules bid $25,000 on a bust of JFK by Salvador Dali and gave it to Eppie for her birthday.

Whether he bought the artwork out of love, or out of guilt, because he had already begun seeing another woman, cannot be determined. But Eppie, unaware of his extramarital activity, was insisting, "My husband finds me fascinating. . . . He thinks he's the luckiest man in the world."

Those who knew Jules and Eppie were quite certain that things weren't all that felicitous. According to friend and psychoanalyst Abe Franzblau, Rose's husband, "All it took was a short time in the Lederers' company to realize Eppie exhibited the classic, text-book traits of a cold, rejecting woman."

Eppie's description of her and Jules's torrid love match and her insistence on the solidity of their relationship alternated be-tween boasting and being maudlin. Perhaps her public statements, a few years before their divorce, reflected her fears and insecurities over her empty marriage. Certainly the continued success of Ann Landers and Eppie's identification with the column namesake did not help her concentrate her energies on Jules. Eppie took pride in instant recognition and enjoyed being the media personality always on stage. "I don't think Eppie knows where Ann Landers stops and Eppie begins," a friend observed.

Agreeing with this assessment, Eppie says, "I don't think Ann Landers and Eppie Lederer are two different people." She contin-ues, "I think that Ann Landers is pretty much what Eppie Lederer is. I am not living two lives."

Supreme Court Justice William O. Douglas and his wife, Cath-leen, met with Eppie for lunch and dinner during the late sixties and early seventies. But whether they saw Eppie in Washington or in Chicago, Jules was not present. "There really is no husband named Jules Lederer, is there?" Cathleen would gently tease Eppie.

Eugene McCarthy, who saw Eppie at Democratic rallies and dinners in Washington and elsewhere, remembers rarely seeing Jules with her. "I didn't really get to know him," he says.

One of the guests at social gatherings hosted by the Lederers reveals, "Sometimes we'd be at cocktail parties at their home. You'd get the feeling she owned the whole house and Jules was just another guest."

Literally, Eppie did own the house. What irritated Jules was that Eppie insisted on buying the fourteen-room apartment while he was fighting for survival at Budget.

"When he sold Budget Rent-A-Car to Transamerica in 1968, he was looking at the world through rose-colored glasses," Eppie would later state in a *Woman's Day* article titled "How Men Feel When Women Wear the Pants." "In 1972, the glasses fell off. He became the victim of that classic greeting, 'Welcome to our conglomerate. You're fired.'

"Jules Lederer was no longer 'Mr. Budget Rent-A-Car.' He had lost his identity. The principal support of his ego structure was shattered. The eternal optimist, the affable, hard-driving dynamo, began to come apart at the seams—and so did our marriage."

Jules realized he wasn't as wealthy as he had hoped. He had made an irrevocable business error when he chose to take Transamerica stock worth $10 million for Budget. The stock had dropped from 33 to 5. In addition, Jules was finding it difficult to accept others' opinions on how to manage Budget, which he still considered his company.

"The entrepreneur just doesn't fit into a large corporation," explained Jules. "It was very hard for a fella like me. I had a thirty-seven-year-old *boy* trying to tell *me* how to run the business I started."

Jules's getting ousted wouldn't have been so hard to take had they not kept on Morrie Mirkin, Jules's buddy and Budget's original founder. A business associate concurs: "Transamerica's firing Jules and keeping Morrie must have been devastating to Jules." Also devastating was that Jules was left holding stock with a plummeting share value. "At one time Jules was way up, and suddenly he's way down," commiserated a friend. Jules joked that he would regain his fortune by writing a book and calling it *I Was a Jewish Millionaire,* with the emphasis on the past tense.

Jules devoted his efforts and depleted funds to a European hamburger franchise all too appropriately called The Great American Disaster. He lost nearly a million dollars on the deal. Another million was lost on an ill-fated health-care-service investment.

Strangely, Jules's sister-in-law took an almost macabre joy in seeing one after another of his ventures fail. Describing Jules's business losses to an acquaintance, Popo ended each anecdote with a heavy intonation of "Too *bad*." Popo seemed awfully hard about her brother-in-law's money problems, the acquaintance thought.

Summing up his business failures, Jules said, "There's an old Las Vegas saying: When the dice are cold, they're *all* cold. Well, the dice were sure cold for me."

Back in Chicago, home life was quickly deteriorating. Eppie dealt with her husband's financial setbacks and personal unhappiness by ignoring his problems. Perhaps because she thought it would cheer him up, she bought the new apartment at the even more prestigious eastern curve of Chicago's Gold Coast. In addition, she spent extravagant sums decorating the fifteenth-floor residence. But the outlay only underscored the difference in their resources. "Jules resisted her splurges," says a Chicago friend. "And he resented her need to live in a facsimile of a European palace just as he was losing his life earnings and going into debt."

"I've never been a pretentious guy in lifestyle," Jules later said. "The mink for the wife, the Jewish hardware, I mean diamonds, that lifestyle is just not a part of me; never was."

The ornate showplace at 209 East Lake Shore Drive is still Eppie's home. Wall panels and sconces imported from a British castle complement the mullioned windows and intricately sculpted ceilings. Recasts of fifteenth-century statuary in the living room, including a covey of kneeling angels Eppie calls "the girls," provide a stunning counterpoint to Louis XV sofas and mother-of-pearl inlaid chairs. Works by Picasso, Renoir, and Dali cover the walls. The perfume-scented living room and dining room serve as a backdrop for some of Eppie's favorite objects, including a fifteenth-century bishop's chair, two Chinese cinnabar vases, and a portrait of Eppie painted by Robert Robles.

In Eppie's office, Windsor-style rocking chairs from all the universities that have bestowed honorary degrees on Ann Landers are lined up along one wall. A corner étagère holds even more plaques and commemoratives. Behind glass cases are keys to many cities, and another paneled wall is covered with lithographs of the nameplates from many of the newspapers that carry the Ann Landers column. Behind her large desk there's a phone and an electric typewriter. Above a wall of bookcases perches a lineup of owls. In Eppie's personal bathroom the toilet is of carved marble with a rococo shell-shaped cover; golden fixtures grace the matching sink. In another bathroom the walls are mirrored, and the marble tub and sink reflect water sprites, nymphs, flying fish, vines, and Neptune in hand-laid mosaics.

Refined and glamorous at the same time, Eppie's apartment mirrored Eppie's success as an influential and top-rated, world-renowned newspaper columnist. There was not a trace of small-town Midwestern to it. Someone who's seen both Eppie's and Popo's homes says, "Eppie has the more cultivated taste, due perhaps to Margo. At some point she persuaded Eppie to start buying good stuff."

Jules was offended by the extraordinary amount of money Eppie was lavishing on their apartment. He was disturbed at his wife's insensitivity to his financial worries. It didn't help when Eppie offered to use her own earnings to pay daily expenses. She told her husband that she worked hard and deserved to live well.

Still blissfully unwilling to address the problems in her relationship with her husband, Eppie was saying, "As far as I know, Jules is well behaved. But if there should be any straying, there'd be no screaming or yelling or threatening from me. But then it's hard to judge, because I never had that kind of problem with my husband."

Eppie wasn't fooling around and didn't suspect Jules was either. But he was, and he had been for some time.

By late 1971, Jules was spending days and weeks at a time in London, Zurich, and other European cities, overseeing Budget's expansion on the continent. "He's away about a third of the time. He's always traveled a lot," Eppie was telling the press in 1974.

Jules's investments in the European hamburger franchise and a factory in Switzerland further justified his spending time overseas. The Lederers bought a townhouse in London, near Hyde Park, and Jules began to prefer that residence to the new apartment in Chicago. He called the fourteen rooms on East Lake Shore Drive the "bowling alley" and saw it as his wife's home, not his.

During one prolonged stay in London, Jules had an infected mosquito bite and had to seek professional care. At the doctor's office, he met Elizabeth Morton, a twenty-five-year-old nurse. Within a few months, the attractive and attentive Englishwoman, six years younger than Jules's daughter, had moved into the Lederers's Hyde Park townhouse.

Few friends who understood the state of the Lederer marriage criticized Jules. "He began to grope and he didn't know in what direction," says one friend. Engrossed in their own lives, Eppie and Margo were indifferent to Jules's needs. Jules felt isolated from his wife and daughter. He no longer played any stable role in family life, except that of breadwinner, and suddenly Eppie had surpassed him in that function. "Jules was having a lot of trouble finding himself, and not having a wife or daughter care about him didn't help," says a sympathetic colleague.

Eppie didn't move to rekindle her marriage. She either ignored or wasn't aware of what Jules was up to. She was having too much fun as Ann Landers. "Eppie hadn't been taking care of Papa," says an acquaintance. "He wasn't getting much comfort from his famous and successful wife. It was certain that some lovely young woman would come into his life."

While Jules carried on with Elizabeth in London, in September 1974 Eppie spent three weeks in China as part of an exchange visit sponsored by the American Medical Association. "I traveled 25,000 miles to learn firsthand about sex—premarital, marital, and extramarital—in the People's Republic of China." Eppie reported on acupuncture and the country's sexual mores and contrasted American and Chinese medical practices. Saying, "It doesn't look like a troubled society," Eppie toured hospitals and factories, learned about divorce and religion, Chinese-style, and dished up quail soup in Peking and went sightseeing along the Great Wall with a delegation of doctors.

Ann Landers' bylined articles didn't disclose that the AMA had picked up the tab for her trip to China. After the breach of ethics became known, journalists and editors lambasted Eppie and Field Enterprises for allowing the columnist to accept an expenses-paid trip from a professional organization, followed by reports favorable to AMA interests. Eppie defended herself by giving the impression that the conflict-of-interest talk was overblown, and that she hadn't done anything wrong.

Back in Chicago, the talk wasn't about Eppie's trip; it was about Jules and Elizabeth. Jules simply wasn't being discreet about his affair. He was seen dining with his live-in companion at posh London restaurants, places the Lederers's affluent and well-traveled friends were certain to frequent. Showing no embarrassment or discomfort, Jules would introduce Elizabeth to his and his wife's friends and invite them to join the party. It was as if Jules were being reckless on purpose, hoping that Eppie would hear about his affair from others and then confront him with the knowledge.

Gossip about the affair had extra zing to it. Jules was cheating on the woman who had set herself up as America's moral conscience for twenty years. If the talk about Jules hadn't reached Eppie yet, it reached Margo, shortly after he confessed to his daughter that he was in love with another woman. On a rainy night in late 1974, Jules showed Margo a picture of his paramour, telling his daughter he wanted to marry Elizabeth. Margo told him he'd better tell his wife, but Jules didn't want or couldn't bring himself to face Eppie about divorce. Within a short time, Margo's fears were confirmed. Everyone but her mother knew about the affair. Margo got a phone call from a friend saying something like, "We were in Spain and we bumped into your father with this other woman. We thought you ought to know."

According to Margo, four months passed and Jules still hadn't confronted Eppie. Margo finally decided to hint to her mother that Jules was unhappy. She urged Eppie to talk to her husband about their marriage. "Margo couldn't stand the whole world laughing at her mother and herself," observes a friend. Margo wanted Eppie to take a stand against Jules's extramarital relationship.

After Margo's visit, Eppie asked Jules if there was anything wrong. He shrugged and said no. The next day, Eppie persisted and asked him again. As Eppie tells it, "One day at dinner, Jules had news that was hard to break. He said, 'I have something to tell you. . . . I'm in love with another woman.' "

Eppie says she believes Jules "was offering to have an 'arrangement,' I guess, but I decided if he could live with that kind of duplicity, it was finished for me. A lot of women accept arrangements because they want to save face, to hang on, to win. I wouldn't." Unlike sister Popo, who thinks arrangements are okay because it may be the only way the wife can keep her head up, Eppie does not condone arrangements for herself, and neither did Jules want to continue his double life. Jules wanted to marry Elizabeth.

Eppie says she was surprised when Jules asked for a divorce. "I was shocked," she says. "I had no idea." But friends believe Eppie suspected Jules's extended stays in London were for reviving more than his failing business ventures.

"She knew for a long time," counters one friend. "She thought it would go away. Eppie did what most other sixty-year-old women would do, she just hoped that Elizabeth was a passing fad of Jules's.' "

Similarly, Popo admits that the night Jules asked her sister for a divorce "was not all that big a shock. She really lost him a long time before. She was so busy with her job that Jules had a lot of time on his hands."

Eppie followed the revised Ann Landers philosophy when she realized that Jules wanted out of their marriage. "If a man wants to escape, you'd better let him. Ugh! Why are some women always clawing and scratching?"

Twenty-Four

After agreeing to the divorce in March 1975, the first thing Eppie did was telephone Popo.

"Come . . . come, Pussy, I nee-e-e-d you," Eppie sobbed, calling her sister by one of her pet names, Pussycat.

"I'm getting the next plane," Popo reassured her.

But Popo couldn't get to her twin's side for a few days. Eppie, needing a trusted friend to speak with, called Father Hesburgh the next morning.

"I'm in trouble, when can I see you?" she asked the kindly and soft-spoken president of Notre Dame University, a man who'd been her close friend and adviser for more than twenty years.

"Right now, if you get down here," Hesburgh told her. "I can't leave because I'm doing some things I have to do here."

Eppie took the next plane to South Bend. As Hesburgh remembers that day, "She was down here in about two hours and we spent the rest of the day talking. . . . We covered a lot of ground." Five hours of conversation with Father Hesburgh in his cozy and cluttered corner office fragrant with the smoke of quality cigars convinced Eppie that she was not to be blamed for the collapse of her marriage.

Eppie remembers him telling her, "Eppie, don't look back. Look forward and move forward. Don't torture yourself with questions like 'Where did I fail?' You did not fail." It was critical to Eppie that she not be held accountable for the breakdown. Eppie announced that her one session with Father Hesburgh made her feel "completely healed, completely whole, no more anxiety, no more doubts."

The fact that Eppie turned to a Catholic priest rather than a rabbi for counseling prompted her to explain her action. "I'm Jewish, and I'm sure some people thought, 'Why not go to a rabbi?' " said Eppie afterward. "But I didn't feel like going to a rabbi."

Hesburgh explains, "I think it was instinctive on her part. I was not just a professional counselor, I'm a good friend. I think it was just natural." In addition to being a close friend of Eppie's, Father Hesburgh knew the whole Lederer family. He says, "There was another thing that may have made a difference. I knew Jules very well too. And I liked Jules. She knew I could be protective of him as well as of her."

In public, Eppie maintained a cheerful front. Behind the façade, Eppie felt dazed and seemed preoccupied, stunned by the discovery that she was unable to juggle a career and a marriage and make them both work. Eppie claims she had only a few bad nights since Jules told her he was leaving. "Not true," says a friend. "She's a crier."

Eppie certainly was weeping when Popo flew in to comfort her. When Popo arrived at O'Hare, Eppie was waiting, but not at the gate as the composed celebrity Ann Landers. Instead, Eppie remained in her darkened limousine so that people would not see her reddened and puffy eyes.

Popo offered her support and the solace that had once nourished their childhood together. But by the time Popo came to her sister's aid, Eppie had already decided what to do. "She had her head together," Popo says. "She didn't need anyone to help her."

Eppie wanted Jules to meet with Bob Stolar, the one trusted friend who had known both of them the longest. Says Stolar, "Eppie claims I can talk to Jules better than anyone else." But Jules was adamant. He was determined to marry Elizabeth Morton.

As Popo sees it, "Jules is not a woman chaser, but he got tired of being 'Mr. Landers,' and he found someone who thought he was great."

Eppie disagrees. "The end of a rich and rewarding thirty-six-year relationship with Jules Lederer had very little to do with Ann Landers and a great deal to do with Budget Rent-A-Car," she later says. "It bothered him not one iota when someone jokingly referred to him as 'Mr. Landers.' "

Father Hesburgh finds some truth to Eppie's perspective. He says, "I think she's just a person that grew a great deal and he was in the business of making money. And they're not quite the same thing."

In 1981, about seven years after her divorce, Eppie makes an observation that seems to refer to her own marital breakup. "I would not hesitate to say that at least half the divorces that have taken place in the last seven years were 'work-related.' "

Poignantly, Eppie chose the couple's thirty-sixth wedding anniversary, July 2, 1975, to reveal in her column, "The lady with all the answers does not know the answers to this one." The end of the Ann Landers column was left blank, "as a memorial to one of the world's best marriages that didn't make it to the finish line."

Rarely did Eppie feel the need to substitute a personal message for the advice in her column. Ironically, the first testimonial on July 2, 1969, marked the occasion of her and Jules's thirtieth wedding anniversary. Complete with a portrait of Eppie and her husband, the open letter to more than 50 million readers stated, "Each year has been better than the last because we have grown together. . . . Thirty years with this unselfish, supportive, responsive man has enabled me to live life as few people get the opportunity to live it."

Disclosing the news about the end of her marriage in the Ann Landers column was solely Eppie's idea. Some of her closest friends advised her against doing so, believing that the column was not an appropriate vehicle for a personal revelation. Stolar says, "I was not in favor of it." In one way, the announcement reveals how closely Eppie identifies with the media character she represents. But it can't be denied that Eppie's decision to air her marital problems was a courageous one. News of the divorce would have reached the public anyway, as soon as she filed the necessary papers. Eppie probably felt it better to go public before the wire services picked up the story and made it official.

Still, Jules was not happy about his wife's public disclosure. "I was always a very private person," he says. "I didn't think, as far as my feelings went, that she should have written the column."

As Eppie suspected, the story was promptly appropriated by the wire services, and details of the breakup appeared on the front pages of American newspapers and in many national news magazines. To some, the dramatic column seemed a last, desperate attempt to ask Jules for a reconciliation.

Following intense publicity and speculation concerning the cause of the separation, Eppie kept a low profile. She did not answer her phone and refused to make public appearances for nearly a year. Her secretaries were instructed to respond "No comment" about divorce inquiries.

The Lederer divorce was granted October 16, 1975, in a Chicago circuit court. Eppie cited "extreme and repeated acts of mental cruelty" and testified that Jules's conduct caused her "embarrassment, humiliation, and anguish." The property settlement went smoothly. After all, Jules had always insisted that Eppie stash her Ann Landers earnings in blue-chip stocks and real estate, in her own name. An acquaintance says, "Jules got screwed. Those fourteen rooms on Lake Shore Drive, that's her dough, and that's only the beginning of it."

Eppie claims she forgot all feelings of bitterness at the time of the divorce. "It was painful for me to sue my former husband for 'cruel and inhuman punishment' when he asked for his freedom," she later says. "He was neither 'cruel' nor 'inhuman.' " Eppie also maintains that she begged Jules to marry quickly so he could be happy. As Jules had asked Eppie for the divorce so that he could marry Elizabeth, the promise Eppie says she extracted from her estranged husband appears to have been unnecessary.

Jules and Elizabeth lost no time, marrying the following month in London. After a brief honeymoon, Jules and Elizabeth returned to the States and settled in at the Sandburg Village complex in Chicago. They found that Eppie had stocked the apartment with food, household items, three dozen pair of black socks, three dozen of brown, and three dozen pair of white boxer shorts.

"I gave him a telephone list, the doctor, the optician, and so on," says Eppie. "I had my chauffeur and housekeeper go to his apartment and stock up the freezer with staples because here was a man who depended on me for such things for thirty-six years." This is her blithe way of explaining her unorthodox generosity. It's not surprising that the new Mrs. Lederer's reaction has gone unrecorded.

Confident that Elizabeth would make a good impression on his friends, Jules said, "A lot of these damn fools think I married a glamorous young cupcake, but the truth is that while she's obviously attractive, she's also extremely mature and plenty bright; she's got a very good head on her shoulders." To Jules's delight, his buddies immediately warmed to his bride. As one friend described her, "She's very attractive, taller than Jules, and, obviously younger. Thankfully, she doesn't appear as aggressive, pushy, or forceful as Eppie."

If that's the kind of woman Jules was looking for, then he found her in Elizabeth. *Aggressive, pushy,* and *forceful* are just some of the adjectives people have used to describe Eppie, knowing well that she didn't get rich and successful being timid and mousey. Besides, there's a positive side to being aggressive. But being compared with the new Mrs. Lederer was of little concern to Eppie. If she had spent the last year worrying about losing her husband, she was now panicky about losing her column. Without Ann Landers, who would Eppie Lederer be?

Media critics were pointing out that perhaps Ann Landers should follow her own advice. Just more than five years earlier, when Margo divorced John Coleman, the columnist announced that she had changed her mind about marriage being forever. It was a gradual process, one that involved self-discovery. Eppie says, "I began to rethink all these old ideas that I grew up with. This was quite a transition for me to make because it was one of the basic concepts that I grew up with."

In her column, Eppie was saying that any separating couple should take several steps before breaking up. "If you realize that the marriage is impossible, and you've gone through counseling and a trial separation, then unload the bum." But neither Eppie nor Jules received counseling, nor did the couple attempt a trial separation before obtaining their decree.

Syndicated columnist Judith Martin poked fun at Eppie's "dignity and mystery" approach to her divorce. Martin noted the incongruity of Eppie's announcing a divorce "after thirty-six years of a perfect marriage." How could an advice columnist not notice that her own marriage was a sham? "What kind of goods are the experts selling?" Martin sniffed.

Eppie expected criticism. "I thought I would lose my career," she admits. "I thought my editor would say he couldn't have an advice columnist who couldn't hold her own marriage together."

She expected more criticism than she got because of her previous holier-than-thou attitude about divorce. John Torinus, writing in the Appleton (Wisconsin) *Post-Crescent,* remembers meeting Eppie for the first time at a dinner party in a minister's home in Green Bay, where one of the other dinner guests happened to be recently divorced.

"During the conversation someone brought up the subject of divorce," recalls Torinus, "and Ann took off on a tirade against selfish men who would abandon their wives and children for the sake of their own pleasure.

"Try as I did, I could not get her to change the subject. I have often wondered since what my friend thought of her performance, but he was too much a gentleman ever to respond. I imagine he must have chuckled some to himself, though, when he read of her divorce."

Emmett Dedmon of Field Enterprises, however, added a note of sanity to Eppie's musings about the consequences of her divorce and dismissed her worries. "We don't think it will have any impact on the column," he said. "We regard it as a personal tragedy."

Her credibility with her syndicate intact, Eppie decided to approach the divorce as a worthwhile learning experience. "This is going to make me stronger," she said. "You *can* turn around tragedies and make them work *for* you. It was an experience from which I've learned." Ever optimistic, Eppie soon announced her divorce was actually helping her career. Now speaking from experience and practicing expert damage control, she declared, "The divorce increased my credibility." She was saying that her readers believed "if it can happen to Ann Landers, it can happen to anyone."

Claiming that her readers sent more than 30,000 letters about her divorce, Eppie was amazed by their compassionate reaction. They were "marvelously supportive," she says. "The people out there were wonderful. Touching, supportive, and beautiful. I treasure that correspondence." Treasure it she does. Eppie keeps those letters close to her, stored in shoeboxes in her bedroom closet.

Twenty-Five

Days after she left her twin's side in March 1975, Popo showed up at the Yugoslavian embassy reception for Prime Minister Dzemal Bijedic in Washington. While in town, Popo lent her support to Senator Birch Bayh's initiative to increase funding to fight juvenile crime and establish a program aimed at curbing alcohol and drug abuse among the nation's youth.

"My late wife, Marvella, met her first, then the four of us became good friends," says Bayh, who got to know Popo and Mort in the mid-sixties, after he won his U.S. Senate seat from Indiana. When Bayh was in the Senate, Popo called him and his staff for expert advice for her column. When he was running for his third term in 1974, Popo helped out. The liberal Democrat had welcomed Popo's support first in the 1968 elections, and she had earned his lifelong friendship.

"Marvella and Abby were very simpatico. She and my wife had a series of large community teas throughout the state," Bayh recalls. "A lot of folks came to see her, I assume, who'd never come to see me. It was an informal kind of thing, where people would ask a question . . . a no-holds-barred kind of situation. Abby got right into the various issues, and you know," Bayh chortles, "she's a ball-buster, nonstop. She's genuine and sincere."

Calling her campaign style "low key, she didn't say anything negative about anybody," Bayh remembers that Popo didn't often campaign for political candidates, and he was flattered she came out for him. "She'd done it for Mark Hatfield and myself, and we were the only two people she'd done it for. That was quite a tribute, I thought, that Abby would be willing to do something like that.

"I think she thought that I was right on the issues. We shared common concerns about problems, and she was willing to risk her reputation," Bayh continues, explaining that Popo was publicly faulted for actively stumping for him. "It was rather a brave thing to do for someone in a position like Abby is. Some of the newspapers which carried her column did not look kindly upon my candidacy or her participation in it. So it was really a very courageous thing for her to do."

In purple ultrasuede or leopard-spotted silk, teetering on five-inch platform sandals of striped silver, basic black, or skyscraper gold, Popo by herself or sometimes with Mort was welcomed from Terre Haute to Pennsylvania Avenue. She attended parties in honor of Bayh, Mark Hatfield, and other senators. When Marie and Walter Ridder gave an anniversary party at their home overlooking the Potomac River for Birch and Marvella, Mort and Popo were there, along with Eppie's friend Mary Lasker, whom Mort made certain to dance with.

Included on Popo's circuit of Washington "must attends" were dinners for visiting dignitaries like Israeli Foreign Minister Moshe Dayan and chief Chinese liaison officer Chai Tse-Min and Madame Li Yu Feng at the swank Madison Hotel, owned by friends Marshall and Jane Coyne. Having come out for Jimmy Carter in the 1976 elections, Popo got to know the president's sister Ruth Carter Stapleton and was appointed to the National Advisory Council on Aging and the White House Council on the Physically Handicapped.

Following her twin's lead, and understanding that most of the business of Washington took place after hours and at social functions, Popo made the city, because of its mix of politicians and diplomats, one of her favored destinations. Convenient stopovers in Chicago or Minneapolis allowed her to spend time with her twin or her grandsons before alighting, all aglitter, on Capitol Hill or Embassy Row to lobby Congress for funding or speak out on causes like ERA, sex education, abortion, and birth control, and issues like child abuse and pornography.

Significantly, many of the issues that Popo championed concerned the rights of individuals, and especially those people who lack the influence to change things for themselves, like children and the infirm. Popo declares that she uses Dear Abby to speak out "for human rights, for the rights of anyone who has been discriminated against for any reason." Of special concern to Popo in the seventies were the needs of the handicapped, perhaps because one of Mort's sisters had been stricken with polio at an early age. She supported the passage of laws to prohibit discrimination against the disabled in employment, education, and health care.

In Washington, Popo must still seem a refreshing voice amid the organized lobbies and strategists who exalt politics over ordinary human relationships. With no hidden agenda, save a philosophy that encourages tolerance, as well as conscious choice and responsibility on the part of the individual, Popo was able to make decision makers listen.

"I don't force my views on other people," says Popo. "I feel very strongly about people telling other people how to live and refusing to let them have something because they think it is bad for everybody. I think people should be able to make up their own minds."

Going political, as Popo did, probably had much to do with her revised perspective on a woman's role in society. Throughout the late seventies, Popo was advocating passage of the Equal Rights Amendment, a measure supported by First Lady Rosalynn Carter and shepherded through Congress by Bayh in 1972. "Women do not have equal rights," she was saying. "We have everything to lose and nothing to gain by saying to the federal government we have all the laws we need."

Popo's liberal stance sounds familiar, yet just ten years earlier, the women's movement confused Popo. She reacted personally to media portrayals of feminists, as many people did in the late sixties. Not yet realizing the congruence between her Democratic beliefs and upcoming issues like the ERA, Popo sounded off against the blurring of traditional sex roles. "Women are becoming much less feminine and more masculine. Women are taking over," claimed an alarmed Popo.

She emphasized the effect the women's movement might have on men. "It's strange how men often feel emasculated if they have a woman for a boss. Some have actually become impotent. They feel unnecessary, which I must admit is how some women want them to feel, women who are saying, 'We don't need men for anything—and we mean anything!' To me, this is terrifying."

Popo's early anti-feminist pronouncements brought criticism from some readers. "They complain I don't come out in public on issues, that I am letting down my sex." In her defense, Popo retaliated by saying, "What I hope is that I am fair, that I represent men as much as women."

Prodded by her grown children's ideas and the atmosphere of Los Angeles, she shifted her beliefs. By the end of the decade Popo was marching in California for ERA alongside Hollywood friends Florence Henderson, Neil Simon, Marsha Mason, Henry Winkler, and Joan Hackett. To her column, a woman wrote, "I am puzzled by your continuing support of the ERA." Dear Abby's response was "You may not be as 'protected' as you think. I believe that the American woman should have the same protection and equality that is guaranteed to men under the highest law in our nation."

Popo used a grieving mother's letter to put a sympathetic slant on the merits of the ERA. The young mother, writing after the death of her child, plaintively explained, "I was given time off from work to recuperate emotionally, but my husband had to go back to work the day after our baby died." Popo thanked the woman, saying, "You also inadvertently gave a boost to the Equal Rights Amendment, which would make discrimination between the sexes illegal under our Constitution. In other words, if a job provided time off to recuperate emotionally after the death of a child, fathers as well as mothers would receive it."

It may have taken Popo some time to support the ERA because she seemed to assume that most women were as privileged as she. When as a Hillsborough housewife Popo wandered through the *Chronicle* offices looking for a job, she had the advantage of not needing the paycheck that went with employment. It probably took Popo many hours and many reader letters to understand what equal rights meant.

Even now, Popo possesses a fractured view of her role as an advice columnist. She denies she has a career. "I really don't consider myself a working woman," she says, neatly sidestepping her position as the country's most successful female columnist. In explaining what the column means to her personally, she sounds as though she were still doing Gray Lady volunteer work in Eau Claire. "Dear Abby is a privilege. . . . I had never worked a day in my life before I became Dear Abby. I'm a very lucky person, who's able to do professionally what I'd have been thrilled to do for nothing."

Popo's twin, who invests all her energy in the Ann Landers column, doesn't view her work as a widely syndicated columnist as a career either. Both women hold onto their image of a "lady" as someone who doesn't work or doesn't have to work. For a long time the twins felt that a woman was unsuccessful as a person if a husband wasn't taking care of her. In addition, they felt money was not a nice topic for ladies to discuss. Popo and Eppie felt above having to earn a living.

"I never went into this for fame or money," explains Popo. "I would pay to do it. Dear Abby is really a hobby that's become successful, just like frosting on a cake."

"It's not really a business," Eppie says. "It is not something we do for a living. She and I have money. We never really needed this to support us."

Before Eppie came out for the ERA in 1973 she questioned whether women really ever were discriminated against on account of their sex primarily because she, like her twin, had never experienced it. "I've never felt discriminated against because I am a woman. I have never found it difficult to be a woman. In fact, on occasion it may have even been an advantage. Because I've never asked for any special privileges, I am able to meet men on their own footing. . . . I work hard and I produce. I'm dedicated, I'm consistent, and I deliver."

Phyllis Schlafly, activist founder of the Eagle Forum, a group overwhelmingly constituted of white, conservative, married women stridently opposed to the ERA, admires Eppie for those qualities of dedication and hard work, as a woman who made it "to the top through hard work, not as a token, not as just another affirmative action statistic collected to placate the government." Schlafly sees Eppie as an example of her oft-quoted slogan, "Opportunities are usually disguised as hard work, so most people don't recognize them."

Eppie's more enviable opportunities, however, happened while she was being cared for and protected first by her father, and later by Jules. Not all women are so fortunate. Just like Popo, her early thinking on equal rights reveals some further misunderstanding and misinformation. "I do not feel that women belong every place," she added. "There are some occupations in which women just don't belong where they're trying to get in. For example . . . heavy construction work." On a roll, Eppie continues, "Don't men have a right to have their own private places? Women do. There are some restaurants that don't admit men."

When responding to a question about whether a woman must decide between a career and a family, she says, "It is more glamorous, let's face it, to put on a girdle and high heels and go to an office. It's much more glamorous than staying home and doing the laundry or listening to the kids yell."

Equality is one thing, glamour something else. Like her sister, the absence of this putative glamour to the early women's movement is probably what initially prompted Eppie to dismiss it, saying feminists looked like "truant officers." She admits, "In the beginning the women's movement turned me off." Defensively, she rationalizes, "They were pushy, aggressive, and anti-male."

Although Popo's children have exerted a liberalizing influence on Dear Abby, Eppie's daughter, Margo, may be partly responsible for Ann Landers' formerly negative assessment of feminists. A self-described "geisha," Margo would use her *Daily News* column to poke fun at "women's libbers," whom she called "roller derby dropouts." However, Margo stated that she did appreciate "the women's movement as a source for column material."

A little investigation into the substance behind the rhetoric, a willingness to look beyond appearances, and, most likely, reflection on her readers' letters led Eppie to change her politics. "But the more I began to think about it the more I realized, yeah, they really have something. Women are not paid what they're worth." Eppie began saying, "I am for the Equal Rights Amendment. I think it is something we have got to have, absolutely."

Both twins admit that they change their opinions. "I'm always changing," says Eppie. "Anyone who doesn't change their ideas over a period of years is either pickled in alcohol or embedded in wood." Popo agrees. "I've gone through a gradual process of loosening my views as my children became adults and they and their friends taught me that maybe I was a little out of step."

In their early years as columnists, both women were staidly predictable, reflecting conventional American morality. By the end of the sixties, both columnists were worried that they were becoming out of date. Over the next ten years the views of these astute women made a quantum jump beyond the traditional patterns of advice giving.

The initial change occurred when they began their careers as advice columnists. They worked with experts who urged them to develop ideas differing from the one-size-fits-all mores they had assimilated as children in Sioux City. Robert Stolar claims he was one of the professionals who influenced the columnists. It took about fifteen years, he says, before Ann or Abby could discuss the subjects he explored with them, such as abortion or obscenity, in their newspaper columns. Popo says, "I hope I'm more tuned in and knowledgeable than I was the day I started. I've had the great opportunity to learn from the experts in various fields."

"I don't know if I've changed as much as the world has changed," says Eppie, who's a little more cautious than her sister. "Twenty-five years ago I would have said no to premarital sex. I don't know what I was thinking about for women who never married. I just thought that all women should be married. Now, I'm not saying that all sex outside of marriage is taboo, but I do believe it takes maturity and commitment."

Eppie's friendship with Supreme Court Justice William O. Douglas perhaps helped speed her transformation into the columnist willing to address social and political issues. Perhaps indirectly so, agrees attorney Cathleen Douglas, the renowned jurist's widow. "Bill was a teacher, not a proselytizer," she says.

A substantial shift in the Ann Landers column is evident after Eppie's divorce in 1975. She began to turn even more toward her friend Father Hesburgh. A civil-rights advocate, Hesburgh has very liberal and outspoken political views that seeped into the Ann Landers column.

"She's a person that learns from experience," says Hesburgh. "As the years went by she learned a lot more in depth about things that were going on. . . . She's got a very quick, open, and inquisitive mind."

"She has changed," admits a Field Enterprise employee. "She was always a very political person, but now she is more political than ever."

Popo explains why her views have changed too. "I haven't changed to be 'with it' or to be popular with young people. But I have changed. I'm less rigid now. That's because my children are grown and I'm not scared to death. They survived a difficult era."

No doubt Popo includes the persuasions of her now former son-in-law, Luke McKissack, who specializes in civil liberties and criminal law cases. And her role as trustee of the Phillips Foundation probably affects gift giving to such organizations as Planned Parenthood and the Lawyers Committee for Civil Rights Under Law.

240 ≈

Popo credits her daughter, Jeannie, who "comes from a different generation, a more enlightened generation than mine," for helping her come to terms with some unpopular stands she's taken, stands that may have cost her readers. "It's never bothered me in the slightest to have opinions my readers might disagree with. I've espoused some very unpopular views—unpopular with some people."

"Some people" even includes her twin, of whom Popo says about the only thing they've ever disagreed on is their attitude toward homosexuals. Despite Eppie's pioneering approach to presenting the homosexual lifestyle as a sexual problem in her column before her sister took up the controversial topic, it is Popo who is more tolerant today of homosexuality as a natural sexual inclination. Eppie has vacillated on the subject.

"From the very beginning, my consultant has always been Dr. Judd Marmor, who has been very supportive of gays," says Popo. "Ann's consultants have not been like-minded people, unfortunately. What a pity!

"Statements perpetuating the theory that homosexuals are 'sick' or emotionally disturbed have been run. Homosexuality is 'unnatural' is what her consultants tell her, and she continues to buy it."

Eppie stands by her guns. "I believe, when an individual prefers a member of his (or her) own sex as an object of physical love, that person suffers from a severe personality disorder." She still says, "If a person is—quote—normal—unquote—and if he is given the choice of a person with whom to have sexual contact, he will select a person of the opposite sex." But despite her opinion, she says, "I was one of the first to fight for homosexual rights."

"Ann's consultants say that if you're gay, you're sick. Well, if they are sick, they're made sick by a society that doesn't understand them," counters Popo. "I think we are all God's children. I think this is the way they go and because we all don't go this way, we can't say they're wrong."

Refusing to pass judgment, Popo sometimes advocates positions contrary to opinions of hard-line traditionalists. For example, she believes it's okay for couples to live together rather than get married. "I try to uphold what I consider moralities. The legal thing isn't always the moral thing. I don't sit and judge people."

Alone, either Popo or Eppie would be a formidable foe to run up against. United behind most causes, the sisters present a double-pronged endorsement of liberal social values. Support of the ERA garnered the twin columnists minor criticism and a mostly favorable response for their shift in attitude. But aside from the ERA, if there's one intensely emotional issue that continues to cause considerable controversy for both columnists and threatens their popularity among their readership, it's abortion.

Twenty-Six

"*I*f I get one more copy of *The Diary of an Unborn Child*, I'll kill myself," says Eppie.

The long-standing support of both Ann Landers and Dear Abby of a woman's right to abortion is well known among the right-to-life organizations and other conservative groups. As early as the late sixties, Abby was stating publicly that "a woman should never be forced by law to have a child she doesn't want." In 1971, Popo as Dear Abby endorsed a mass demonstration and march held simultaneously in San Francisco and Washington on behalf of "a woman's right to choose."

In response to a reader who decried abortion because "that poor child will never see a butterfly. Or a rainbow. A waterfall. A smile. A dog wagging his tail," Popo said, "But neither will an unborn child feel the pain of poverty. Or prejudice. A Hiroshima. A holocaust."

Eppie's pro-choice stand as Ann Landers riled right-to-lifers in many quarters. When St. Johns College in North Windham, Maine, offered Ann Landers an honorary degree, complaints from angry alumni quickly prompted its president to rescind the invitation to speak at the school's 1973 commencement. "When it came to light that Miss Landers favored abortion on demand we felt it necessary to rescind the offer," said the college administrator.

"At first, I was stunned," says Eppie. "Then I was puzzled. Now I'm amused."

Eppie early on chose to emphasize the discriminatory nature of abortion laws. "If a woman wants to have an abortion because of an unwanted pregnancy, she should be free to do so. It should not be up to the state or the church or anybody else to tell her whether or not she can have one.

"I have repeatedly stated that I am for abortion on demand, and I think the abortion laws are discriminatory against the poor. Rich people can go to Japan or Europe or wherever they have to go to pay a doctor in their own town. Poor people can't do it. And I feel that in this area there should be no equivocation."

Despite its costing her popularity with some of her readers, Eppie holds fast to her stance on abortion. Over the years she has become ever more adamant in her support of legalized abortion. In 1981, two columns were devoted exclusively to testimony given before a U.S. Senate subcommittee on the popularly termed "Human Life Amendment." She chose to print the testimony of George Ryan, M.D., former president of the American College of Obstetrics and Gynecologists, followed by a tagline: "And now, readers, a final statement from Ann Landers."

Dramatically, Eppie as Ann Landers warned that there existed a "dangerous element" in the right-to-life groups that "poses a serious threat to our domestic way of life. . . . We must not allow this to happen."

The right-to-life groups were incensed. Terming them dangerous would alone have engendered a commotion, but the major irritant was Eppie's neglect of testimony given by other expert witnesses before the Senate subcommittee. The hearing itself had been criticized even by pro-choice groups who labeled it one-sided for inviting only one sympathetic witness, George Ryan, the only person Eppie quoted.

American Pro-Life Lobby wrote Ann Landers a two-page letter and provided her with pro-life Senate testimony. The Pro-Life Action League requested a meeting with Eppie to present its view. She neither responded to nor acknowledged the correspondence and ignored the request. Letters and phone calls to her office went unanswered.

Readers also thought the columns were slanted. "Ann Landers deliberately withheld information from her readership by only presenting expert testimony and viewpoints she agreed with," wrote a reader in a letter to the editor of a Minneapolis newspaper.

Her bias apparent even to readers, only one newspaper had decided not to run the columns. The *Daily News* of Whittier, California, told its readers that the missing Ann Landers feature would appear when she balanced her views with the other side of the abortion issue. *Daily News* subscribers protested and charged the newspaper with censorship. But the paper didn't budge.

A letter from the columnist herself requesting, "Will you take another look at the situation and print these columns?" didn't work. Eppie's rationale to the *Daily News* for her failure to present the right-to-life arguments was lack of information. A reader had sent Ryan's testimony to Ann Landers, and she ran only the pro-choice argument because she "had no other side to work with."

The next month, Eppie printed three letters from readers espousing the pro-life line. But her seeming fairness in presenting opposing viewpoints was tainted when she told readers, "The majority of those who wrote in to disagree with me were threatening, hysterical, and vituperative." To emphasize her point, one of the three letters printed was addressed, "You murderess," and ended with, "I hope you burn in hell."

The National Right to Life Committee objected to Eppie's choice of rebuttal material. None of the three letters was from a doctor or a person whose professional esteem was equivalent to Ryan's. "By omitting to print a qualified medical rebuttal in your column," the Committee wrote, you make "one doubt your sincerity and fairness."

American Life Lobby summarized, "Ann Landers has a tendency to consider anyone who disagrees with her on the abortion subject a nut."

After giving the other side its say, Eppie appeared on NBC's "Today" show to announce she would "take on" the right-to-life movement. She ran another column supporting the right to an abortion and claimed that her mail ran two-to-one in support of her own viewpoint.

The Pro-Life Action League, perhaps the most vociferous of the anti-abortion groups, officially urged its members in late 1981 to join a "Dump Ann Landers" movement. "I didn't want to start a Dump Ann Landers movement until I had talked to her on the phone," says Pro-Life director Joseph Schindler. "But she would never return my phone calls or respond to my letters."

Why only Ann and not Abby too? As on many issues, Eppie has always been a trifle more pious and more willing than her sister to continue the fight once she's made her position known. It's the part of her personality that gets reflected in her column, because Eppie is the more serious-minded of the twins. Popo, by contrast, is less academic in her approach in her column. Rarely would Popo reprint Senate testimony on any subject. Although she supports a woman's right to an abortion, she endorses causes in her column far less often than her sister. Instead, she responds to issues on a more individualized basis, by discussing the issue in response to a particular reader letter.

Several state and national so-called pro-family as well as right-to-life groups like American Life Lobby joined the campaign. Dubbing the boycott "Can Ann," one of these groups told its members, "Ann Landers will not stop using her column to place her particular brand of moral beliefs before the nation, and so we must do everything we can to see to it that newspapers simply do not carry her column. Please write and ask your local newspaper to discontinue her column."

Phyllis Schlafly's group, the Eagle Forum, while not formally a part of the coordinated Dump Ann campaign, finds the political viewpoints of Ann Landers and Dear Abby offensive. Says a spokesperson, "Our members have written them at great length, particularly on issues of abortion and the ERA." The Eagle Forum recommends that its members complain to their newspaper editor and stop buying the papers that carry the Ann or Abby columns. "The only recourse you have is against the newspaper," explains the spokesperson.

In the face of mounting pressure against her abortion position, Eppie agreed to the request from her good friend and confidante Mary Lasker, a philanthropist who has endowed the National Abortion Rights Action League (NARAL) and through her foundation awards the prestigious Lasker Prize for exemplary medical research, to appear as Ann Landers in advertisements to aid the pro-choice cause. Headed "Ann Landers on Abortion," the full-page ads ran in newspapers throughout the country at the same time the U.S. Senate was voting on the proposed human life amendment in February 1982. The ad reprinted the controversial Ann Landers column accompanied by a picture of Eppie prominently displayed. At the bottom was a clip-and-mail coupon targeted for a specific senator.

NARAL spokeswoman Marguerite Beck-Rex was asked why Ann Landers appeared in the ad. She says that extensive research shows that influential persons, such as doctors, are needed to back the pro-choice opinions. Ann Landers may not be a doctor, but her influence with the average American makes her a natural to plug NARAL and its goals.

After the appearance of the ad, the Dump Ann campaign gathered momentum. NARAL staff considered ways to undermine the effort but finally decided that the Can Ann movement was no serious menace to the columnist. "If it looked like a real threat, of course, we would have helped Ann, because she stuck her neck out for us," says Beck-Rex.

The Dump Ann proponents claim they have help cut down the number of columns devoted to abortion. Local pro-life and pro-family newsletters continually encourage their readers to protest Ann Landers and her views. When one such newsletter arrived at the Fort Worth *Star-Telegram,* columnist Bill Youngblood called Eppie to get her reaction.

"I've had a few such letters from Fort Worth," she said, "but there doesn't appear to be any national movement or anything."

When told of the advice columnist's denial, Pro-Life Action League director Joseph Schindler snorted, "It is a national campaign, and she knows about it and is bothered by it. She's on my mailing list and I send her press releases. She knows what's going on."

Schindler attributes Eppie's pro-abortion stance to, of all people, her friend and adviser Father Hesburgh. Hesburgh says of course it's not true. Speaking of Eppie, he says, "She doesn't necessarily follow your advice. She and I don't agree on a number of things, like abortion, for example. . . . We agree to disagree, but she still wants to know what you think about it and why . . . you can disagree without being disagreeable."

If the Ann and Abby columns are the ideological targets of certain groups, these groups' efforts have been, to date, particularly unsuccessful. But the columnists have other critics, people who may not be actively organizing to have Ann and Abby dropped from the daily paper. These people and their organizations feel that the twin columnists' views and power actually threaten the fabric of American life.

Twenty-Seven

"There are a lot of problems in the world, and Ann and Abby are one of them," concludes Howard Phillips, national director of the Conservative Caucus Foundation. "They have a bad influence on people."

The American Life Lobby concurs: "Ann and Abby represent a typically liberal viewpoint and one which is in increasing disrepute among serious conservatives."

Howard Phillips reiterates, "The tragedy is that there are a lot of impressionable people who may not reflect on these things and who have much more ready access to a columnist than a member of the clergy. It does have an unfortunate influence, but that's for the people to decide."

Ann and Abby do not appear to be intimidated by their critics. "Some people think I'm too liberal," Eppie readily acknowledges. "I think I have a liberal point of view," says Popo. Both assert they have chosen to wield their considerable prestige to sway the American public's opinions. They know their messages have a significant impact on the average reader.

Cal Thomas, the former spokesman for the Moral Majority, spelled out his group's objections, as well as its anxiety over how

Ann and Abby have come to reflect the changing face of American culture. Agreeing that the columnists' views have shifted over the past fifteen years, he says, "You see more of an attempt on Ann and Abby's part to conform to the current culture rather than rely on traditional values."

Similarly, the American Life Lobby has noticed the transformation in the columnists' perspective. "Ann has gotten softer on traditional family values," says James Kappas. "Now Abby is off the traditional family path."

"There may be an occasional sop to the old-line values," concedes Cal Thomas. But the Moral Majority was contending that any support for old-fashioned values was couched in language that limited its wide application to all readers. "It's almost like they're saying, well, there's our thing for traditional values."

Conservative organizations are angry that the advice columnists use their syndicated networks, freely and consciously, to advance selected political and social opinions. The views that Eppie and Popo express in their columns contrast sharply with those of the political right on sex education in schools, open access to birth control for teenagers, nuclear disarmament, government funding of social programs, homosexual rights, gun control, affirmative action, divorce, and many other issues.

What many of these spokespeople for conservative groups object to is the extent of the columnists' influence and their exposure to the public. Frankly, they sound envious.

Eppie and Popo acknowledge their own power. "I can form public opinion," states Eppie. "I am in a position where I can make my weight felt. I can count."

"Listen," says Popo, "if you stand for something, you cannot have everyone love you. But that's okay, because I think I'm doing a lot of good for a lot of people. In fact, I know I am."

Misuse of their power is a concern of the columnists' critics. "Abby wrote something that specifically attacked Moral Majority and Jerry Falwell," says Cal Thomas, annoyed by what he viewed as Popo's lack of accountability. "And it was wrong. It asserted a position we do not hold. In fact, it was the antithesis of something we believe.

"I wrote Abby a letter and said, 'We don't mind your criticizing us legitimately. There's plenty of room for discussion and debate. But don't accuse us of something we're not guilty of.' " Knowing that the columnists say they answer all correspondence, the Moral Majority expected a response from Popo. "We never heard back," says Thomas. "I was amazed."

Eppie and Popo have strong views on the organization that was founded by Jerry Falwell, and now, because of its finances and diminishing public image, has been rechristened the Liberty Lobby.

"I am probably on the Moral Majority's hit list," says Popo. "I guess I'm the immoral minority. If that's what I am, I suppose I should be proud of it."

Former Bishop James Shannon supports the twins' "shared deep conviction of basic moral teachings. These two women are an enormously potent source of morality, teaching service, kindness, civility." Terming the columnists' critics the "moral minority," Shannon believes that any slight deviation from conservative beliefs means that "you don't pass their purity test."

"They're neither moral, nor are they the majority," concurs Eppie, who, with her tendency to see issues in terms of absolutes, challenged the Moral Majority. She compared the questioning of her column's bias by groups like Falwell's to the repressive era of McCarthyism in the fifties. "I see a similarity between McCarthy and the Moral Majority. These people are saying, 'If you don't believe the way I believe then you must be punished.' "

Popo, who on occasion shifts her opinions more easily than her twin, tends to see more gray areas, but she also criticizes the hard-line conservative groups. "I think they're people telling other people, 'If you don't think the way I do, you're wrong.' "

When public schools use either twin's column as a teaching aid, conservatives and their organizations really get riled. In Texas, parents complained about a teacher's use of the Ann Landers teen-age-sex questionnaire. In North Carolina, a newsletter devoted to conservative causes criticized a classroom exercise that involved composing a letter to Dear Abby.

Occasionally, a newspaper will delete portions of an Ann or Abby column thought to be offensive. A Wisconsin paper refused to run the annual Ann Landers teenage-sex survey. One of the questions to adolescents was: "Even though you are straight, would you go kinky to see what it's like?"

The newspaper editor defended his action, saying, "The column was in no way an instrument to educate our teenagers or anyone else. As far as we are concerned, there was no purpose or value to this test."

It is this sort of teen-sex question that makes the Conservative Caucus regard the Ann Landers column as tawdry. Says Howard Phillips, "If I were a newspaper publisher, I would not run their columns, because the advice they give out is trashy. I don't think any serious person looks to them as a source of good judgment."

Eppie pooh-poohs detractors who call her column repugnant. She says her intentions are honorable. "I'm always direct. There's no obscenity, no pornographic overtones, and no attempt at sensationalism.

"I don't just come out with a story about transvestites or masturbation. Mine is just a response to a person who is troubled over something."

Popo sees much of her criticism coming from people who have hidden anxiety over the very problems she addresses. Things haven't changed all that much, she seems to be saying, and people who complain about subverting "traditional values" are trying to affirm a state of affairs that speaks more of personal longing than reality. "People have the same problems now," she says, "but we're more vocal about them than we were twenty years ago. People weren't talking about sexual dysfunction, or homosexuality, or the problems of the elderly.

"Of course, I was on to incest twenty years ago. People would write Dear Abby about things they would never tell anyone else. A great deal of it was going on, but it was hushed up. Now, we're letting kids know they don't have to deal with it. They can talk about it."

The columnists' more avid detractors have resorted to personal attacks on the women. Both have been labeled or called every conceivable derogatory term, usually anonymously. When Eppie ran a column blasting chiropractors, she was sent a photograph of a bulletin board with the message "DID YOU READ WHAT THE JEWISH BITCH SAID ABOUT CHIROPRACTORS NOW?"

"Let me tell you the difference between being a tough broad, and a bitch," says Eppie. "You can talk to one hundred people who know me, you will never hear me described as a bitch. . . . Yeah, I'm a tough broad when it comes to principles. When it comes to standing up for what I believe in, when it comes to speaking for people who have no voice, when it comes to issues I think are important, I am a tough broad. But I'm not a bitch. I'm not unreasonable. I'm willing to listen."

Disagreeing, the gun lobby claims that Eppie is not willing to listen. "She knows nothing about existing gun laws and apparently prefers it that way," says Ashley Halsey, editor of *American Rifleman*. After the Ann Landers column contained errors about federal gun laws, the National Rifle Association repeatedly wrote Eppie so that she could correct the misinformation, but to no avail.

"The standards that one would expect from a journalist are not demanded of her," gripes John Aquilino, formerly of the NRA.

Eppie's characterization of gun owners as "nuts" bothered some readers. After the column had been run in papers throughout the country, Handgun Control, the anti-gun lobby, received a call from Eppie's syndicate. They were concerned with the accuracy of the statements in the column and wanted to check on the facts.

Eppie's friend Father Hesburgh notes, "It takes a strong person to take on the NRA. She's got very strong convictions on gun control. I wouldn't want to have her on my back. If she goes after them, she can cause them trouble, and I hope she does."

Popo explains both her own and Eppie's reason for risking their popularity by taking up social and political causes in their columns: The twins have always been leaders, not followers, and they recognize the virtue of boldness. "Strong stands on anything bring you criticism," she says. "If you don't take a stand on anything, you stand for nothing."

Twenty-Eight

*P*opo's support at the time of Eppie's divorce rekindled the harmony between the twins. Ten years earlier, the sisters had been pleased to receive honorary degrees from Morningside College. Because they weren't speaking, they accepted their degrees at different times. Now, together again, the two women carefully prepared for their first public appearance side by side in years. The 1976 occasion the famed pair chose was an appropriately sentimental one, the fortieth anniversary of their Central High School graduation.

"We just want to go home as the Friedman twins," Popo modestly protested, putting her best profile forward. Once in Sioux City, however, the twins attracted the kind of attention usually reserved for visiting royalty.

Eppie, always trying to make the most of her talents and her looks, and, believing in plastic surgery, had decided, après divorce, to be a new woman. Along with a face lift, she had extensive body surgery. Popo, for her part, may protest that she hasn't indulged in any cosmetic sculpting, but she too looked svelte, and a mite more held together than her former classmates. Margo states that her aunt has had her eyes done and her thighs slimmed.

During the reunion banquet, wherever the Friedman twins went, autographing old yearbook pictures and signing souvenir programs, cameras and reporters followed. Not lingering very long after the Spornitz Band tuned up with dance music, the twins, on their way out, agreed on the advice they'd give anyone undecided about attending a class reunion. "Go," they sang in unison. "It's like an extra facet on a diamond. It'll make all your memories even more precious."

Days after her return from Sioux City, Eppie was off again, this time to Mary Lasker's all-white Long Island beach house, which has a large framed photograph of her good friend Eppie Lederer in the living room. Ever since the early days of her separation from Jules, Eppie has spent nearly every Independence Day holiday, which coincides with both her birthday and wedding anniversary, in privacy at one of the Lasker homes, sometimes among a close circle of friends that includes Walter and Betsy Cronkite and Art and Ann Buchwald.

Back in Chicago, family life was getting bumpy again. Margo told her mother that not only was she divorcing her second husband, Jules Furth, but she was not planning on marrying again, ever. Eppie, respecting her daughter's decision, confidently proclaimed, "I don't think a clinker marriage or two is the end of the world."

Aunt Popo, however, wasn't so sympathetic. She and her niece barely tolerated each other. Once, when a friend of Margo's got a job at her aunt's syndicate, she warned him not to let on he knew her, because Popo would then take an immediate dislike to him. When six months later Margo announced she was marrying for a third time, Popo became even more snide about what she viewed as Margo's deficiencies.

Margo met the actor Ken Howard in December 1976 during a four-hour lunch interview. She had resumed her lightweight column writing for the *Chicago Daily News,* the afternoon paper, and was assigned to interview the 6'6" basketball aficionado who was playing the psychiatrist in a local production of *Equus.* "In three days we knew we were in love," says Margo, and after a three-month courtship they were married under a tree at the Chicago Art Institute.

"People say having three children is a liability for a woman who wants to remarry, but I really think the kids were quite an attraction," says Margo. "He was very brave to marry the Zsa Zsa Gabor of Lake Michigan."

Eppie called Ken "The Gorgeous Goy" and "a marvelous guy, solid, a real *mensch*" and trotted out her by then familiar line, "This is one of the most beautiful marriages I know."

Passing lightly over any concerns she may have had about her new son-in-law's religion, Eppie acknowledged that a couple did not necessarily have to share a religion to have a successful marriage. "My own daughter married first in her faith and is now married to a Congregationalist," she says. "I couldn't be more pleased. If anyone had told me twenty-five years ago that my attitude would be so different, I would not have believed it."

Eppie says, "I consider my Jewishness very important to me, and I believe my daughter feels the same way." It's a small point of honor, but Eppie dislikes the thought of people believing that she hides behind a gentile-sounding pseudonym. "Sometimes I almost create an opportunity to say I'm Jewish," she says.

With her daughter's remarriage, and being single herself after thirty-six years of marriage, Eppie started dating. She talked about the type of man who would interest her. "Someone in good physical condition, bright, stimulating, honest, preferably a nondrinker, nonsmoker, someone who cerebrates at a very high level. . . . Frankly, I'd have to be turned on by him.

"Only the best," she was saying. "I'd need a man with some measure of achievement of his own and one who could tolerate being married to Ann Landers. It's something to put up with."

A suitable husband would not only have to be someone unawed by her celebrity status but also someone who would respect her. "In some respects, I'm still a 'Shirley,' still a nice Jewish girl who believes in saving it for marriage. Some men respect this; others, well, they're not for me."

Eppie feels that finding a husband who measures up isn't going to be an easy task. "It's gonna take a helluva man to marry me," she says, "but I had me one once, and I'll have me another." And she's determined. "I intend to find him. I must. I need to share what is otherwise a wonderful life. Right now, not being married is like trying to clap with one hand."

Clapping with only one hand, Eppie discovered she could still make a lot of noise. In 1977, her unsolicited advice ranged from the subject of Richard Nixon—"The war and the Nixon administration did more to undermine morality in this country than anything I can think of"—to "that Anita Bryant dame," of whom she was saying, "Boy, if there's one thing I distrust, it's a person who thinks God talks directly to her."

On top of her column writing and speaking engagements, Eppie wanted to maintain an active presence in politics. A friend of Boston Mayor Kevin White's, she accompanied him to Chicago Mayor Richard Daley's funeral and later flew to White's side to join him in a march to support nonviolent desegregation in Boston's south end.

Eppie liked visiting with Connecticut Governor Ella Grasso, the nation's first female governor elected in her own right, and counted many of the House and Senate's Democratic leadership as close friends, including Florida Congressman Claude Pepper, who got Eppie appointed to a House panel studying health issues.

In Washington, Eppie thrived. Being recognized in the hallways of the House and Senate office buildings, or short-stopping lunch conversation in the Congressional dining rooms, Eppie had discovered a community to which she felt she truly belonged. What's more, she was welcomed in the city's power corridors by many of its most notable habitués.

"She knows most of the big Democratic senators," says Father Hesburgh. "It's amazing, if you walk through the House of Representatives or the Senate, how many of those people know her. She knows where the power is, and I think she's got her finger on it.

"One classic example was during the Nixon administration," recounts Hesburgh. "I happened to be in the Senate on a civil-rights purpose just after she had done a column supporting the Cancer Act."

Eppie's 1971 column message was succinct: Cancer is killing more Americans each year than had died in World War II. It is killing "more children under fifteen years of age than any other illness." The bill to speed up research on cancer was stalled in the Senate, and the year before, President Nixon had vetoed a measure that would have substantially increased the federal funding available for medical research. Eppie told her readers to write their senators.

"She had all the facts and figures because of all her advisers," says Hesburgh. "They were bringing in the letters literally by the truckload. They were coming in sack after sack. I think they got 60,000 letters a day just because of that column. Believe me, that made an impact. They got $100 million for that Act. It went through—zing—because Ann Landers said write your Senator."

On a first-name basis with almost every chief executive since Harry Truman, Eppie was no stranger to presidential politics either. Having supported Jimmy Carter in the 1976 election, she met him and Rosalynn several times and was a guest at White House dinners. "I like both of them very much, and have had good talks with them," she said.

President Carter delivered the eulogy for Senator Hubert Humphrey at the Church of St. Hope in St. Paul. Both Eppie and Popo attended the February 1978 services for their long-time friend and were deeply moved by the tribute the president delivered.

Before he died, Eppie had asked Humphrey to write an article on politics and the rewards of public life for a book she was compiling, *The Ann Landers Encyclopedia A to Z*. Eppie attributes the idea for the book to Mary Lasker. "We just sat down one day and listed all the subjects we thought troubled people. People don't even know where to get help these days; that in itself is extraordinary."

In addition to Senator Humphrey, Eppie pressed many of her friends and recent acquaintances into service. An article on forgiving was contributed by Father Hesburgh, one on crime by Dr. Karl Menninger, and another on heart surgery by Dr. Michael DeBakey, the surgeon with whom she had worked on Congressman Claude Pepper's health panel. Mike Royko, a colleague at the *Sun-Times,* contributed a light-hearted piece on hangovers, while old friend Art Buchwald wrote on unreturned phone calls, a slight vignette that Eppie, in her introduction, charitably called funny.

Of all the contributions to her book, Eppie says the "piece closest to my heart" was Senator Humphrey's. "That magnificent man wrote the piece during the last days of his illness. He phoned repeatedly to say, 'Don't worry, Eppie, it's coming. I'm just putting on the finishing touches.' "

Eppie also was thankful to Popo for delaying publication of a book she was working on that would have competed for the same reading audience. "My sister was preparing a book similar to my *Encyclopedia,*" she explains. "But she graciously decided to hold off on hers until I got mine out."

Calling the hefty, 1,212-page volume of advice and infotainment "the work of a lifetime," Eppie says, caressing her leather-bound copy, "I'm proud of it. Because if anyone would have said to me twenty-four years ago that I'd someday be putting together an encyclopedia, I'd have laughed. I'd never have thought it possible."

Twenty-Nine

The appearance on all national best-seller lists of sister Eppie's *Encyclopedia* accelerated Popo's thinking about her next business move. She was evaluating how her current syndicate, the Tribune Company, was promoting her. Even Mort became involved in some of the money issues, says Popo's Tribune Company editor, Don Michaels.

During Popo's tenure at the Tribune Company from 1966 to 1980, she profited from an increase in subscribers. Three columnists were locked into the top syndication spots. As before, Dear Abby was a more popular advice columnist than Ann Landers. Together, the twins' columns, along with Jack Anderson's column of political commentary, were entrenched in the first three positions.

Popo's discussions with Tribune Company executives were friendly and thoughtful, but she advised them in late 1979 that she was looking for a new home for Dear Abby. One of the competing syndicates Popo courted was Universal Press. Transformed from selling only Roman Catholic features, Universal was eager to acquire a big name like Dear Abby.

"Abby had talked to some people and was intrigued," remembers John McMeel, the syndicate president and one of its founders, who knows both sisters and calls Popo "Abby" and Eppie "Eppie." "We had a chance to meet with her. It was a love affair, at least from this end.

"Abby was not at a point where she said, 'I'm coming to you because you'll give me a better piece of the action,' " says McMeel. "Her arrangements with the Tribune syndicate are the arrangements we accepted. It's a very handsome contract, but it's good for both parties.

"Her former syndicate is a great operation," continues McMeel, speaking well of his company's competition, "but we brought something that she saw was kind of exciting. . . . When she called, we said we'd hop on the bus and come out, we were so excited," he chuckles. "There was a chemistry, an identification. And we were going to prove her confidence in us was well placed."

After weeks of tinkering over the terms of Popo's new contract, McMeel was ready to announce that Dear Abby had become "the crowning jewel in Universal Press's tenth anniversary celebration." Mustering company pride, McMeel continued, "In a year when we've added heavyweights like William Buckley, James Kilpatrick, Mary McGrory, and Hugh Sidey, the addition of Dear Abby is a tribute to our sales and marketing staff." McMeel also announced the start of a national campaign to add client newspapers to the Dear Abby roster.

Popo not only gained a new sales force, dedicated to picking up more newspapers and increasing the column's going rate, but more importantly, according to syndicate expert Richard Weiner, Popo's share of column billings shot up to an unprecedented ratio of more than 90 percent. There was yet another factor that no doubt persuaded Popo to move Dear Abby to Universal.

Ever ambitious, Popo was assembling old columns to turn into a book. She wisely chose a syndicate that had its own publishing house. The package deal Popo worked out with Universal included both the column and the book. Recognizing that a book credited to Abigail Van Buren would be a best-seller, and also realizing that her column could increase sales of the book and that her book sales could increase sales of her column, Universal was delighted.

"My God, there are people who want to put you on the shelf, Abby," McMeel remembers telling his star client. "There are just too many people out there who tear out Dear Abby and keep it, and we should have a book."

"John, that takes a lot of effort, but I'll do it right," said a determined Popo.

"Anything you want to do, go ahead," encouraged McMeel.

As with her decision to join Universal, Mort was involved. "Abby doesn't move without Mort," says McMeel. "He's solid and he's patient and considerate, and he's firm. Abby is very wise that she wants Mort to be involved with everything that's very important in her life. . . . Abby always introduces me as her boss. *Nobody* is Abby's boss except Mort. Mort is really the one who's Abby's boss."

The Best of Dear Abby was published in October 1981, three years after *The Ann Landers Encyclopedia.* In January 1981, Popo had celebrated the twenty-fifth anniversary of Dear Abby with a column of thanks to those who had helped her. She ended with a paragraph of gratitude to her readers, saying, "I am eternally grateful [to you] for providing me daily with a treasury of letters so human, so poignant and so outrageously funny that at times the column practically writes itself."

Like her three earlier works, Popo's *Best of* consisted primarily of a rehash of reader letters, and she unabashedly plugged the book in her column. Although some newspapers delete their syndicated columnists' self-serving advertisements, others don't. Popo told readers to send directly for her book. "It's available by sending $9.95 plus $1 for postage and handling. Make checks payable to Universal Press Syndicate."

To boost sales, Popo got dressed up as Dear Abby and hit the road. From Portland to Detroit, from the "Today" show to a Focus interview on WJR Atlanta, for as long as Popo's lop-sided grin and last bristle of sprayed and blow-dried hair kept pace, reporters, sales clerks, book buyers, and broadcasters were treated to the wit, wisdom, and wiliness of America's pre-eminent advice queen.

Accompanied by Cloyd Koop, her hairdresser, and as many as four others, including a publicist, a news reporter, and a couple of publisher's representatives, breathing space in the black, white, burgundy, or gold limo was at a premium. Along with advice, Popo peppered her presentations with tidbits of personal whimsy, revealing, mostly, her feelings for Mort.

About Mort, "He's my Rock of Gibraltar. I'm very lucky." Again, about Mort, "The deeper you go, the better he gets." And again, about Mort, "My husband is a loving, sensitive, considerate man who's my personal advisor, my guiding light, my live-in editor. How could you not love a man like that and not give him everything you've got?"

Gushing, "I have one of the better marriages," Popo may have been contrasting her marital status with that of her twin, who obviously didn't. Or perhaps her repeated public declarations of her affection for Mort were an attempt to convince herself of her happy marriage and acknowledge that because she was attached so blissfully, she wasn't missing out on anything.

Popo explains to reporters how she keeps her slim figure, while sidling up to the Godiva chocolates counter and ordering a bagful for immediate consumption. "I used to exercise by standing in front of an open window and winding my watch," she says playfully. "But now I watch Donahue. Our house has a hallway that forms a square, so I put on my Adidas shoes and walk around the house at a fast clip for an hour. All four TVs are tuned in to Donahue, so wherever I am, I can see it. I don't miss anything."

In her hotel room, reporter present, she orders tea from room service, singing into the phone, "Tea, for two, and two, for tea. . . ." In a Detroit bookstore, doffing a full-length sable coat, saying she "trapped it under the kitchen sink," Popo is aghast to find her book under Psychology, right next to one by Dr. Joyce Brothers. "Delma!" she hollers at the store manager, picking up all the copies of her book, carrying them to the front of the store and plopping them down alongside the cash register, "Better order some more!"

Koop, along not only to comb Popo out, but to keep her out of trouble—"Cloyd Koop is not only my hairdresser, he's a good friend and traveling companion," says Popo—spots her, between bookstores, ogling a pair of purple, thigh-high, heeled boots in a store window. "Do you know what you look like in boots?" asks Koop, taking Popo by the arm. "Yeah, like I'm walking in a hole," she winks. "I really wanted those purple boots, but I didn't have the courage," she later adds. "Can you see me with a baton and those boots?"

Performing for her public, whether at Marshall Field's Old Orchard store in Skokie or at a question-and-answer session at a suburban high school where she reveals she once tried marijuana and "zonked out," Popo couldn't avoid the one question that hounded her in every city. Snapping at whoever asked whether she spoke with her sister, whether they were friends, Popo repeatedly stated in every city she visited that their feud had ended almost two decades before, and yes, she and Eppie were close and loving.

Popo would add that she resented the stories, and that they were inaccurate and damaging. That's why she added a slight, eleven-page autobiographical sketch to the beginning of *The Best of Dear Abby*—to set the record straight.

"My sister called me when she read it," Popo remembers, saying Eppie was misty-eyed, "and she said, you're right, that's exactly the way it happened!"

The feud story may once have been old news, and had it stayed old news, it might not have continually threatened to eclipse the gaiety of Popo's publicity tour. But it was topical again, not because the press was being spiteful or envious or downright mean, as Popo insists. But thanks to Popo herself.

Back in December 1979, *Ladies' Home Journal* had run an interview with Eppie in which she briefly referred to how her twin stepped in on her success with a copycat Dear Abby column. Eppie's mention of Popo was almost parenthetical, and her relationship with her twin was not discussed in detail. The focus of the article, stemming from writer Cliff Jahr's four or five talks with Eppie over a few days, concerned her intimate feelings about her divorce from Jules. The article itself was sensitive and touching, and Eppie's candor about "the major tragedy of my life" revealed her inner strength and upbeat sensibility.

Publicly, Popo made no comment about the *Journal* piece. For more than a year, she refused Jahr's requests to chat about her life and career.

Then, in the spring of 1981, Popo appeared on "The Charlie Rose Show," a syndicated television program based in Washington, D.C. On the air, Rose asked his guest if she read her sister's column. "Of course!" Popo replied, looking exasperated, as if to imply that Rose's question was not only trivial and annoying but also impertinent.

"And does Ann Landers read Dear Abby?" Rose asked, as he leaned forward, intentionally baiting Popo.

Popo looked angry as she nodded in affirmation and clutched a lace handkerchief.

"Let's see what Ann has to say," purred Rose. On the bottom right of the screen, an earlier telecast with Eppie appeared. In the clip, Rose asks, "Ann, do you read Dear Abby's column?"

Eppie stiffened her back, clenched her teeth, smugly and unhesitatingly replying, "No." After a pause, she continued, "It runs in a Chicago paper which . . . I . . . do . . . not . . . read."

The studio audience and TV viewers watched both Eppie's taped words and Popo's live reaction. Popo's mouth started to drop open; she appeared distraught and unbelieving, no doubt angry over Rose's prepared stunt. When she realized she was still on camera, Popo quickly closed her mouth, gulped, and attempted to compose her features. The frilly handkerchief was a wadded ball in her hand.

"I read her column every day," Popo sharply stated. "I don't care what paper it's in. I wouldn't miss it for the world."

Luckily for Jahr, his next call to Popo was shortly after her Charlie Rose encounter. "Yes," Popo told Jahr. "I'm ready for the interview."

The subsequent *Journal* article, appearing in August 1981, two months before the publication of *The Best of Dear Abby,* revealed to the public that the conflicts between the twins still hadn't been resolved. At age sixty-three, Popo, seventeen years after their unsisterly differences had supposedly been put to rest, recited a litany of imperfections attributable to her twin.

Sounding off on Eppie's plastic surgery, Popo said, "If she looked old, if she needed a face-lift, believe me it's because she needed it. I'm quite opposed to chopping myself up, but it was her right. Why not? When you cry a lot," she continued, alluding to Eppie's divorce, "it's got to show."

On the infamous feud, Popo said, "She kept that chip on her shoulder for eight years. . . . She really gave me a heck of a beating and what for? For what?" On Eppie's interest in money, "Look, she needs a lot of reinforcement," on Jules, "He got tired of being Mr. Landers," and on her sister's chances of getting married again, "She's looking for a man with Jules's spark, and she ain't going to find him."

The one remark Eppie had made to Jahr a year and a half earlier about the feud and her sister starting the Dear Abby column, ("It was not all that bitter. There was a problem at first—she didn't tell me and I was surprised and disappointed—but I soon forgot about it,") Popo said she thought was "improper—indeed upsetting."

Jahr recalls that Popo's motives for the interview became readily apparent as soon as he met her. "I arrived at Popo's house and not five minutes had passed before, unasked, she was showing photos of her sister with remarks like, 'Oh, of course these are before Eppie had her face lifted.' My God, I wondered, what's going on here?"

An experienced celebrity interviewer, Jahr was surprised by Popo's unprompted outbursts. Over the next several hours Popo continued to make unflattering remarks about Eppie. Only in a few instances did she add, half-heartedly, "But that's not for the story." Yet she then repeated the same comments about her sister sometimes three and four times over more than fifteen hours of interviewing, without the caution.

"She's a smart, tough, and charming lady," notes Jahr, "a hilarious storyteller, and I like her enormously. But I realized she had to know what she was doing. She wanted the Eppie revelations to get out, at least subconsciously, while at the same time she wanted to be able to disown the deed. 'Oh, I was misquoted, I would never say such things.' It was either that," Jahr continues, "or she was out of control."

Realizing that the interview with Popo would make a wire-service story, Jahr wanted to make sure Popo understood that what she was relating was to be on the record.

"Every once in a while I'd say, 'Popo, what would you tell my five million *Journal* ladies?' I was reminding her, 'Hey gal, I love you, but we're working here and, remember, this tape machine is going.' "

But Popo persisted, continuing with references to old slights and past animosities. Naturally, some of the material, like Popo's boasting that she had pulled strings to let Eppie enroll in Eau Claire's Gray Ladies forty years earlier, was too trivial to put in the *Journal* story.

Jahr was proven correct. Highlights from his chat with Popo hit the major wires in time to give nearly every columnist returning from a Labor Day weekend a topic to write about. PR Newswire ran as its lead-in, "Abby Van Buren today revealed that she ghost-wrote many of her twin sister Ann Landers' initial advice columns in 1956 before she started her own column eighty-five days later." The same wire story continued with direct quotes that revealed Popo at her venomous best.

Syndicated columnist Laura Berman commented that Popo seemed happy "because she won the contest. She writes a nationally syndicated column like her sister, but she doesn't need a face-lift and is still married." Berman continued, "After reading this interview, solutions from either of these advice queens should have as much credibility as a lecture on ethics from Richard Nixon."

A Louisville, Kentucky, reporter suggested that Dear Abby receive counseling "after she has both her faces lifted."

Eppie, cresting above the furor created by the article, remained sequestered in her Chicago high-rise and made no public statement. Popo, on her cross-country *Best of* book trek over the next several months, was compelled to respond to her own statements.

Ultimately, Popo called Jahr and blamed him for publicly rekindling the twins' feud. On tour, during a stopover in Pennsylvania, a manifestly contrite Popo proclaimed, "The press has always played up an alleged feud, and sometimes I have been too trusting." Throughout Florida, Popo said, "Our differences have been greatly exaggerated. We get along fine," and in San Francisco, "We made up in 1964!"

Phil Donahue proved to be a match for Popo. On his television talk show, he asked her to explain why she had been so critical of her sister.

"I was quoted out of context," Popo emphasized. Members of the Donahue audience could be heard taking in a quick breath, then murmuring to one another.

"Sometimes it means you're sorry that you said what you said," Donahue quickly rejoined.

The audience laughed. Popo looked embarrassed, forced a smile, and nodded her head slightly. "With me, it often . . . it often means that," she stuttered.

Popo's explanation did not make a true believer of her twin. Furious over Popo's remarks, Eppie tried to obtain the *Journal* interview tapes. She was determined to hear the unpublished disclosures that Popo had made to Jahr. Unable to get them, Eppie instead called Popo. The tense phone call between the two women reported by a man who knows them both brought little relief for either twin.

"I'm sure you're angry and you have every right to be furious with me," said Popo. "But I've been misquoted," she protested. "Jahr got it all wrong. I didn't say any of that stuff."

"Don't give me that!" Eppie quickly replied. "I know Cliff Jahr very well. I know how careful he is, how accurate he is. Remember he interviewed me a year ago and I had no problem with that story.

"I bet you said all that stuff," Eppie continued. "In fact, his article said that you revealed a lot more. What more did you say?"

Popo denied any wrongdoing. "No, it's just not true."

Eppie hung up and wrote Popo a note: "I forgive you, sister, now forgive yourself."

Later, Eppie explained why she forgave Popo. "The alternative is to write her off. I can't do it. It's too painful. . . . I refuse to allow myself to be miserable."

Popo's children and friends didn't provide her with their usual support. Jeannie and Eddie's reaction was livid. "Mother, how could you?" they both exclaimed.

Mort, for once, chastised his wife. "If these are twin sisters," he said, "I'll take cobras."

Even Popo's syndicate head was surprised. "I'm not sure what happened either," McMeel states.

Angered but not surprised, Margo said, "Forget they are sisters. A friend wouldn't say the things she said."

Ken Howard chimed in with, "They are as theatrical as movie stars."

Jules offered to support Eppie publicly, but she talked him out of making a statement to the press.

The twins' older sisters were dumbstruck. Both Kenny and Dubbie scolded Popo, but they also blamed Eppie for starting the clamor with her comment about her sister in the first *Journal* interview. The family, closing ranks, finally rallied about both sisters and refused to talk about it.

Popo's reasons for opening up and striking out at Eppie are uncertain, probably even to herself. Clearly, for Popo, the sisterly rivalry was still an emotional topic. A man who knows both twins suggests, "Popo made a subconscious and misguided judgment that she could reach out to her sister with this sensational interview." Popo may have wanted to force some warmth into her relationship with Eppie, but initially, she accomplished the opposite. The aftermath, the reconciliation between the sisters, has perhaps buried the issue once and for all.

Because the twins hadn't completely worked out their troubles, resentments between the two hadn't been directly expressed. Popo's feelings, expressed through the *Journal* piece, finally brought the unspoken hostility out in the open. The article acted as a catalyst for communication. Eppie, forgiving her sister, more or less ter-

270 ≈

minated the conversation. It's entirely possible that both sisters will never again feel a need to speak out on the subject.

"It had to come out eventually," says Robert Stolar. "I think Eppie accepts the twin relationship emotionally. I don't know about Popo."

Eppie, confirming Stolar's assessment of her feelings, refuses to indulge in the sisterly carping. In her first full-length profile since the appearance of the *Journal* article, Eppie cut her interviewer short when the subject of Popo's unkind jabs cropped up. "I don't talk about it. There are many more interesting things to talk about. We get along fine."

When pressed with Popo's claim that she ghosted early Ann Landers columns, Eppie responded, "Everything that appears in my column is totally mine. I think ghost-writing is a fraud."

"Eppie Lederer, if she were left alone by Popo, would have been fine," Stolar continues, "because we worked at it rather closely and at length for fifteen years."

Another friend of Eppie's agrees. "Eppie has worked it through. She's a strong person for having been through so many problems."

Thirty

*I*gnoring the fallout from Popo's interview with Jahr, Eppie resumed her about-town appearances. Months before, she had cruised around Manhattan on Malcolm Forbes's yacht, *The Highlander,* and showed up at the wedding of New York Governor Hugh Carey and Chicago real estate magnate Evangeline Gouletas. Eppie wasn't going to let Popo's public statements stop her from making an appearance at the White House. A month after the August issue of the *Ladies' Home Journal* hit the stands, Eppie sat between Michael Deaver and Mort Sahl at a state dinner for Israeli Prime Minister Menachem Begin.

A few weeks later, Eppie was back in Washington, this time for Nancy Reagan's thank-you reception and White House tour for donors to the refurbishing fund. "It was an incredible renovation," remarked Eppie on the $730,000 spent on some twenty rooms in the executive mansion; "the place hasn't had a paintbrush laid on it for ten years."

Though both sisters had supported Jimmy Carter in 1976, and Eppie met him at O'Hare to show her support to news reporters and photographers alerted by Carter's advance team, only Popo supported the president again in 1980. Eppie, the arch Democrat, switched allegiances and voted for Ronald Reagan. "I met him and Nancy at the Annenbergs' "—that's Walter Annenberg, former U.S. ambassador to Great Britain, and Eppie's friend Lee. Eppie continues, "We spent a weekend together in Palm Springs. Now that was before he was elected and I told him I was a dyed-in-the-wool Democrat and could never vote for him. He took it good-naturedly, but before the election I decided the country couldn't stand another four years of Carter."

Back in stride, Eppie was lecturing again, at $10,000 per talk. Dragging her mink through the lobby of the Diplomat Hotel in Fort Lauderdale, where she was addressing a wholesale pharmaceutical convention, Eppie didn't look, act, or, by her account, feel all of sixty-three.

"Hey, lady, your coat is on the floor," yelled a hotel guest.

"That's okay, dear. It's four years old," twinkled Eppie.

Hissing, "They call this a suite?" at the sight of her hotel room, Eppie provided a reporter with a slew of opinions on everything from room service to "the horrors of sun-caused skin damage."

Before her talk, Eppie had explained many times why she hasn't attempted to change the jarring quality of her voice, with its nasal intonation and pronounced sibilance. "I seriously considered speech lessons years ago when someone asked me if I was born in this country. Several knowledgeable friends in communication advised against it. One well-known TV anchorman said, 'Your voice is very distinctive, and this can be a great asset. Let it alone.' "

In the coffee shop after her convention speech, people came up to Eppie and "tend to genuflect before her," reported the Fort Lauderdale *News*. "They kneel alongside her and lower their voices confidentially. They seek absolution and brush her cheek with their lips when they get it."

"This is rewarding to me because it lets me know I'm getting through," Eppie says about the people who read her column, people she has never ever muttered anything against, or ever attempted to belittle.

Gratified that her public still believes in her, single but dating, alone but not lonely, Eppie felt good about her life and her work.

In good health, and with everything that democracy could provide, Eppie was squeezing the best out of life. "Life for me is very good," she emphasizes. "Very good."

"I realize that I am not the common, garden-variety divorcée. I have good health. I've got my looks. I'm financially secure. There are no kids to worry about. I have good friends. I have many interesting men friends and I meet plenty of people. Many doors are open to me. I understand this."

In October 1981, Eppie appeared on a Boston-based talk show hosted by Tom Cottle, who knew her from his years at Francis Parker with Margo. Eppie, with long, shiny red nails, hair freshly coiffed, and a wrinkle-free, glowing-peach complexion, looked a lot more youthful than sixty-three while chatting about being middle-aged. "I have no intention of being middle-aged," she stated. "I have no use for age. . . . To me age means absolutely nothing. . . . I want to be ageless. I expect to get older, but I don't expect to get old.

"I don't want to know from arthritis, I don't want to know from any kind of physical disabilities," she continued, nodding and grinning. "I am not programmed for arthritis, I am not programmed for boredom. I don't program myself for hostility, for anger. I don't want to have anything to do with these, what I consider, negative things. . . . I am energetic. I feel young. I feel well. I feel good. These are things that generally go along with being youthful."

In addition to keeping "three weeks ahead of the gray as long as the band plays," staying youthful means to Eppie that she doesn't dwell in the past, especially on former hurts and bad experiences. She believes the best years of her life are yet to come. "To me the present is the best. And there will be other best moments to come."

At the same time, Eppie tells Cottle that she hasn't ever been let down, by anyone, not even by Jules when he asked her for a divorce. She says she refused to let it "knock me out, or to flatten me. . . . I'm not in that self-pity camp. I don't hang out with divorced women who spend their whole afternoon knocking the ex-husband, yelling about the other woman, saying, 'Argh, look what happened to me after all I did for him.' "

So willing is Eppie to smooth out the curves in her life that she can look back and express some lingering affection for the man who left her after thirty-six years of marriage. "I thought, gee, he was a good guy. He was adorable. He was great. He was good to me. He was loving, he was affectionate, he was all the good things. I had no complaints. It was good."

When her marriage was over, Eppie says she was able not only to deal with it but also to grow from it. "I had a choice, I could either collapse and go to pieces, or I could say this is going to make me stronger, because I believe for everything that happens that may seem at that moment like a catastrophe or a tragedy, you can turn it around and make it work for you. . . . It was an experience from which I've learned."

For Eppie, that's not just talk-show-circuit patter. The astounding equanimity she summons forth isn't on hold until she's in front of an audience. Certainly, however, the passage of seven years had blunted some of the sting of her divorce. The retelling of her story must be easier for her after she's lived through it and had the time to reflect on it. Yet there's always the suspicion that there's much more she's *not* telling.

Eppie knows the one thing that underpins her influence, her public trust, her popularity, the fame and the fanfare is her credibility. She says, "Being true to myself. Saying what I feel. Being upfront about what I am" are what's important to her. To protect that public trust, to keep people believing in her and her advice, Eppie defends her integrity at all costs. In Eppie's handling of her column, however, lurked strains on her equanimity and credibility.

Barbara Sandken, a conscientious part-time reporter for the Pontiac (Illinois) *Daily Leader*, was culling through old Ann Landers columns for the daily "Remember" feature. Though she occasionally sensed she'd already read a particular letter, it wasn't until late April 1982 when one phrase in a letter made her realize she'd seen it only days before in a recent column. After comparing other columns over a span of fifteen years, she was ready to reveal her suspicions to the *Leader* management.

"I was out of town on business the day Mrs. Sandken brought her findings to the attention of our managing editor," says James Pearre, the assistant publisher of the *Leader*. "It was his decision to call in the AP because he felt we might not have the resources to conduct the necessary research."

Because the *Leader* is a small-circulation daily, it lacked the means to verify Sandken's findings. The Associated Press, with access to extensive microfilm files, could evaluate the accuracy of Sandken's discovery, and the extent to which Eppie had indulged in reprinting Ann Landers columns without informing her readers, her syndicate, or her subscribing newspapers. AP and the *Leader* found that thirty-three letters published in 1981 and 1982 alone were copied from 1963 columns, with only a few superficial changes.

Pearre knew he was privy to a serious breach of ethics. Newspapers do not pay as much as $1,000 a month or more for fresh features to receive twenty-year-old reprints. If Eppie had chosen to rerun old material without labeling it as such, the misrepresentation carried with it overtones of deceit.

In order to make certain he wasn't overlooking a legitimate explanation for her actions, Pearre called the Ann Landers office to request an interview. Without divulging his reason for calling, Pearre casually reminded Kathie Mitchell, Eppie's top assistant, that his paper had subscribed to Ann Landers for twenty-four years.

"Mrs. Lederer is out of town this week," Mitchell told him. "We will get back to you next week."

When no return call came from either Mitchell or Eppie, Pearre called back. Once more he was given a vague promise. "Mrs. Lederer is out of town. Call back Monday morning."

Pearre, along with James Litke of the AP bureau in Chicago, decided that it was time to force the issue. Pearre flew to Chicago to meet with Litke, and the two men called the Landers office early Monday. Pearre repeated his request for a meeting with Eppie, but this time he specified that he wanted it to be that morning.

≈ 277

Mitchell admitted that her employer was at home, but said that the columnist "never consents to morning interviews ever," and that Eppie forbade her staff to call her before 10:00 A.M.

"By this point," says Pearre, "we were pressing, saying it was rather urgent to see her that day."

A few minutes past 10:00 A.M., an apologetic Mitchell phoned Pearre. Eppie was sending her regrets: She was going out of town again and had no time for an interview that day or that week. In fact, Mitchell added, it would be very difficult to make time for a personal interview at all.

Pearre then told Mitchell why he was in Chicago. He said he had proof that Eppie was "fortifying her column over the past year with occasional letters she had selected and slightly rewritten from columns published fifteen years ago."

"Well, that's very interesting," Mitchell calmly responded, indicating she'd mention the matter to Eppie.

Within minutes Pearre had a return phone call, this time not from Mitchell but from Eppie. She told Pearre she could explain why she reused old material and invited Pearre and Litke to her apartment.

Forty-five minutes later, an immaculately groomed Eppie was offering coffee and soft drinks to Pearre and Litke in the living room of her spacious apartment. How long had the *Leader* carried her column? she asked. Twenty-four years, Pearre told her. "Well, I've been at this twenty-six years now," Eppie remarked, saying she was proud of the fact that she writes the column herself, "every word" of it.

Presented with evidence of her recycled columns, Eppie explained that she had reprinted a few worthy letters and responses she had come across while reviewing material for the Dial Ann Landers project for Illinois Bell she had started in 1981. She saw nothing wrong with the practice, she asserted, of superficially altering the letters and answers and turning them in as new.

Pearre, aware that on some days all three letters in her column were repeats, suspected that much of her work was not fresh. He asked Eppie what proportion of her daily work was not original.

"My credibility is very important," Eppie reminded the two men, ignoring many of their questions. "I'm afraid that what you're suggesting here is that I'm doing something that is not honorable."

Crossing the thick beige pile carpet to her study to show the men bundles of letters she was sorting through for column material, Eppie hinted that the *Leader* and AP should keep silent about their discovery. But she stopped short of actually asking the two men not to announce their findings. Readers might misinterpret the news reports, Eppie implied several times. Tabloids like the *National Enquirer* or the *Star* would likely distort the story, she said.

Eppie suddenly turned to Litke and asked him for the name of his boss at AP. "We were both taken aback at her question," says Pearre. Although Litke supplied the name, Eppie didn't call, apparently realizing that an attempt to intercede might cause further damage.

Appearing disoriented and confused, Eppie asked Pearre to explain again how he had uncovered the rerun columns. Listening closely to his account, Eppie led the two men to her bedroom and one of her clothes closets, where, in a storage habit that's a throwback to her Sioux City days, she began searching for shoeboxes of old mail.

"She stooped over and rummaged through the closet recesses to retrieve more bundles of letters," recalls Pearre. "These were the only letters she has saved over the years, she told us. They are letters she received in 1975 consoling and supporting her at the time of her divorce."

Puzzled by her actions, Pearre and Litke realized that the interview was over. As the men left her apartment, Eppie pressed her unlisted phone number into Pearre's hand. "Call me if you have any more questions," she implored. "Only my close friends have this number."

Because Eppie's explanations were flimsy and her reasons for the recycling of letters from her readers implausible, AP and the *Leader* released the story. ANN LANDERS MISLEADING HER READERS became a front-page headline across the country. Television and radio stations interrupted their programming to announce that Ann

Landers was involved in a scandal. That a small-town newspaper had taken on one of the nation's top personalities added a delightful hook to the story. Soon Barbara Sandken, an Illinois farm wife, was being interviewed by ABC, CBS, and WGN television for their nightly newscasts.

"I'm appalled at the ruckus this has raised," charged Eppie, saying the issue of recycled columns was a "tempest in a teacup" and "has been blown out of proportion." Repeating letters, she said, enabled her to present valuable information her readers may have missed the first time.

Considering that one of the recycled letters that tipped off the *Leader* concerned a woman who washed bananas after peeling them to ensure their cleanliness, Eppie's claim that her advice was worthy of repetition doesn't quite hold up.

Eppie didn't acknowledge the chronology of her repeats. The match between the original and recycled letters was in exact sequence, indicating that Eppie plowed through a stack of old columns in the order of their initial publication. In fact, a letter that first appeared on February 22, 1967, was reprinted on that same date in 1982.

"I was not trying to put anything over on anyone," Eppie protested. Yet she had no consistent explanation as to why she didn't label her columns as previously printed material. She attempted to explain the variations by saying she changed the readers' names to protect their anonymity. Reporters quickly countered by pointing out that even the original column did not carry the writer's name.

Eppie then offered another explanation. She altered the letters, she said, "for my own amusement." Soon, she offered a third explanation. "The changes were not deliberate. I sometimes rewrite a column three times and sometimes I do it too quickly." Eppie, finally, was saying she had made a mistake.

"I wasn't trying to slip in something as new as some wackos make out," she said, underscoring her contempt for her critics. "If I had wanted to do that, I would have done a much better job of disguising the columns.

"I was stupid to do this. It would have been so simple to do it and put in a statement that this material appeared at such and such time. Who would care? The fact that I didn't do it was stupid."

Executives at Field's newspaper syndicate were asked about Eppie's warmed-over columns. President Steve Jehorek said, "I've never had any knowledge of it whatsoever." Then he seemed to contradict himself. "And Ann Landers always denied it."

Jehorek excused the syndicate's editorial laxity by saying that an experienced columnist like Ann Landers was given a "freer hand" than other writers. She should have labeled her material as a repeat, said her boss, but he downplayed the criticism by saying, "It's a minor transgression."

Summoning a flock of decoys, Eppie tried to take the heat off herself and force the spotlight on others. Daughter Margo tried to help by stating mysteriously, "There were some shady politics involved." Eppie was more specific. "It boils down to a television hatchet job," she claimed, overlooking that the disclosure was made public by one of her own subscribing newspapers. "Television has been vicious," she repeated. Professing her honesty through false modesty, Eppie was saying, "Some people may say I'm dim-witted, but I'm not crooked."

Finally, the ruckus was blamed on activist groups identified with conservative causes. The people who want newspapers to drop Ann Landers because of the recycling, asserted Eppie, are members of the pro-gun lobby and anti-abortion forces.

Criticism wasn't limited to single-issue groups. One newspaper editor scorned Eppie's defense that she had no formal journalism training and wasn't aware she was committing an impropriety. "At age sixty-three, and after twenty-six years in the newspaper business, such 'Who, me?' innocence rings a bit hollow," insisted the editor.

"If Miss Landers refuses to see the moral principle involved here, let us come down to street level and put it as charitably as we know how: Editors are loath to pay twice for material they paid for once."

News editors across the country agreed that a reporter who pulled such a recycling stunt would be summarily dismissed. Even the editor of Eppie's hometown newspaper, the *Sioux City Journal,* stated, "If she worked on my staff, I'd fire her."

"I'm sure anyone who writes an advice column does this sort of thing," said Eppie, perhaps expecting Popo to confess that she too, had recycled columns.

If sisterly support was what Eppie was seeking, she must have been sorely disappointed by Popo's bland, for-the-record comment to the press. "Oh dear, that's incredible. I'm sorry about that. She's always been the soul of integrity as far as I'm concerned."

Popo's public championing of her twin was tepid, but Eppie claimed that Popo gave her strong support. "She thought what they are doing to me is terrible," said Eppie. "She said she was with me all the way."

Not surprisingly, everyone wanted to know whether Dear Abby recycled her letters too. "If Abby reruns items, they are clearly labeled as such," affirmed Popo's assistant Katie Beal.

Popo's public play of innocence over her twin's predicament backfired eight days later, after the Universal Press Syndicate staunchly claimed that any rerun Dear Abby letters are clearly identified. The end of the syndicate press release, however, disclosed that some letters were run a second time, "without necessarily identifying every one."

The *Cherokee Daily Times,* a small-circulation Idaho paper, revealed that Dear Abby makes extensive use of recycled, unlabeled columns. Popo was quick to respond, "I usually, but not always, identify them as reruns."

"Abby had not done what Ann Landers has done," intoned Universal Press Syndicate, loyally defending its star columnist. Popo, through her syndicate, issued a statement saying she labeled reprints, except for "special holiday subjects or special subjects, but henceforth there will be no exceptions."

"*Et tu,* Abby?" jibed the press, viewing the twins' transgressions as identical. Popo's silence during her sister's difficulties earned her the disdain of most editors. "Couldn't you at least have set the record straight when Ann had her troubles?" asked one editor.

Popo's niece Margo pointed out, "Why it didn't occur to her when this started with my mother that they would be looking at her next, I'm not sure."

"As soon as this thing with Eppie surfaced," counters John McMeel, head of Universal Press, "naturally they looked at Abby. There are classic columns that you just go ahead and rerun," he insists. " 'From now on, let's identify it as a reprint,' " he remembers suggesting to his star columnist. "From that point forward, even though they're classic columns, we put 'reprinted at this time.' "

"I talked to Abby this morning, and she had been doing the same thing I was," said an almost giddy Eppie, feeling partially vindicated. "I just hope her readers and editors and publishers will give her as much support as mine have given me."

Nearly a dozen editors cancelled their Dear Abby and Ann Landers contracts, only to reinstate them when a small but vocal number of readers howled in protest. Every one of the cancellations was rescinded. In fact, Eppie claimed that she acquired a new subscribing paper in Idaho.

If Eppie and Popo learned anything from the recycling uproar, it's that having one of the nation's more loyal reading audiences doesn't mean a columnist, even an advice columnist imparting specialized information, can rest on past successes. With the enormous amount of mail Eppie and Popo receive, it's inconceivable why they would ever need to reprint any letter. Perhaps it's as some editors have suggested, that the problem was not a lack of material, but "obviously was lack of time and those kinds of pressures. . . ."

Although publishers were outraged that women paid an estimated million dollars a year each resorted to copying old columns, they admitted that they were obliged to retain the advice columns, against their professional judgment. Ann Landers and Dear Abby are undisputably among the nation's most popular newspaper features. Concedes one editor, "Ann Landers and Dear Abby have their readers pegged."

Eppie may have conquered her critics and walked right through her professional crisis virtually unscathed, but she still had to reckon with a few disenchanted fans and the tenacity of Jim Pearre.

Pearre was soon receiving letters from readers around the country charging Ann Landers with rerunning material for more than twenty years, not just an eighteen-month period. Some of the readers enclosed clippings to prove their accusations. Investigating the charges, the *Leader* found that a significant portion of the Ann Landers columns, beginning in the early sixties, was not original material.

Pearre's research, which has never been publicly released, indicates that many of the Ann Landers columns have been recycled for two decades, and there have been at least half a dozen letters that have seen print on three different dates.

Pearre says that Eppie "had not been entirely candid and forthright with us." He was determined to see her held accountable for her statements. A letter detailing the paper's newest findings was sent to Eppie. Contact your subscribing publishers, he suggested, and tell them the full truth.

After a three-week silence, Pearre dialed the unlisted phone number Eppie had given him at their initial meeting.

When Eppie answered, Pearre identified himself. There was a pause at the other end of the line. Then Eppie said angrily, "This number on which you called me is a number I give out only to my close friends. I no longer consider you a friend, and I would appreciate it very much if you never again used this number." With that, Eppie hung up.

Thirty-One

onservative chic didn't suit Popo. Even if Eppie had decided to buddy up to the Reagan administration, hoping perhaps to influence its policy on social programs, Popo didn't want any part of it. What she saw was a claque of politicos hell-bent on axing essential social services while a coterie of that inner elite trumpeted its own affluence. Popo, if she so desired, would take her baby vegetables, veal chop, and raspberry tartlet apart from the circle of power-hungry parvenus who figured that, somehow, a few crumbs might fall to the poor, the homeless, and the truly needy.

Popo used her column to tell her readers, "I hope you support the party that best takes care of its poor and elderly." In a June 1982 interview she cited government cuts in social programs as the worst problem in America today.

"It's a tragedy," she was saying. "I used to be able to refer people to their Legal Aid Society—many have closed down. What's the poor person to do? Lord knows we need mental health clinics . . . education, medicine, programs for the elderly, the poor.

"I'd say vote in an administration that will be more caring, that will take care of its people."

Back on her soapbox, Popo was preaching consideration and kindness and working to encourage financial assistance from any source, government, private, or corporate. "Mort and Abby do so much for philanthropy that's never mentioned," says John Mc-Meel. "I know it from our association and through a third party. They never talk about it, but Mort and Abby's generosity is there."

Social responsibility extended to other aspects of family affairs. Under son Eddie's stewardship, the Phillipses' liquor company was spending considerable sums on newspaper and radio advertising advocating the common-sense use of alcohol, with the message directed especially at teenagers.

"I've gotten a lot of praise from them," says Eddie about his parents' reaction to the public service campaign. "My mother applauds me, saying I am showing a correct social approach to business. She occupies a dual position, that of a mother, and that of a confidante and close friend."

Eddie, in early 1983, was confiding in his mother that his marriage of eleven years to Dee-Dee was failing. This was a shock to Popo because daughter Jeannie and Luke McKissack were seeking a quiet divorce in Los Angeles. Jeannie's childless marriage ended amicably, and Popo still holds her daughter's former husband in high esteem. However, Eddie and Dee-Dee's break-up made headlines from the moment papers were filed in Minneapolis.

Hennepin County family court hearings dragged on as Dee-Dee maintained that the alimony and financial assets Eddie was willing to settle on her were inadequate for her needs. "The amount of money is contested, highly contested," stated her Minneapolis lawyer, Edward Winer.

Dee-Dee was demanding a monthly allowance of $19,000—that's $228,000 a year—as well as a share of the couples' combined assets. "I've become accustomed to a high standard of living since I married Eddie," explained Dee-Dee.

Playing hardball, Dee-Dee sought the counsel of Hollywood "palimony" attorney Marvin Mitchelson, who had gained notoriety in representing Michelle Triola Marvin in her suit against actor Lee Marvin and whose roster of clients included Bianca Jagger and the wives of Marlon Brando and Peter Pulitzer. In addition to the yearly quarter-million-dollar allowance, Mitchelson announced that Dee-Dee should be awarded half the couple's assets, which he conservatively estimated at $10 million. "I think it's much more," he speculated.

What disturbed Dee-Dee during the prolonged hearings was her mother-in-law's attitude toward her grandsons. Shortly after the battle over money began, Popo ended communication with Dee-Dee's children. Dee-Dee says she still felt maternal toward Eddie despite the divorce proceedings, and was at a loss to explain Popo's atypical grandmotherly behavior. Once the suit was settled, and Eddie saw to it that he would be with his sons, Popo no longer masked her concern for her grandchildren.

The judge eventually reduced Dee-Dee's request to $9,000 of temporary monthly support, terming the interim settlement "what the court would like to believe is a dose of reality." Property settlement was left to negotiation.

"My client is pleased about it," reported Mitchelson.

Pleased too, was Popo, clucking about her grandsons and advising Eddie on single parenting. Eddie, unpretentious and easygoing, inherited his parent's social conscience and is well thought of in Minneapolis. "Eddie is very community minded, just a wonderful fellow," says Rabbi Max Shapiro of Temple Israel, where Eddie's a member. Eddie's lead in AMICUS, a group of civic leaders who counsel ex-convicts and help them find jobs, has brought the Phillips family much praise.

Rabbi Shapiro recalls, "Mort and Popo attended the bar mitzvahs of their grandsons," and the party afterward was hardly elaborate. "Just the normal kind," says the rabbi. "We don't have spectacular parties here."

The spectacular parties Popo was attending were taking place elsewhere. Getting ready for a round of parties and charity benefits for the fall season in 1982, Popo was encouraged by daughter Jeannie to change her hairstyle. As they were going out to dinner one evening, says Popo, "My hair was a mess. So I tucked my hair under a short, close-fitting wig."

"Mother, you're a knockout," said Jeannie. "You look 20 years younger."

Cloyd Koop admits he panicked when Popo announced that she wanted a new look.

"I saw Lana Turner when she appeared on 'Falcon Crest' and liked her hair," says Popo. "She wrote me the dearest letter giving me the name and telephone number of her stylist."

Koop cut Popo's hair with instructions from Lana's stylist. Popo still showed as much forehead with the new style, but her hair was cropped closer on the sides and on top, and the flip was gone. Apparently Popo wasn't completely satisfied with the new hairdo for she soon went back to her former look, updated for the eighties with less rise and a subtler side sweep.

On the board of the United World Colleges, along with Armand Hammer, Popo showed up at a Palm Beach dinner in honor of the Prince and Princess of Wales. Prince Charles had assumed the title of international president of the UWC upon the death of his great-uncle Lord Mountbatten. Calling the Prince of Wales "the epitome of a gentleman, but more important, a gentle man," Popo then followed Prince Charles to the dedication ceremony for the newest campus of the UWC in Montezuma, New Mexico, where during dinner she met up with her close friends Cary and Barbara Grant.

The goal of the UWC is fostering world peace. It's an objective that both Popo and Eppie have made a commitment to, but in different ways. Eppie, for her part, has taken a more activist role in working toward that goal, including advocating nuclear disarmament.

Ground Zero, an anti-nuclear proliferation group, was planning nationwide rallies in April 1982. Local leaders in Chicago didn't alone have the influence to convince Eppie to join the rally, but one organizer was a trustee of Notre Dame. Because the university's president, Father Hesburgh, is strongly opposed to nuclear weapons and was willing to speak at the Ground Zero rally, it was an easy task enlisting Eppie's assistance.

At the rally, Eppie limited her involvement to a five-minute introduction of Hesburgh. Ground Zero organizers were aware that Eppie's participation was based on friendship, not shared ideology. Hesburgh remembers, "We were in Chicago and I gave a talk and she came to it. Then I gave a very strong anti-nuclear talk to the Council on Foreign Relations and she came to that. Two or three times she came to my talks.

"I told her, in my judgment, it's the number-one primordial moral problem facing humanity. If we don't solve this problem, we can forget the rest of them because there will be no human beings and no human problems."

From then on, Eppie was convinced. She chose to run a letter detailing a reader's fear of nuclear war. "You are more than an advice columnist," stated the letter writer. "You mold public opinion. People believe in you. For the love of mankind and its survival, please address yourself to this issue."

In her response, Eppie echoed the Ground Zero handouts and urged her readers to write President Reagan. It was clear to rally organizers that within a month's time, Eppie had moved from being uninformed to being a leading spokesperson for the anti-nuclear cause.

According to the White House Press Office, the Ann Landers column persuaded 100,000 writers to respond to the May 1982 column. Enough letters were received to prompt a reply from President Reagan that Eppie printed in her column.

"Ann," the personal reply began, "we have tried many times since World War II to persuade the Russians to join us in reducing or even eliminating nuclear weapons, with little success. Perhaps instead of sending your copies to me, your readers should send copies of your column to Soviet President Leonid Brezhnev."

As a follow-up, Eppie printed a column describing the horrors of nuclear war, saying she hoped the Soviet leader would get to read a copy of the column. Quick thinking on Eppie's part made it possible. She arranged for an unnamed "industrialist" to deliver the column. The industrialist was none other than Popo's fellow director on the UWC board, Armand Hammer.

* * *

"Because it's a good story, and it's *my* story," says Margo, defending the spring 1982 publication of her hybrid and faintly revisionist biography/autobiography, *Eppie, The Story of Ann Landers.* "There were some things she would have preferred that I left out, but for the most part, she thought it was fair."

For the record, Eppie publicized her daughter's book by devoting her column to it. "I felt it was a thoroughly honest account of Margo's struggle with the events in my life that affected her deeply," she said. "There are parts of *Eppie* I would have deleted if I had anything to say about it.

"I felt that she was a bit too hard on my sister, and that she went too far and revealed too much about my divorce from Jules Lederer."

In her book, which sometimes is more about Margo than about her mother, Margo describes her aunt's behavior to her "not at all like warfare . . . more like being nibbled to death by ducks." Throughout her narrative she takes swipes at Popo whenever she can. Conveniently, Margo was finishing the book when Popo's *Ladies' Home Journal* interview came out. For Margo, her aunt's tactless remarks only confirmed what she'd been remembering all along.

"She handed me the last chapter," says Margo. "We never got along. . . . I have no wish to be unkind to Popo, but she's not a favorite aunt."

Margo divulged that her father began drinking heavily when his career at Budget was failing, and that the reason for her estrangement from him is not the divorce, but that he's interested only in money. She shrugged off his anger over her revelations, saying, "I've heard he's not pleased about the book."

Her public posture aside, friends say that privately, Eppie wasn't so pleased with *Eppie* either.

"There's some strain there because of the book," says a friend. "Margo used up Eppie's material and damn it, her daughter monkeyed around with it."

But publicly, what's done is done, Eppie seemed to be saying, and no matter how self-serving on Margo's part the gesture seemed, she was still her daughter.

"That's part of her strength of will, the no-comment part," says Margo. She doesn't "step into my life, with both hands and feet—buy my clothes, plan my menus, raise my children. I was quite touched by her answer."

It was the only answer Eppie was willing or could bring herself to give. And the end-of-her-column publicity for her daughter's book speaks more of a mother's unconditional love than of her unqualified approval.

"Parts of *Eppie* are hilarious," Eppie says, "but I'm certain there were tears in the ink when she wrote some of it—and when a daughter weeps, so does her mother. What more can I say?"

The twins celebrated their sixty-fifth birthday on July 4, 1983, a continent apart. Popo had just returned from Europe and spent the day with Mort and family and a few close friends in Beverly Hills.

"Becoming sixty-five doesn't make any difference to me," said Popo. "I feel terrific. Reaching sixty-five is just like turning fifty-five or sixty. I hope I turn a few more. You are as young as you look, as young as you feel."

Eppie flew from Chicago to the east coast to be with Mary Lasker at her Greenwich, Connecticut, home. Eppie had spent her past eight birthdays since her divorce from Jules in 1975 with Lasker. Poolside, with a handful of friends, Eppie wouldn't disclose the guest list, saying, "I wouldn't want to create any hard feelings in dear friends who were not included."

No doubt one of the guests was Warren Bennis, a former college president now teaching at the University of Southern California. Though she had met him twenty years before while married to Jules, it wasn't until they got together again, alone, that romance bloomed. "Meeting him, it was as if I were meeting him for the first time," says Eppie.

"It's wonderful to have someone in your life. That's enhancing. Fascinating. He's very bright. Very interesting. Wonderful company. I try to keep everything in its place. . . . For my time of life, this arrangement is just lovely."

The next evening Eppie was off to Manhattan for a birthday dinner hosted by her producer friend Morton Gottlieb in the Ambassador Grill of the United Nations Plaza Hotel.

"Eppie must be in love, she looks so radiant," beamed Gottlieb.

"I'm sixty-five, why lie?" she announced to all present. "It's a source of embarrassment to me that people can never forget the day. Barbara Walters always sends me something, and I don't even know when hers is."

Asked if she were "besieged by advice seekers at dinner parties," Eppie answered, "In the powder room, that's when I get the questions." Sure enough, when Eppie headed for the ladies' room after dessert, she was trailed by several of the female guests.

A month after the twins' birthday, and six years since they'd all been there together, all four of the Friedman sisters descended on Sioux City for a cousin's wedding. "The four of us are here together, and we're having great fun," said Popo. "Of course my twin and I get together the most, either in Los Angeles or Chicago. We criss-cross a lot."

Actually, Popo also sees a lot of Dubbie, the middle sister, because she has a house in Palm Springs. Mort's parents, Jay and Rose Phillips, spend the winter at their Palm Springs home beginning December 15, and Popo and Mort go there often to visit.

Visiting friends Walter and Helen Cronkite on Martha's Vineyard, and a frequent guest of Art and Ann Buchwald's at their retreat on that island off Cape Cod, Eppie admitted that her conception of how to take time off had changed. "I used to go to Paris or Rome or London. Now I can go anywhere I want to, but I have no interest in going to Vienna or Madrid," Eppie was saying. "I'd go to a place like Martha's Vineyard, someplace quiet where I could go barefoot, and I wouldn't have to dress up or get my hair fixed."

In the eighties, Eppie and Popo were making more time for family and friends, visiting Sioux City occasionally, and being more selective about their public appearances. As a form of stress management, they both were saying that their lives had become much easier once they'd learned how to say "No." Yet talk of retirement was being dismissed by Popo, who said, "Mother Confessors don't retire, they just turn up the volume on their hearing aids.

"I'd like to continue as I am, being blessed with good health so that I can do what I'm doing. I don't look to the future too much. I make every day count. I do as much as I can with the time on hand."

Yet Popo may be thinking of turning the column over to Jeannie some time in the future. Muses John McMeel, "It would be great, like mother, like daughter. Those genes, I'm sure they're there. They are very close, and I know they want to be involved in one way or another together. They have some kind of professional relationship but I'm not privy to what type. . . . It would be terrific for newspaper subscribers."

Eppie says, "Two things that are irreplaceable are time and energy. When they're gone they are gone." But Eppie still has time and energy in good measure. She echoes Popo, saying she can't ever imagine retiring, "I can't imagine why I would. People usually retire to do what they really want to do and I'm already doing that."

Eppie sparkled at the champagne reception held in her honor in the ornate twentieth-floor ballroom at Chicago's wedding-cake white, lacey landmark, the Tribune Tower. "It's a joy to be here. It's a right decision for me, something I did with a full heart," proclaimed Eppie about switching her column from the *Chicago Sun-Times* to its in-town rival, the *Tribune*. Eppie had good reason to bubble. The February 1987 sale of her News America Syndicate to King Features freed her from her restrictive contract. Finally able to negotiate a new contract elsewhere, she worked out a deal with the Los Angeles Times Syndicate and Creators Syndicate under which she, just like sister Popo, will own all rights to her own work.

There's no mistaking Eppie's devotion to her work, or her humility, but at the same time, she enjoys being the celebrated columnist Ann Landers. She confesses that one of her fears is of stepping off a plane and finding no one in the terminal to greet her. Restaurant owners on Chicago's North Side note that Eppie likes entering quietly, and then, when seated, smiling and glancing around at the other diners. "She loves to be recognized," says one of the restaurant owners.

On a nonstop flight from Los Angeles to Washington's Dulles airport, men go up to her and ask her to autograph their boarding passes.

"Are you Abby or . . .?"

"Ann!" declares Eppie, delighted to be recognized but miffed at still being confused with her twin. When the plane lands, the men are back at her side, asking if they can help her with her luggage.

In Beverly Hills, Popo avoids tourists as much as she can. "Popo doesn't want to be recognized by those yahoos from Ohio looking at the homes of the stars," says a friend.

When Eppie visits, Popo sometimes gets irritated when they go out together. Popo puts on a big hat and dark glasses, sometimes will wear a wig, and avoids eye contact with stargazers and tourists. When Popo notices that Eppie is no longer at her side she need only turn around to see Eppie mesmerizing out-of-towners with her Ann Landers act.

Friends say Popo's not comfortable going out all the time as a celebrity. She guards her privacy. Because Mort's away a lot, Popo often finds she needs an escort when she does go out. But she doesn't seek the company of other celebrities. Many of her escorts are attractive, younger unattached men who enjoy her sense of humor and her notoriety.

"It isn't as if I'm trying to impress anyone. A person in my position has got to meet a few people," says Popo. "But you must appreciate that most of the neatest people I know you never heard of."

At parties in people's homes Popo sometimes becomes a traveling mother confessor. "She quietly and privately takes each guest aside to root out problems and discuss them. She isn't pushy about it, but very sincere and trying to be helpful," says a close friend.

294 ≈

Zeroing in on where they believe they can do the most good, the twins continue their appeals for funding for mental health and medical research, knowing full well that politically, the fight is mainly a battle over dollars. As early as 1983 both women tackled AIDS when research on the illness was still in its infancy. Even though Eppie is more critical of the homosexual lifestyle, she, like her sister, refused to see AIDS as solely a gay disease, finding the sentiment that homosexuals had somehow collaborated in contracting it truly offensive.

Popo made AIDS her primary target for worry, counseling caution and warning about the social consequences and emotional impact of irrational fear. Eppie, active trustee or advisory board member of the Harvard Medical School, National Cancer Institute, Menninger Foundation, and Mayo Clinic, took a decidedly more academic approach, citing statistics, describing symptoms, and finally, pleading for compassion for those afflicted with the disease.

"It's a very frightening disease," says Eppie. "It's a horrible disease. In addition to having the disease, people shouldn't be ostracized. It should not be a moral issue. It should be a health issue."

One of the things Popo is proudest of is "making people aware of The Living Will—urging that no heroic measures be utilized to keep them alive when there is no hope of recovery." In early 1984 she appeared before the House and Senate to support "living will" legislation that would make signing the document legally binding. "Now between 8 and 10 million people in this country have signed it," she said of the document she began writing about in 1959.

The pattern repeats itself. When more than a year later Popo printed a letter from the actor Kirk Douglas railing about the sad state of care for the elderly, she received 15,000 letters in response. Nursing-home abuse became a big issue, and Popo insisted, "The answer does lie in funding nursing homes. . . . It can be improved."

Earlier in 1986, sister Eppie had caused a similar stir on Capitol Hill when she printed a column on unfit medical practitioners. Senator John Glenn, responding to the column, wrote saying that doctors and others deprived of medical licenses in one state simply move to another state, and he introduced legislation to keep track of unfit medical professionals. According to a Senate staffer, the proposal gained momentum only after Eppie took up the issue in her column.

While their positions on many issues are identical, and they may both support the same nationally recognized groups, such as the National Cancer Institute, the twin columnists do not endorse the same struggling self-help groups. If Ann Landers recognizes a new group in her column, Dear Abby will not follow suit. And vice versa.

The twins' resolve not to retire is dictated by their continuing usefulness. "My only worry is one that many older people have. It's the fear of falling out of touch. In my line of work, that would be disastrous," says Eppie.

"Nothing is forever," agrees Popo, "but I guess I will go on as long as I'm able. And if I'm not able, I'm sure someone will tell me, 'Hey, get off the stage. You've had it, sister.' "

More than thirty years of advice giving is long enough for any mortal. Being the subject of public scrutiny, both personally and professionally, while taking on the task of counseling others is in many ways an unenviable lot. But both Eppie and Popo possess a natural endurance, an improbable combination of the uncannily perceptive and the comfortingly practical that lingers long after the klieg light moves on.

"It's a great privilege for me to introduce one of the most famous Americans who has had a real long run of stardom," began Popo's introduction by Charles Z. Wick, head of the United States Information Agency, before a gathering of eighteen foreign journalists representing as many foreign countries at the Foreign Press Center in Los Angeles in late July 1985, "probably one of the best-known people in America and also in many parts of the world."

On May 30, 1986, at a gala black-tie dinner in honor of Popo's thirty years of advice giving, Erma Bombeck began her tribute to Popo, "There is a lot to admire about her. She's a professional, she makes deadlines, and she is one of a handful of human beings who roam this earth who have the patience, time, and compassion just to listen. That indeed is very rare."

Twin Eppie chose not to be present to share in the tribute to Popo and the benefit for the Los Angeles Suicide Prevention Center. Refusing to acknowledge each other's professional success is an accommodation the sisters worked out long ago. Stellar attendees among the 750 included the Cary Grants, Henry Winkler, Rhonda Fleming and Ted Mann, Donald O'Connor, and Charles Nelson Reilly. Following the conga line, a Dear Abby Delight of heart-shaped chocolate, and entertainment by Marvin Hamlisch, a wide range of friends, including June Allyson and Dr. Judd Marmor, paraded to the lectern to praise Popo.

Back at their seats, guests were thumbing through a sixty-page program of tribute. "Dear Abby," chum Bombeck wrote, "I took your crummy advice. I am in hock for a new dress, touched up roots, and three estrogen jokes for this dinner. It's a good thing I love you."

Echoing as many as thirty newspaper editors and publishers who wrote thanking a special lady for their fruitful and happy association, Charles Kilpatrick of the San Antonio Express-News Corporation reminisced, "I remember my first contact with Abby almost a quarter-century ago as if it were yesterday." Telling of his decision as a twenty-seven-year-old editor to acquire Dear Abby from a competing, larger-circulation daily and Popo's phone call upon finding out, "She presented me with her views in terms of conviction that I had not heard since the day at Parris Island when my Marine drill sergeant noticed my bootlace had come loose in the middle of a parade.

"She peppered me with more promotional ideas than an aggressive beer distributor would have all summer. . . . If all our columnists wrote so wisely and understood the value of salesmanship so well, it wouldn't have taken me nearly so long to wrest the circulation from my competitor."

Rising amid the unrestrained bonhomie, Popo, in a beaded, pale-blue cocktail sheath with big shoulders and pouf sleeves and matching high heels, gazed out over her loyal following and thanked them for their devotion, their kindness, and their unguarded and sentimental appreciation.

"The lady who for thirty years has been solving people's problems has a few of her own. How can I thank my friend Erma Bombeck whom I called four months ago to be emcee," said Popo, singling out her long-time buddy. And last but not least, "Morton Phillips, my husband, lover, and live-in editor who believed in me, guided me and pushed me, but best of all loved me for nearly fifty years." Having mentioned many many dear friends, Popo concluded, "Believe me to be deeply grateful."

Being one of the world's best listeners is its own reward, says Popo, who can't recount the times someone's written back telling her how she's wrought a positive change in their life. "The personal rewards are enormous, beyond price, beyond any small fame I might have achieved. Every day I get letters from people who say, 'You changed my life. Thank you.' "

Popo modestly admits, "I have liberated a lot of people, and I feel very good about that. . . . You can't turn back the clock no matter how many people would like you to do that.

"I think we've made great strides in human dignity and in understanding people who are unlike ourselves, and I will do all I can, until my typewriter falls apart, to make progress, to be even more liberal. To be liberal is to be willing to listen to a great number of people, not to be constricted by somebody else's view of what is morally right and what is morally wrong."

"Givers get the most," says Eppie, explaining what has kept her motivated to provide the best advice she can, day in, day out, for more than three decades. There are some readers she's communicated with for most of those years, counseling them as teenagers, and later on marriage, raising kids, divorce, and as grandparents. "I feel like I'm part of their family," says Eppie. "It's almost as though they have an in-house counselor."

Eppie agrees with Popo that the rewards are personal, a feeling of fulfillment, of having done the best that she possibly can for her fellow human beings. "It makes me feel as though I'm doing something valuable," she emphasizes.

True concern for their fellow man, the kind that's more than mere kindness, is what both twins are esteemed for. Probably, it's how they'd like to be remembered. "This will sound too corny, but it comes back to me every time," says John McMeel about Popo. "I can never get over her caring.

"I was skeptical at first, but she cares about her fellow human beings. She cares about the small person. She's got power and she uses it right. She really is a concerned, caring person. There's nothing phony about her."

"I don't suppose she'd mind me using an example from the New Testament," says former Senator Birch Bayh of Popo. " 'Do unto others as you would have them do unto you.' She's the kind of gentle person who wants to ease the burden in the hearts and minds of people generally and individuals, specifically. She's such a dear soul. No axe to grind at all. Just a dear genuine soul."

Eppie, Father Ted Hesburgh says, "likes to feel that she's someone who can be turned to by those who are most abandoned in our society." It's a commitment Eppie made long ago. "If she weren't doing this, she'd be doing something else. She's a person with a lot of energy, a lot of ideas, who wants to make a difference in the world," says Hesburgh. "It's her own kind of personal mission, of mercy."

Home Again

Thirty-Two

"Abigail Van Buren and her sister, what's her name, are going to be in town this weekend," announces the Hertz girl at the Sioux City airport.

Friday night at the in-town Hilton, where Central High's class of 1936 has been gathering for a week's end of fifty-year-reunion activities, the lobby is abuzz with talk of "the twins."

Four white-haired ladies with white handbags and white shoes are resting after a day of intensive reminiscing.

"I bet they don't get to see each other so often," says one of the ladies.

"I'll bet they see each other whenever they want to," says another.

"Probably just as much as I see of my sister," says a third.

"I'll have to make a special trip to see 'em, because I'm not working on Saturday," says the barmaid in the lobby's Pub, eyeing the flowers for Mrs. Lederer perched at the front desk since noon-time.

"No, not yet," answers the friendly but wearied desk clerk about whether either Mrs. Lederer or Mrs. Phillips has checked in, getting the eerie feeling that in Sioux City, anyway, the Friedman twins had somehow passed into legend, or folklore.

Skipping the Thursday evening of dinner theater, Friday's Dutch Treat luncheon, and that evening's Garden Party Picnic, as well as the tour of the old high school building, since closed, and Saturday's champagne brunch, Eppie and Popo limoed up from Omaha where they'd been visiting with sister Kenny and arrived in Sioux City at 3:00 P.M.

"We've been anonymous and we've been famous," says Popo, bustling up to the front desk, "and it's more fun famous."

Featured speakers at the Saturday-night banquet, the twins were hurrying to get ready. "Sissie, get your duds on and I'll help you zip up, dear," hollers Popo across the hallway. The twins are together again in the same suite they shared ten years before at their forty-year reunion.

Descending to banquet level, Popo in raspberry Norman Norell, darker raspberry platform heels, beaded clutch of raspberry and black, and big, big diamond, big enough to skate on, Eppie in cream and pink beaded Alfred Bosand, white hose, little gold clutch and big pearl earrings, move closer together and giggle.

"Oh there they are, bless their hearts," says a voice in the crowd.

"You look terrific," says Popo, embracing a classmate, having decided to forget any slights she may have received, long ago.

"We won't know who you are without your name tags," jokes another classmate.

Time out for the first of many photos.

Side by side on a couch, Eppie nudges Popo, "Slit on the left?"

"Slit on the left," nods Popo as two twin legs sling over, slits part, and Popo slides her arm around her sister.

Flash. "I don't do lunch," says Eppie, in response to a reporter's question. Flash again. "I don't think it's strange we ended up doing the same thing," says Popo, patting her twin on the wrist.

"Mrs. Phillips?" asks a reporter.

"Call me Abby," commands Popo, patting the reporter on the wrist.

On their way into the ballroom: "Ann, could I get one of you, please?" motions a classmate with an Instamatic.

Together at the head table, Popo points out classmates among the 310 reuniongoers—172 from the class of 1936—filling every table in the packed ballroom.

"She's a nice lady; I've always liked her," murmurs one woman as Popo starts her "remember when" address. Comparing 1936 with the present, Popo says, "In 1936 we had the CCC, the NRA, and the FBI, but we never even heard of the ERA, the CIA, or the IUD. . . . That was before surrogate mothers, vasectomies, penile implants, bypass surgery, silicone boobs, and the Pill."

While Popo manages to get a chuckle out of her audience, Eppie chooses a more serious and in many ways more moving topic for her speech. She speaks convincingly of her father, saying, "He had a loving wife and four children who adored him. He helped his relatives, his friends, and his neighbors. He worked for Catholic charities, for Protestant charities, as well as for Jewish causes. He was a good citizen and he loved Sioux City. In return, Sioux City loved him."

Defining success, she continues, her audience listening closely to every word, "If you have a good name, if you are right more often than you are wrong, if your children respect you, if your grandchildren are glad to see you, if your friends can count on you and you can count on them in time of trouble, if you can face your God and say I have done my best, then you are a success."

By all measures, Eppie and Popo are successful. When asked how she celebrates her success, how she enjoys it, Eppie responds, "By not thinking too much about it. Just going on and seeing if I can turn out as good a column every day as I can."

Eppie says, "I always remember Eleanor Roosevelt saying how important it was to forget about money, fame, and glory. Just do the best job you can do and the rest will come. And it has."

Unlike some people who experience a long arc of success, neither Eppie nor Popo seems to be a prisoner of the stories they told at the beginning. Yet after being the overshadowed twin in

Sioux City, and later, to a degree dependent on her sister's standing in Eau Claire, Eppie appears freer and more comfortable with her life than her twin. In one of life's reversals, in the end, Eppie ends up with the leverage in the twin relationship. Popo's the more vulnerable.

Eppie worked through her relationship with her sister and came to terms with it. Popo, on the other hand, needed her sister's forgiveness after she lashed out at her and is more unsettled at the mention of an uneasy truce. As one friend has pointed out, "Eppie would be perfectly content going to her grave never reconciling with her sister, but it would gnaw at Popo the rest of her life."

Both women are talented and tough survivors of personal and professional battles. Neither twin got famous by accident. In looking back, however, in each of their lives there's only a few rough spots. Eppie grew up in the more talented Popo's shadow. Then, she finally accomplished something she thought was hers alone— being an advice columnist. Again she was outdistanced when twin Popo began a similar advice column.

For Eppie it's also her divorce that stands out, while for Popo it's dealing with her sister's initial success as Ann Landers, and her inability to understand and deal with Eppie's sensitive needs and feelings. For both of them, it's coping with their children's divorces, and the constant public and professional attention that comes with being history's most famous twins.

For the most part, the lives of both twins have been a series of small epiphanies, the kind that make life worth living. Elevating themselves beyond the traditional role granted housewives, and then, advice columnists, the Friedman twins are perceived as fallible, yet possessing innate wisdom, insight, and virtue.

The twins share a passion for understanding, something they learned from Abe and Becky, and they derive great personal and professional satisfaction from their work. Delivering counsel and advice, through their columns, or in person, with a down-home accent that's all lisp and hiss, people listen. "America belongs to me," Eppie crows. Both sisters are masters at organizing, summarizing, and transmitting information and other people's more considered opinions, refracted by their own biases.

There are "oh, so many times," says Eppie, that she has thought how wonderful it would be to share her success with her parents. "Both my parents died before I became involved in my career. . . . They would have had so much *naches,* which means pleasure in Yiddish. . . . They were very proud of anything their children did."

Popo, too, wishes that after all she's done, all that's happened to Popo Friedman over the years, she wishes only that one thing be different. "My one regret is that my parents didn't live to see me become Dear Abby. They were dear, sweet, adorable, lovable, charitable people. They saw me married, but they never lived to see their kids become celebrities."

Up close, Popo looks more like a well-groomed Jewish grandmother, a favorite aunt, than a celebrity. Even when she's all sequinned-up in a dark raspberry gown, matching raspberry platform pumps, and a Brazilian cut-diamond covering the lower half of her ring finger, she projects a huggable, endearing quality in spite of all the finery.

Twin Eppie, after having established herself at the center of America's moral conscience for more than thirty years, declares she's still the original square Jewish lady from Sioux City, Iowa, who's small town at heart. And Popo agrees, taking it as the supreme compliment. "I'm still the same person I always was, and the kindest thing people can say to me is that I haven't changed."

Notes

Primary sources for *Dear Ann, Dear Abby* are the interviews conducted by the authors and an exhaustive review of all print and nonprint materials covering the life and careers of Eppie Lederer (Ann Landers) and Popo Phillips (Dear Abby). Throughout these notes *we* refers to either Jan Pottker or Bob Speziale, or both of us.

The authors conducted several hundred interviews with friends and colleagues of Eppie Lederer and Popo Phillips. All but a few of the interviews were taped.

Dr. Robert Stolar, Dr. Abraham Franzblau, and Father Theodore Hesburgh all granted us interviews. These three men are among the twins' oldest and closest friends. In addition to conversations with people who knew the columnists, individuals with expert knowledge in areas relevant to our research were contacted. We spoke with representatives from newspaper syndicates, philanthropic organizations, political action committees, single-issue groups, and others.

One of the patterns that emerged during our research is that often Eppie has one story to tell about an incident, and Popo has a slightly different version. Colleagues or friends of the twins provide a third version of the event. We attempt to present each version as it was told to us or as we found it elsewhere from independent sources, so the reader is provided with all available information.

Eppie and Popo have been public figures for more than thirty years. Masters at publicity, they have granted hundreds of interviews each year. Eppie writes 365 columns a year; Popo appears in newspapers at least six days a week. They have written hundreds of articles and pamphlets and more than a dozen books. Even though the twins did not grant us interviews, there was no lack of material coming directly from the twins themselves on the life and career of Eppie Lederer or Popo Phillips.

Quotations in *Dear Ann, Dear Abby* are direct quotations from the people we interviewed or from written sources or nonprint media. Sources for the Eppie and Popo quotations are from the columnists themselves and include their print and nonprint interviews, speeches, and writings.

We reviewed all available print and nonprint material on Eppie Lederer and Popo Phillips. Briefly, we have read every book published by either sister, their mail-order pamphlets, and virtually every magazine article written by them. We have reviewed their daily columns for the last twelve years and a sampling of their columns dating back to 1955.

Research files on the twins were obtained from the Minneapolis Public Library, Chippewa Valley Museum, L. E. Phillips Memorial Library, Sioux City Public Library, and Morningside College Library. Morgue files were obtained from the twins' former flagship papers, the *Chicago Sun-Times* and the *San Francisco Chronicle,* as well as from numerous other newspapers, including the Eau Claire (Wisconsin) *Leader-Telegram* and the Waukegan (Illinois) *News-Sun.* The files included material unavailable to the public, such as reporters' notes, publicity releases, stories that were not printed, and the like.

A clipping service provided us with all articles published on the sisters in an American daily newspaper, selected weekly newspapers, and trade journals. We have more than a thousand news/features and a hundred magazine articles on Ann and Abby. We obtained any story ever published about the twins in an American magazine or newspaper that is indexed.

We also viewed many videotapes and 16mm films of the columnists. Tapes of radio broadcasts were obtained. Among the films and tapes reviewed the most helpful included those from CBS News, NBC News, National Public Radio, "The Tom Cottle Show" (WBGH Boston), "The Charlie Rose Show" (Washington, D.C.), and "Chicago Feedback with John Callaway" (WTTG Chicago).

One

The twins' return to Sioux City for the forty-year reunion of their Central High School class is well remembered by their classmates. Charles Lindsay, who headed the 1976 reunion committee, and his wife, Margaret (a Central High graduate and herself a twin), spent an evening with us, discussing the preparations necessary for the columnists' attendance and describing the celebration. Mr. Lindsay shared reunion photos and other memorabilia. Classmates provided their impressions of the event. The weekend festivities were given extensive coverage in the national press, magazines such as *People,* "The Friedman Twins Find You Can Go Home Again, Especially if You're Ann Landers and Dear Abby" by Linda Witt, July 1976, and especially the twins' hometown paper, the *Sioux City Journal.*

Two events, integral to the Ann and Abby story, are first mentioned in the opening chapter. How and why Popo became Dear Abby and the seven-year period of open hostility between the columnists offer perhaps the best examples of the twins' selective memories.

Popo claims in many interviews and in her book *The Best of Dear Abby* (Andrews and McMeel, 1981) that there never was a period of silence between the sisters. On the other hand, Eppie admits to years of silence. So does every person we interviewed who knew either or both sisters. Popo insists that the press was to blame for hyping the feud; she says it again in *Best of.*

Two

The Ann and Abby columns reflect the values Eppie and Popo learned growing up as the daughters of immigrant parents in the Midwest. Nearly all of Abe and Becky Friedman's contemporaries had died by the time we began our research. However, we did correspond with Rabbi H. R. Rabinowitz, the family rabbi, and talked with his daughter, Shirley Rabinowitz Givot. She told us, "The girls attended Sunday school but that was it. They weren't that involved in synagogue activities."

We also talked with Irma James, who was a young woman teaching in the Sioux City schools when Abe Friedman went from chicken peddler to theater owner. Irma recalled how Abe liked to gamble. "Quite a gambler. Elks Club. Every afternoon he sat there in a poker game. He won more than he lost."

Don Stone, barely out of his teens when he approached Abe for advice on beginning a radio career (Abe was already in "the show business"), provided us with a vivid and loving description. Stone concurs that although Abe was a successful businessman and did well for himself considering his beginnings, he was hardly the "philanthropist" the twins remember. Says Stone about the Friedmans, "Sioux City used to have a Mardi Gras for charity, big social event of the season. They would not have participated in that, I'm sure. They did not move at that rank."

The teenage John Gruenberg II, who was in love with Popo (Chapter 4), met the Friedmans through his uncle, Arthur Sanford, Abe's business partner. Gruenberg compared Abe's stature as a small businessman with his uncle's more extensive business interests.

Many of Eppie and Popo's childhood friends have remained in Sioux City and shared their memories of the twins with us.

Rabbi Martin J. Berman of Shaare Zion synagogue kindly gave us permission to go through synagogue scrapbooks and donor cards and helped us interpret what we found. We visited the Jewish Federation of Sioux City and spoke with its director, Joseph Bluestein.

Louise Zerschling, historian at the *Sioux City Journal,* helped us picture Depression-era Sioux City. At the public library, we unearthed histories of the period and obtained a copy of *History of the Sioux City Jewish Community.* This book lists every prominent Jewish business and civic leader during Abe's lifetime. Abe Friedman is not listed. In addition, contemporaries of Eppie and Popo, Jewish and Christian, male and female, high school and college, described Abe's first theater, The World, as marginal. *Easy Street* (Dial Press, 1981), Susan Berman's biography of her gangster father, Davie Berman, portrayed the neighborhood called The Bottoms and some of the town's less illustrious citizens during Prohibition.

Three

Virtually every graduate of Central High's class of 1936 had stories of Eppie and Popo's school days. Graduates were candid in talking about the religious schism in 1930s Sioux City schools. Some classmates who themselves were twins commented on how Abe and Becky raised their twin daughters. The Sioux City library has preserved Central High memorabilia and yearbooks.

We consulted several dozen references on twin bonding and psychology. The more notable include *Twins: An Uncanny Relationship,* Peter Watson (Viking Press, 1981); *Parallels: A Look at Twins,* Harvey Stein and Ted Wolner (Dutton, 1979); *Twins on Twins,* Kathryn McLaughlin Abbe and Frances McLaughlin Gill (Clarkson Potter, 1980); *Identical Twins Reared Apart,* Susan L. Farber (Basic, 1981); *Individual and Environment: Monozygotic Twins Reared Apart,* Niels Juel-Nielsen (International Universities Press, 1981); *First Child, Second Child,* Bradford Wilson and George Edington (McGraw-Hill, 1981); "Identical Twins Reared Apart," *Science,* March 21, 1980, and "Nova: *Twins,*" number 820, first airdate December 6, 1981, PBS, WGBH Transcripts.

Over the years Eppie has discussed with Dr. Robert Stolar her childhood in Sioux City and especially the stress she and Popo felt as Jews in a predominantly Christian setting. She recounted her feelings with Stolar about how the sorority rebuffed her.

Four

Morningside College classmates shared their memories of the "robust but choice" twins.

John Seward, who dated Eppie for several years, and James Olson, who dated Popo and is now the president of the University of Missouri, related many anecdotes of their college years.

Five

The growth of the Phillips liquor fortune is documented in the business pages of Wisconsin and Minnesota newspapers. City papers provided files on Ed Phillips and Sons, Inc., Presto Industries, Jay Phillips, and L. E. Phillips. Diane Olson of the L. E. Phillips Public Library helped us locate information.

Dale Peterson of the Eau Claire *Leader-Telegram* ran down many years of publicity releases issued by the Phillipses' public relations firm. Of course, by the late 1950s Presto had become a household word. Because it is known especially for the manufacture of pressure cookers, Popo has joked that husband Mort "is the man who put a pot roast into orbit."

Popo's father-in-law, Jay Phillips, is a leading philanthropist in the upper Midwest as well as one of the area's top businessmen. Gregarious and sociable, he has been interviewed at length many times. *Time* presented the Time Magazine Distinguished Wholesaler Award to Phillips in 1977, and Beryl Leffler supplied us with additional information on him.

Harold Senecker of *Forbes,* the senior editor responsible for the annual newswire story of the "Four Hundred Richest People in the U.S.," shared his insights on how to research family wealth and his knowledge of some of the Phillips men and their companies.

In an unlikely pairing, the autobiographies of U.S. Senator Hubert H. Humphrey, *The Education of a Public Man* (Doubleday, 1976), and convicted felon Alvin Karpis, *The Alvin Karpis Story* (Coward McCann, 1971), provided background on anti-Semitism in Minnesota and Wisconsin. The Karpis autobiography also describes the Jewish underworld in the Midwest during Prohibition.

The Foundation Center, Washington, D.C., keeps tabs on the Phillips Foundation and retains microfilm copies of the Internal Revenue Service records on the Phillips Foundation, including members and officers, assets, sources of assets, and recipients of funds.

Six

Guests who attended the twins' double wedding related their impressions.

Shirley Rabinowitz Givot provided her backstage look at the excitement. Her father, Rabbi Rabinowitz, who officiated at Shaare Zion, also described the wedding to us.

The Friedman twins' engagement and wedding were documented in the Morningside College scrapbook for 1939, and the *Sioux City Journal* covered the event in excruciating detail, from every nip and tuck with "quaint ties of velvet ribbon" to necklines of "sweetheart decolletage."

Seven

Dr. Robert Stolar described how he first met Eppie and discussed his attraction to her energy and strong character. He also discussed with us her plastic surgery, her need to fit in with a new group of people, and her early attempts at mothering.

Jules Lederer has described his formative years and early sales ventures in many published interviews. Initially leery about ringing doorbells, Jules said he soon learned, "Hey, there are some nice people behind those doors. And I discovered I *loved* to sell."

Eight

Staff at the Chippewa Valley Museum and the Eau Claire Chamber of Commerce provided material on the region, its history, and its businesses. Particularly helpful was *The River Flows On: A Record of Eau Claire from 1910 to 1960* by Louis Barland.

Eppie Lederer and Popo Phillips have always led typically middle-class lives. Their friends and neighbors are counted among Eau Claire's more productive and respectable citizens. Several dozen of these friends, colleagues, and neighbors of the twins provided a portrait of Eppie and Popo during the early years of their marriage. Rosemary Bloedorn conducted many of these interviews in Eau Claire.

Several people spoke of the twins' speech "defect," the distinctive way they talk. One said that Popo's was worse than Eppie's; another said the opposite. It's clear that their speech has been distinctive all their lives, but it may not have been as noticeable when they were children as other Sioux City residents also may have had strong regional accents.

Nine

The reminiscences of the late forties and early fifties were shared by friends and fellow volunteers of the twins. Some of Eppie's and Popo's considerable volunteer work was captured in the local paper, the Eau Claire *Leader-Telegram.*

The *Life* article by Paul O'Neil, "Twin Lovelorn Advisers Torn Asunder by Success," April 17, 1958, highlighted the Bishop Fulton Sheen friendship, and Rabbi Rabinowitz told us that he expressed his concern at the time over the twins' interest in Catholicism.

Marshall Atkinson, publisher of the *Leader-Telegram,* gave his oral history to the Chippewa Valley Museum. He speaks at length about Eppie and Popo.

Members of the Campus School faculty told us about Eppie and Popo as young mothers and characterized their children for us.

Ten

Professor Arthur Henning, retired from the political science department of the University of Wisconsin, Eau Claire, and former local party head, supplied a general background on the regional activities of the Democratic party. Although a close friend of Eppie's at the time, he gave us an impartial assessment of her political activities. Professor Martin Cypress also gave us a broad perspective on Eppie Lederer and Eau Claire Democratic party politics.

Josephine Schneider, a librarian, was active in politics with Eppie and shared memories of Eppie's involvement. Mrs. Schneider's late husband, John, was also well known in local party circles.

Lawrence Wahlstrom provided his recollections of Eppie's introduction to party politics. Edwin Larkin is the attorney who chaired the

Democratic meeting at which Eppie won her first political election. More background was provided by Senator Humphrey's autobiography, and articles and clippings were sent to us by the State Historical Society of Wisconsin. Professor Henning allowed us to see a student paper, "The Democratic Party in Eau Claire County, 1946–1958" by Sylvia Schilling, unpublished.

The Eau Claire County clerk supplied records of election results and party membership counts.

Eleven

Although Homs Schwahn is deceased, we located Kenneth Nispel by following a lead and calling every Nispel phone listing in Colorado. Eppie's election was more than thirty years ago, yet it is vividly remembered by both her political friends and opponents. Her perseverance and political canniness, combined with the unusual circumstances surrounding this election, make it stand out in the minds of current and former Eau Claire residents.

Marshall Atkinson's oral history and clippings from the *Leader-Telegram* were particularly helpful, especially "Democratic County Election Challenged," January 22, 1954; "County Democrats Prepare for Showdown Battle for Control," March 5, 1954; "Mrs. Lederer Wins Democratic Chairmanship, Losers May Appeal," March 8, 1954; and "Tactics in Last County Election Deplored by Losing Group," March 11, 1954.

Twelve

Eppie was eager for publicity when she began her Ann Landers career. There are countless photographs of her in almost every room of her Lake Shore Drive apartment. We even know that she lined her display cabinets with paper lace doilies.

Olga Pottker, a retired news editor at the Waukegan (Illinois) *News-Sun,* worked with people who worked with Eppie. In addition, living in Highland Park, a bedroom suburb of Chicago, and through various personal ties, Olga knew people who knew Jules and Eppie. Olga's knowledge of Chicago, its newspapers, and its politics was extremely helpful.

Art Henning recounted Jake Arvey's reaction to the former Eau Claire housewife's ambitions, and Eppie herself has told how she was quickly dismissed by the sophisticated and powerful Cook County Democratic party machine.

Several Chicago-area women, among them Peg (Mrs. Lewis) Pollock, were struck by Eppie's unusual aspirations and recall Eppie's pre-Ann Landers restlessness. Lewis Pollock was a salesman and executive at Autopoint under Jules and vividly described Jules and his work style. Lew was the salesman challenged by Jules as not being "man enough" to sell the 100,000 pens. Luckily, Lew was able to prove his manhood on that sale. Also, the Ann Landers thank-you note (Chapter 18) was to Lewis Pollock.

The executive who succeeded Jules as Autopoint president, Sol Shulman, augmented the descriptions of Jules we obtained from top Autopoint managers. Autopoint business correspondence and internal memoranda issued by Jules also were obtained from them.

Sterling "Red" Quinlan, formerly vice president of ABC, gave us a sympathetic picture of Eppie and her career ambitions. Eppie sought advice from Quinlan on whether she needed speech therapy for TV work. (He said no.)

One of the twenty-eight contenders for the Ann Landers spot talked with us about the competition. She has requested anonymity. Eppie has explained the workings of the contest too.

There's an interesting parallel between the conflicting stories on the origination of the Ann Landers name and how the Dear Abby column name was created (Chapter 14). William Steven, who has held various positions at the *Chicago Daily News* (a Field paper) and the *Minneapolis Star & Tribune,* and is now retired spoke to us from his home in Sarasota, Florida. He was a good friend of Larry Fanning's and told us of Fanning's impact on Eppie. Also a good friend of Eppie's, he pointed out that Eppie knew when she had a good thing going. "Eppie never let anyone edit her column who wasn't damn good," said Steven. He also remembered how much Ann Landers meant to the newspapers he worked on. "Eppie was the star in the kennel and we took good care of her. If you get a winner like that, that's your first order of business."

Professor Stanley Ned Rosenbaum of the religion department at Dickinson College, Carlisle, Pennsylvania, discussed with us the role of advice givers throughout Jewish history. He told us about "The Bintel Brief" (literally, bundle of letters), which was published for seventy-five years in New York's Yiddish newspaper, the *Jewish Daily Forward.* Earlier, mail sent by Jews isolated in ghettos to Jewish scholars in distant lands and called "responsa literature" figured in Jewish history. It's not surprising that the late advice columnist Dr. Rose Franzblau and the current columnists Dr. Joyce Brothers and Eppie and Popo are all Jewish women.

We are indebted to Dr. Joyce Brothers for discussing advice columns with us. Although Dr. Brothers stopped short of analyzing the Ann Landers and Dear Abby advice columns, she did tell us enough about her own work for us to contrast it with how the twins operate. "I have two rooms full of nothing but cross-indexed files," she says. Furthermore, "My training at Columbia University was in experimental psychology, so I'm able to sort out those results which are not valid by looking at the original experimental design."

Thirteen

Confirming the veracity of Eppie's stories on how she came to win the Ann Landers column was an interesting task. First, we found that Eppie has alternately described one of the three contest letters as dealing with either apples, chestnuts, or walnuts. That's an insignificant discrepancy. More fascinating and meaningful was how there was little to back up Eppie's story of calling on supersonic advisers at the beginning of her career.

Our opinion is that she did not consult U.S. Supreme Court Justice William O. Douglas since neither his former wife Mercedes (now Mrs. Robert Eicholtz), who was married to Douglas at the time of the contest, nor his widow, Cathleen, remember any such story. In addition, the justice himself was quoted as saying "No, no, no, *no* . . ." in *The Love Doctors* by Patrick M. McGrady Jr. (Macmillan, 1972) about his involvement in the Ann Landers column.

Eppie did call Dr. Robert Stolar, a dermatologist; we wondered why she once felt it necessary to claim that she had called the head of the Mayo Clinic. Similarly, her call to a local parish priest about a marriage annulment was later construed as a personal answer from the president of the University of Notre Dame, Father Theodore Hesburgh. Although Father Hesburgh's knowledge and connections were later used for column advice, he told us in an interview in his South Bend, Indiana, office that he had no memory of this incident. At least once, Eppie has said that she received help on this question from Bishop Fulton Sheen.

Katherine Fanning is the executive editor of *The Christian Science Monitor*. She spoke with us about Eppie Lederer's burgeoning career as Ann Landers. Mrs. Fanning provided a unique perspective because she was married to two of Eppie's bosses.

Chicago Sun-Times staffers emphasized the importance of Larry Fanning's influence on the Ann Landers column. They said it's true that he served as Eppie's mentor and should also receive credit for encouraging Eppie to call on professionals for expert advice. Fanning did not want to limit the column to merely what former housewife Eppie Lederer knew from experience.

Information on the first Ann Landers, the late Ruth Holt Crowley, was obtained from her family, notably her daughter, Diane Crowley, and articles written by her niece, Patricia Holt, a journalist at the *San Francisco Chronicle*. Diane Crowley, who in June 1987 succeeded Eppie as the *Sun-Times's* advice columnist, also checked with her brother John Crowley on factual material.

Ms. Crowley wrote to us from Springfield, Massachusetts, "Let me first say how happy my brothers and I are that you are doing such thorough research before writing your book. . . . there has been some distortion of fact over the years since our mother's death."

Since loving relatives can sometimes be biased, we checked the tenor of Ruth Crowley's advice by obtaining some of the Ann Landers columns she wrote in the forties and early fifties. *Sun-Times* reporters familiar with both Eppie's and Crowley's authorship confirmed that it was Crowley who initiated the zippy and blunt approach.

Fourteen

Popo's Hillsborough home was described by friends and colleagues, and details were confirmed through photographs. Many magazine articles and newspaper interviews with the twins or about them discuss their beginning column days. Staff at the *Sun-Times* and the *Chronicle,* both editors and reporters, provided their eyewitness accounts of the first few weeks of Ann and Abby on the job.

Stanleigh "Auk" Arnold of the *Chronicle* and J. H. Clinton of the *San Mateo Times* recounted their first meeting with Popo. Arnold remains friends with Popo and Mort today and spoke affectionately of Popo.

We first heard from Arnold himself that many women were petitioning the *Chronicle* in 1955 and 1956. Popo does not volunteer the information that her column beginning was somewhat similar to her twin's in that there was a general competition for the advice-columnist spot going on when she breezed into Arnold's office. *Chronicle* management had decided that Arnold needed to find a replacement for the

≈ 319

Molly Mayfield column, a replacement who could write very much like the new *Sun-Times* columnist Ann Landers.

Arnold emphatically states he did not know that Popo was Eppie's twin. He says he would have been struck by this revelation if Popo had told him initially because he had been charged with finding "another" Ann Landers. Arnold disputes what Margo, Eppie's daughter, has implied, claiming her Aunt Popo sold herself to Arnold by capitalizing on the fact she was Eppie's twin.

Popo has repeated her "Blessed is thy advice, O Abigail" story hundreds of times in television, radio, newspaper, and magazine interviews. She has even written about it. Arnold casts suspicion on Popo's insisting that she is the sole creator of the Abigail Van Buren name. He refused to confirm Popo's "official" story, although he would not give any details concerning why he didn't want to talk about the name's creation. In fact, Arnold was downright uncomfortable being asked about it.

Fifteen

Eppie's morgue file from the *Sun-Times* contained old editions of that paper's in-house newsletter, which revealed early syndication figures. The figures reported within the *Sun-Times* family during that period were significantly lower than those publicly stated by Eppie herself.

Trade publications, especially *Editor & Publisher,* were the first to report on the beginnings of the seven-year freeze between Eppie and Popo, including its start at the news editors' annual convention.

Charles McAdam Jr. spoke to us at length about Popo's first decade as a syndicated advice columnist under contract with the McNaught Syndicate. McAdam's father should be credited with picking up the Dear Abby column and helping to shape it into the top-rated feature it is today. Follow-up to the McAdam version of the Dear Abby trademark story was done at the U.S. Patent Office, Department of the Interior, Arlington, Virginia.

The Love Doctors, which profiles Ann and Abby among advice givers and sex therapists who have "clarified many problems of a society that has alienated itself from the grace of love" and includes profiles of William H. Masters and Virginia E. Johnson, Dr. Joyce Brothers, David Reuben, M.D., Dr. Rose Franzblau, Eugene Schoenfeld, Menie Gregoire, and Inge and Sten Hegeler, among others, mentions the sisters' nascent rivalry over market share and bickering over exposure in New York City newspapers.

Notes

Sixteen

A 16mm film of Popo and her family interviewed by Edward R. Murrow on his live broadcast of "People to People" was provided by CBS News.

The first detailed public airing of the twins' bitterness appeared in the November 1957 *McCall's,* "Dear Abby vs. Dear Ann" by Elizabeth Pope. The April 1958 *Life* article picked up the feuding-twin theme and elaborated on it. The quarrel and subsequent silence haunted both sisters in all news media stories for the next thirty years.

Before his death in late 1982, Dr. Abraham Franzblau spoke with us at length about Eppie and Popo. Although Dr. Franzblau knew both Eppie and Popo, he and his wife, Rose, regarded Popo and not Eppie as a good friend.

Dr. Robert Stolar again freely discussed how he helped Eppie admit that her rivalry with Popo affected her deeply, and how Eppie and Popo attempted to resolve their feelings about each other.

Popo's posture that her career as Dear Abby is actually her hobby continued over the next three decades. As can be seen in Chapter 25, it was difficult for both twins to abandon their generation's expectations concerning women. If, as they believed, women were not expected to achieve beyond the roles supposedly granted them by anatomy, then both twins may have wisely determined not to let their readers know just how important their careers have been to them. Of course, it's entirely possible that Eppie and Popo themselves have not been able to acknowledge the degree to which their careers have shaped their own lives and character.

Seventeen

Eppie's early successes were recounted by *Sun-Times* staffers and by Kay Fanning.

Both Dr. Stolar and Father Hesburgh told us of Eppie's wanting to make something more of her column, wanting to break out of the "agony columnist" mode.

Variously headlined ANN LANDERS IN RUSSIA or ANN LANDERS VISITS THE RUSSIAN PEOPLE, the twelve installments of Eppie's trip to Moscow were syndicated in the *Sun-Times* in September 1959.

Eighteen

Conversations with Dr. Stolar, Mrs. Eicholtz, and Father Hesburgh are the sources for some of the remarks in this chapter.

Jules Lederer talked about how he formed Budget Rent-A-Car in *Los Angeles* magazine.

Margo's life at Brandeis was related by Eppie to Tom Cottle on his Boston talk show. She said she regretted not going to Selma. Father Hesburgh mentioned to us his conversations with Eppie about civil rights during this period.

John Coleman was profiled in a December 6, 1982, *New York* magazine article, "Putting on the Ritz" by Anthony Haden-Guest. Coleman discussed his adoption and feelings about Judaism. Significantly, many of Eppie's friends were puzzled by Margo's interest in him.

Nineteen

Rose Franzblau was the first advice columnist to present basic psychiatric principles to newspaper readers. Her column, called "Human Relations," began in 1948 at the New York *Star* and continued at the *Post* until her retirement in 1976.

Although Rose Franzblau died before we began our work, Dr. Abraham Franzblau talked freely with us about his wife and her friendship with Popo. Rose's statement "Who does Ann Landers think she is . . ." was told to us by her husband.

We also had a conversation with the Franzblaus' son, Dr. Michael Franzblau, a Beverly Hills psychoanalyst.

Eddie Phillips's confessed ambivalence over his family's wealth was quoted in *Corporate Report–Minnesota,* a regional business magazine.

Development office administrators at Morningside College spoke with us about the honorary awards given to the twins at separate times.

Jeannie talked about her personal problems growing up in *The Love Doctors.*

Twenty

Although Eppie is reluctant to discuss the ending of the seven-year sisterly silence, Popo is not. Her olive-branch story is mentioned in many interviews and in her book *The Best of Dear Abby.* No one we spoke with, however, backed up Popo's contention, "There was never a time we weren't speaking with each other." Even Eppie says differently.

Richard Weiner wrote of columnists, their profits, and their syndicates in his book *Syndicated Columnists* (Weiner, 1977).

Don Michaels, then senior editor of the Tribune New York News Syndicate, spoke with us about Popo's arrival from McNaught and Mort's role in guiding her career. Michaels, along with Charles McAdam of McNaught, spotlighted the crucial and unpublicized role Mort Phillips has played in turning Dear Abby into the country's most popular advice column.

Twenty-One

Twin Cities newspapers reported that area police withheld reports of the Phillipses' River Drive robbery.

Popo discussed her female fan with the man's haircut in a newspaper interview.

Barbara Flanagan, a columnist for the Minneapolis *Star and Tribune,* chatted with us about Popo, the Phillipses, and social life in the Twin Cities.

Mrs. Flanagan also gave us leads to many of the current and former Minneapolis and St. Paul residents, "quite a fascinating and eclectic collection of friends that crossed a lot of lines, including the archbishop of the Catholic diocese, university presidents, and titans of industry," who knew Popo and the Phillips family but wanted their comments to remain confidential.

James Shannon, a St. Paul bishop active in various liberal social causes, eventually relinquished his standing in the Roman Catholic hierarchy and St. Paul archdiocese to marry. He is now director of the General Mills Foundation and is familiar with the philanthropic gestures of the Phillipses. He retains a "firm friendship" with Eddie, Popo, and Mort.

John G. Trezevant, executive vice-president of the *Sun-Times* and *Daily News,* was quoted by Judith Wax in her 1973 *New York Times Magazine* article, "Ann Landers: Is Incest Hereditary?" as saying, "Her policies and replies are all her own though I urge her to stay out of such political things as specific endorsements of candidates or pending legislation."

Although Eppie was cautioned about turning Ann Landers into a political and social action column by her editors, Kay Fanning supposes that Eppie's reluctance to be publicly involved in causes she personally believed in was more typical of celebrities in those days (fifties, early sixties) than it is now.

Eppie's two reports on her trip to Vietnam were serialized in the *Sun-Times* on May 25 and June 1, 1967.

The New York Times story about celebrity visits to Vietnam, "Flood of V.I.P. Visitors Harries Saigon Officials" (June 8, 1967), specifically cited Eppie's visit as counterproductive to the U.S. armed forces because it diverted the attention of top military leaders like General Westmoreland from more pressing matters. The article criticized civilian visitors and politicos who "like to enliven Washington cocktail parties with 'I just talked to Westy in Saigon and he says. . . .'" Also, Admiral Elmo Zumwalt, who was in charge of naval operations in Vietnam, has since written in *My Father, My Son* (Macmillan, 1986) of the negative impact of celebrity visits on military operations.

A conversation with Institute for Policy Studies co-director Richard Barnet revealed Eppie's lack of involvement in the sixties' antiwar movement.

Senator Eugene McCarthy first met Eppie in Wisconsin in the early fifties when he was a congressman from Minnesota, and even though Popo "lived in Minneapolis when I was a congressman from St. Paul, we didn't cross over very much," and he got to know Eppie better. "She was more involved in politics than Mrs. Phillips," said McCarthy, even though he characterized both women to us as "identifiable Democrats." The Phillips family has also "contributed some" to McCarthy's campaigns, although "they were not principles of my campaigns. They supported Democrats generally."

Senator McCarthy was clear and emphatic that Eppie did not play a part in the public protest against the war in southeast Asia, nor did she support his 1968 presidential bid. He thinks highly of Eppie, and when told of her "early dove" claim, he replied very slowly, carefully choosing his words, "I think she was against the war all right, but . . . [he paused and spoke even more slowly] I believe if she says that, it's probably true, but she was not involved in my campaign."

Eppie has made several claims about political involvement for which it is difficult to find support. The first was that she was actively involved in the fight against McCarthyism in the early fifties, which has not been confirmed by her Eau Claire Democratic friends of the era, and the second claim concerns her antiwar activities, which also is not supported. She has placed some of her friends who knew her during these periods in embarrassing situations when they've been asked to support her claims and find that they cannot.

Twenty-Two

Eppie's high-toned social activities at the same time as the Lincoln Park head bashings were reported by the Chicago press.

The New York Times listed Mort Phillips as a large contributor to Vice President Hubert Humphrey's presidential campaign and a contributor to the special fund to clear up his campaign debt. When told of this financial support, Senator McCarthy wryly responded, "I don't think they gave any money to help clean up *my* debt."

The late sixties serves as the turning point for Eppie and Popo's involvement in the world beyond Mother of the Year awards. Although Eppie traveled as a reporter to the USSR and to Vietnam, her newspaper accounts of her trips contained mostly sanitized observations chock full of domestic details calculated not to startle her column readers. Their willingness to take on controversial issues and risk making some enemies began to emerge in the late sixties.

Popo's angered treatment of mail she received which supported the Vietnam war was reported in *The Love Doctors.*

The current Dun and Bradstreet financial ratings and history of the Phillips family firms helped estimate their wealth.

We visited the U.S. Securities and Exchange Commission to use its vast files and examined corporate and financial information on National Presto Industries, Inc., and the Westland Corporation. The federal forms detailed shares owned by the Phillips family members, their status as officers, their trust funds, and so on. Activities and defense contracts of Presto during the Vietnam War were mentioned in news clippings, corporate documents, and U.S. Department of Justice documents from 1966 to date. Presto was generous enough to send us back issues of its annual reports, which are the source of the Presto quotations in this chapter. We also talked with Stuart E. Schiffer, Deputy Assistant Attorney General, U.S. Department of Justice, who gave us background on this case and who confirmed the amount of money the government eventually released to Presto.

The Illinois attorney general's questions about the A.B. Foundation established by Jules and Eppie were duly noted by the Chicago press.

The faux pas with the pontiff was reported in the *Minneapolis Tribune.* Ambassador to Italy Max Rabb; his secretary, Katherine M. Astala; Michael Hornblow of the Office of the Personal Envoy of the President of the United States of America to the Vatican; and Reverend Karlheinz Hoffman, S.J., undersecretary of the Pontificia Commissione per le Communicazioni Sociali were very helpful in running this story down for us.

Michael Kernan's extraordinarily insightful March 10, 1974, article "Advice from Ann Landers" in the *Washington Post* is the source of the "We get along fine. . . ." quotation. Eppie castigated Kernan for his audacity in asking her secretary what she thought of her boss. The response which set Eppie off? "I think she's just great. I love her." Kernan is one of the very few reporters who tried to probe deeper into Eppie's Ann Landers image.

We were fascinated by Margo's naming her children after Ann Landers advice column advisers Bob Stolar and Ted Hesburgh, both childless men who were justifiably proud of the compliment. Father Hesburgh said to us, "I thought it was kind of nice, although I never heard of Andrea Ted before."

Margo's assessment of Eppie's grandmotherly instincts was reported by Judith Wax in her 1973 *New York Times Magazine* story.

John Coleman discussed his Menninger Foundation stay with *New York* magazine. Financial information on Coleman keeps popping up, none of it favorable. Coleman was served notice by the D.C. government for $1.4 million in delinquent taxes and has had "difficulties" with the Johnson Properties Inc./Ritz-Carlton Co. over his use of the Ritz-Carlton name on his Washington, D.C., hotel. His bankruptcy filing was reported in major east coast and Chicago papers, including the *Washington Post, The New York Times,* and the *Chicago Tribune.*

Margo's sometime column of social commentary was bought for syndication by her mother's syndicate (Field Enterprises) shortly after its appearance in the competing Chicago newspaper, the *Tribune,* which had declined to syndicate the feature. The Field syndicate managed to sell it to some sixty newspapers. Said William Steven about Margo's column and why his Minneapolis newspaper ran it, "She wrote some pretty good stuff. We were desperately trying for anything that would stir a nickel into the circulation box."

The suit against Margo by Dr. David Reuben was well publicized at the time.

Twenty-Three

Wedding guests at Deanna and Eddie's marriage ceremony and guests at Jeannie and Luke's wedding shared their recollections of the happy affairs with us. Also, the weddings were reported in the Minneapolis/St. Paul and Los Angeles newspapers.

Notes

Luke McKissack's professional status was obtained from interviews with civil liberties attorneys on both coasts.

We obtained the Alco annual reports and Westland annual reports and looked at their files at the SEC. Viewing the links between the directors of Alco, Westland, and the Phillips Foundation confirmed certain family ties and friendships.

Chicago friends, colleagues, and acquaintances of Eppie and Jules provided background to the Lederer marital breakdown. In addition, comments of Dr. Abraham Franzblau, Dr. Robert Stolar, Father Hesburgh, Cathleen Douglas, and Senator Eugene McCarthy indicated, sometimes inadvertently, that Jules Lederer was not a major part of Eppie's life by the early seventies. For example, Senator McCarthy calls himself a good friend of Eppie's since the early fifties, yet says of Jules: "I didn't really know him." These types of comments from a variety of unrelated sources indicated to us the Lederer marriage was not what Eppie idealized it to be.

Jules's fall from grace at Transamerica was documented in local papers, business articles, and magazines.

Eppie's story of her trip to China was serialized in her column during September 1974 and later ran as one article in other publications, such as *The Saturday Evening Post,* which attempted to sensationalize the rather tame piece by titling it, "Sex Behind the Bamboo Curtain."

Newspapers carried reporters' concern over the trip's being in violation of journalistic ethics. Like the USSR and the Vietnam trips, Eppie's international forays seem superficial and not well thought out, leaving her vulnerable to criticism.

Twenty-Four

Father Hesburgh reviewed for us Eppie's phone call and visit to him about her impending divorce when we saw him in South Bend. He emphasized how he counseled her as an educated friend, not as a priest, and how his friendship with Jules allowed him to be fair to Jules when talking with Eppie. Dr. Stolar recounted to us how he counseled both Jules and Eppie separately.

Jules's statement, "I didn't think . . . that she should have written the column" appeared in *Los Angeles* magazine.

Twenty-Five

Senator Birch Bayh took the time to speak with us about his friendship with Popo and Mort, and Popo's stumping for him in Indiana. Stressing that it was Popo who turned out the voters in his 1968 and 1974 Senate races, Bayh laughed, "My ego can stand it." He also emphasized that Popo put Dear Abby on the line for him during a tough and unpleasant campaign.

We were mystified and, admittedly, amused at seeing Eppie and Popo say, year after year, that they didn't really work for a living. Their comments probably reflect both their generation's attitude regarding married middle-class women who work as well as their own reservations over being seen as independent and wealthy career women.

Phyllis Schlafly was quoted in *The Sweetheart of the Silent Majority* by Carol Felsenthal (Doubleday, 1981).

The Phillips Foundation gifts are listed on their IRS forms and were viewed at the Foundation Center, Washington, D.C.

The actor Henry Winkler talked with us about his ERA walk with Popo and his admiration for her. Later, he was an honored guest at Popo's thirtieth-anniversary tribute.

Twenty-Six

Withdrawing the offer of an honorary degree to Eppie by St. Joseph's College was widely reported in the media. However, not all alumni found the action justifiable. One graduate, now a priest and a professor of psychology at Loyola University, pointed out, "To fail to recognize the enormous good Ann Landers has done, always with sensitivity to Catholic needs, is a truly small and sad judgment."

We spoke with national pro-life and pro-choice organizations, including James Kappas at American Life Lobby; Joseph Schindler at the Pro Life Action League; the Eagle Forum; National Right to Life Committee; and Marguerite Beck-Rex at the National Abortion Rights Action League (NARAL).

Joseph Schindler told us that Eppie was pro-choice because she "has one foot in Father Hesburgh," whom he characterized as a liberal priest. Hesburgh emphatically told us that he (1) is against abortion, and (2) disagreed strongly with Eppie on this issue.

The strength of the anti-abortion feeling in this country and the pro-life groups' anger at Eppie Lederer's supporting a woman's right to abortion should not be discounted. Once we began our investigation on this issue, we began receiving impassioned letters from the members of these anti-abortion groups telling us to spend our time writing a biography of a "worthy" person, not Eppie Lederer. These letters were usually accompanied by vivid photos of bloody fetuses.

Notes

Twenty-Seven

We spoke with Howard Phillips, director of the Conservative Caucus Foundation; James Kappas, American Life Lobby; and Cal Thomas of the group formerly called the Moral Majority.

The handgun organizations we spoke with are: John Snider at the Citizens Committee for the Right to Keep and Bear Arms; John D. Aquilino Jr., formerly with the National Rifle Association; Ashley Halsey at *American Rifleman;* Barbara Lautman at Handgun Control; and Abbe Jolles with the National Coalition to Ban Handguns. It was Lautman who told us that the Field Syndicate called to check on Eppie's "facts" after the Ann Landers column had already run. We also spoke with staffers at Accuracy in Media about presentation of factual data in the Ann Landers and Dear Abby advice columns.

We discussed pressure brought by different interest groups on Ann Landers and Dear Abby and columnists in general with Leanne Katz at the National Coalition Against Censorship and with a staffer at People for the American Way.

The vehemence of Eppie's detractors and the fury of the response from chiropractors were detailed in *The New York Times Magazine* profile by Judith Wax.

Twenty-Eight

As described earlier, Central High classmates of Eppie and Popo's revived the forty-year class reunion for us.

Dr. Robert Stolar discussed the twins' cosmetic surgery. Popo talked to Cliff Jahr about Eppie's extensive surgery, and Margo has reported on her Aunt Popo's surgery.

Twenty-Nine

Don Michaels, then senior editor of the Tribune Company, talked with us about Popo's switch of syndicates.

John McMeel, president of Universal Press Syndicate and Popo's current "boss," very kindly granted us a lengthy interview. He gave us thoughtful answers to our many questions about Popo and the Dear Abby column. Interestingly, McMeel "had the good fortune of knowing both women. For four years before Field bought Publishers Hall I had the job of selling Ann Landers."

McMeel is perhaps the only person in the enviable position of being able to say, "I guess I'm the only one who has been privy to both the list of Ann Landers papers and Dear Abby papers." He continued, "Eppie has got a tremendous list of newspapers . . . and her syndicate has done a good job of continuing to add to her list. But when I saw the Abby list, the initial one, the numbers there! The numbers were just *amazing.* As I say, Abby has so many of the smaller papers. Between Ann and Abby, the market is taken, and that's why no one else has been able to penetrate."

Both McMeel and Michaels concurred that Popo's syndicate switch was not predicated by money. Both of them stressed Mort's involvement with the financial and contractual Dear Abby agreements. "He sure *is* a good businessman," said McMeel. John McMeel also ventured to characterize Popo and Mort's marriage. "He never meddles. She wants him involved and I do too, because he always has a better idea and he doesn't shove it down your throat. . . . I love to have dinner with Abby alone, but I also want Mort there, too, because of what he adds and what he's all about."

When sizing up the twins' lives we couldn't help but compare the differences in their marriages—not just that Popo remains married while Eppie endured a very public divorce, but that the quality of their marriages has been so different. Despite Eppie's proclamations of a wonderful relationship, it's obvious that Popo has a real partner, personal and professional, in Mort. We speculated that Eppie's reliance on a few advisers (Father Hesburgh and Dr. Stolar come to mind immediately) helped substitute for a man she could talk to about the issues she was interested in. Hesburgh told us, "I've heard it said you've got three kinds of conversations. You can talk about things or friends or ideas. She's interested in the latter. We talk about ideas." Jules may have shown little interest in Eppie's ideas.

The writer Cliff Jahr generously related to us his different experiences in interviewing Eppie and Popo. In addition, he flipped through his notes from his meetings with them and reviewed some of the material cut by his *Ladies' Home Journal* editor for the two articles, "Ann Landers, America's Confidante" (January 1980) and "Dear Abby Speaks Out on Marriage, Success and Ann Landers" (September 1981).

Transcripts of "The Phil Donahue Show" with Popo as guest were provided by Multimedia Entertainment, Inc., Cincinnati, Ohio.

Columnist Liz Smith reported Mort's comment, "If these are twin sisters, I'll take cobras."

Margo quoted her husband, Ken Howard, as saying, "They are as theatrical as movie stars," on a New York talk show.

Thirty

Tom Cottle talked with us about what Eppie Lederer was like when he knew her just as another mother of one of his friends at Francis Parker School in Chicago. A psychologist and a skilled interviewer, he drew Eppie out on his talk show in a way no other talk-show host has done. WGBH Boston provided us with a videotape of "The Tom Cottle Show."

James Pearre, assistant publisher of the *Leader,* which broke the recycling story, talked with us about his encounters with Eppie and her view of him as her adversary. He detailed the unusual meeting he had with her, her eccentric behavior, and the time she hung up on him.

In addition, Pearre provided original research which showed that Eppie has reprinted column material for many years more than she has admitted. Incredibly, he and his staff found that Eppie has printed the same material three times, not just twice as she has confessed. Fatigued by the media uproar and disappointed by what he considers the unprofessional reaction of a top-rated columnist, he hasn't published his newer findings.

One example of Ann Landers's triple exposure concerned a man who insisted he could not hear his wife's voice.

THE MAN'S LETTER(S)

December 29, 1966	*June 21, 1976*	*December 30, 1981*
We argue a lot lately because my wife says I don't answer her when she talks to me.	We argue a lot because she says I ignore her.	Lately my wife and I argue a lot because she claims I don't answer her when she speaks to me.
I have told her repeatedly that I don't hear her.	I've told her time and again that I don't hear well and that she should talk louder.	I told her I answer when I hear her.
She says I don't hear her because I don't *want* to hear her.	She insists that I "tune her out" on purpose.	She says I hear what I want to hear and I am just being difficult.

≈ 331

Notes

December 29, 1966

I suspect she doesn't speak up so she will have an excuse to chew at me about something. She used to nag me to death about my smoking, but now that I have quit she needs a new subject.

June 21, 1976

Now I'm beginning to think she speaks softly so she will have something to pick at me about. She used to nag me about my cigar smoking, but since I gave up tobacco, she needs a new topic.

December 30, 1981

For years, she nagged me about my smelly cigars. Now that I've quit, she needs a new subject.

RESPONSE FROM ANN LANDERS

December 29, 1966

Yes, I have had the problem before and my ear experts tell me that the male sometimes loses the ability to hear high-pitched sounds as he grows older—especially if the sound is his wife's voice.

Ask her to try to speak in a lower register, and you try to listen a little harder, Bub.

June 21, 1976

Husbands often lose the ability to hear a high-pitched voice, especially if it's the wife's.

Suggest that she speak in a lower register—and you listen a little harder, Buster.

December 30, 1981

According to the experts, males sometimes lose the ability to hear high-pitched sounds as they grow older—especially if the sound is a wife's voice.

Ask her nicely to speak in a lower register. And listen a little harder, Mister.

We obtained hundreds of stories, editorials, and editorial cartoons on Ann Landers' practice of recycling letters, as well as reader responses to these stories.

Editors were overwhelmingly critical of Eppie and her alleged innocence, while the Ann Landers readers viewed the whole fiasco as a minor goof. John McMeel spoke of the criticism received by Popo for recycling letters in the Dear Abby column, and his response to this. Popo's expressed astonishment over her twin's actions and her own implied innocence is interesting in light of her handling of the Dear Abby column.

332 ≈

Notes

Thirty-One

Deanna's lawyer, Edward Winer (Mitchelson's colleague), spoke with us about Deanna's divorce from Eddie, and Popo's reaction to Deanna. Deanna also spoke with us about her divorce.

National and Chicago Ground Zero leaders told us of Eppie's anti-nuclear activities that came about from her friendship with Father Hesburgh. Father Hesburgh also confirmed that Eppie's involvement was a result of their friendship.

John McMeel graciously had his syndicate provide us with material on Popo's thirty-year tribute. As a thank-you gesture, Popo had a few friends and syndicate staffers to dinner in her Bel Air home the following evening. Popo usually prefers to entertain in restaurants.

Rabbi Max Shapiro, spiritual leader of Temple Israel in Minneapolis, spoke with genuine admiration of the Phillipses and especially the generosity of Jay Phillips.

Jim McConnell found himself seated across the aisle from Ann Landers in the first-class compartment of an American Airlines flight from Los Angeles to Washington, D.C., and overheard her conversation.

Thirty-Two

We attended the festive fifty-year reunion of the Central High class of 1936 along with Eppie and Popo and observed firsthand the twins' activities during the Saturday afternoon and evening celebration at the Sioux City Hilton. Some anecdotes were provided by Elizabeth Kastor in her *Washington Post* feature story, "The Weekend with the Friedman Twins" (June 23, 1986.)

Index

Index